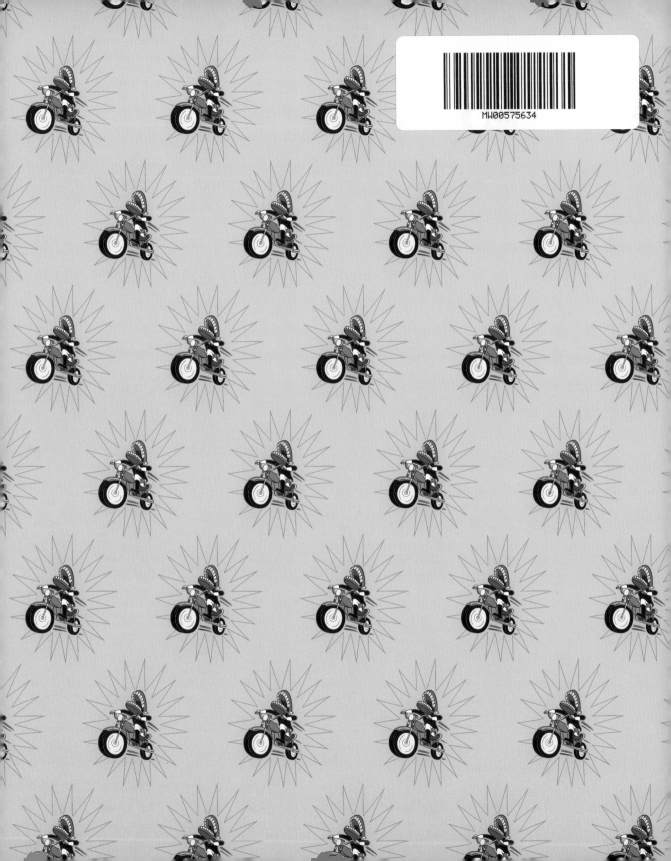

COMEDY BANG! BANG!

THE PODCAST

(THE BOOK)

EDITED BY SCOTT AUKERMAN

ABRAMS IMAGE, NEW YORK

TABLE OF

CONTENTS

BY THE EDITOR

And with that, I put down my Peterson pipe, tapping the chamber upon my armrest,[1] chuckling mightily. "Ha ha ha," I muttered. "A most entertaining way to spend the afternoon."

Augustina, the charwoman with whom I had been having an affair, had stormed out angrily that Tuesday, taking the Dutch oven with her. The aroma of beef barley bake still lingered, reminding me of both my sorrow and the fact that I hadn't eaten in six days.

But before her melodramatic exit (and the ill-tempered soliloquy that came with it), Augustina had mislaid her mobile telephone device, and I eventually found it in the furnace room, amongst some oily rags.

Not possessing one myself, I was curious as to what fascinated her so much about this rectangular marvel. She was known to spend upward of twenty-two hours a day staring at its face (while she barely gave mine a second look).

I tapped at it, much like a bear paws away at a branch, hoping a dead bird will fall down that it can devour. And eventually, I was able to power the blasted thing on.

And there, staring up at me, like a filthy, bedraggled orphan, hoping to be chosen by a loving set of parents, was a square—an "app" as they call it—with the title "Podcasts."

. . . And so, my adventures began.

I cannot remember the name of whatever I listened to (I suspect the contents had something to do with the serialized accounting of a local murder). But, O! Such diversion awaited me. I had fallen in love with a medium. How ironic that the departure of one love had been supplanted with another![2]

Grunting mightily, I struggled to rise. My kyphosis had contributed to my vague feelings of unease. Back to my chambers, to be sure. Yet, for some reason, I paused.

"What IF," I stealthily muttered, "what IF I tried my hand at this emerging art form?"

Until then, I had enjoyed some success as the author of a popular book series, *The Damaged, Quaint Midriffs*.[3] They were as thrilling as they were most likely hallucinated.

But something about these iPod broadcasts called to me—like a man yelling instructions to another man regarding how to safely disentangle his arm from a tortilla machine.[4]

Of course, the rest is history (much like the majority of what has transpired in the course of human events). I was an immediate success in my chosen field, and you currently hold this book in your hand(s). Who could have foreseen this? Certainly not I.

Since the inception of *Comedy Bang! Bang!*, over a decade has passed, full of laughter and the occasional silent breaking of wind. I hope this publication acts as both a souvenir of your interest in the program, and as something that will reside in your home for a few years, until your spouse tosses it into the waste bin.

Therefore, let us tarry no longer. Introductions are to be read by the young! Time is slipping away! I welcome you to this tome and sincerely apologize for its contents.

Scottrick Q. Aukerland
Criehaven Island, just of the coast of Maine, summer 1977

1. I later found that the draught hole had become clogged, and a certain amount of tobacco had seeped into the shank and mortise. "Nothing more than a minor inconvenience," I thought to myself. "I shall have this pipe thrown into the garbage at first rising of the sun upon the morrow."

2. The similarities end there, as Augustina happened to wear a size XXL.

3. Eventually turned into somewhat more enjoyable film adaptations—the tetralogy *A Ha'penny for Junior, Ten Ha'pennies to a Nickel, Life Upon Ha'penny Bridge,* and *Bikini Daze 2: A Sphincter's Tale.*

4. A "viral" video I watched on another app—"YouTube," I believe, immediately upon finishing the podcast.

LIN-MANUEL MIRANDA

Comedy Bang Bang! If you're a fan like me, just saying these words aloud will set Reggie Watts's immortal theme humming in your ears. For over a decade, this radio-show-turned-podcast-turned-cultural-phenomenon has been the ground floor for countless comedy legends.

Scott Aukerman's "open-door policy" has introduced us many unique characters and catchphrases: Paul F. Tompkins's Lord Andrew Lloyd Webber (and his "composing by dreams" technique, a gift I truly envy); Scott's nephew Todd, played by Lauren Lapkus; Bobby Bottleservice by Nick Kroll; and of course, Jason Mantzoukas, created by the great Jeffrey Characterwheaties. Whether you're a new fan of the podcast, or you edit the increasingly Byzantine Comedy Bang Bang Wiki page in your spare time, this book has much to enthrall you. Read on!

Heynong man,

Lin-Manuel Miranda

"WEIRD AL" YANKOVIC

Scott Aukerman personally asked me to write something for this book, and so naturally I felt somewhat obligated to do so. But then I read the introduction that was supposed to come directly before mine, and, well . . . I don't think I can continue without addressing a few things about that dumpster fire first.

Look, Lin-Manuel is one of my dearest friends, and he's a true genius, but I can't let him get away with this sycophantic crap. I mean, come on.

First of all, he says he's a fan, but then he doesn't put an exclamation point after both *Bangs* in *Comedy Bang! Bang!*? If you don't know the manual of style for the title of one of your supposedly favorite shows, you're not a fan, you're a freakin' noob.

Then he has the nerve to say the radio show went from "podcast" to "cultural phenomenon." I can only assume when he says "cultural phenomenon" he's referring to the fifth season of the *Comedy Bang! Bang!* television show on IFC (the one where I costarred as Scott's bandleader). Now, I certainly won't argue with the fact that my season was the high point of the series, but it's kind of a huge slap in the face to Reggie Watts and Kid Cudi, who were both, you know . . . fine. Rude, Lin. Rude.

Okay, and then he writes that the show "has introduced us many unique characters and catchphrases." WHAT?? I'm pretty sure he meant to say "has introduced us TO many unique characters and catchphrases." Hey, I know Lin-Manuel Miranda's a busy guy, he's got a lot on his plate . . . but if he can't even be bothered to proofread his own stinking two-paragraph introduction, I think what he's really trying to say between the lines is that he hates the show. I'm sorry you all had to find out this way.

Look, I could go on, but I don't feel like I have the strength after slogging through that lazy, ill-conceived trash heap of sentences. Again, I love Lin like a brother, I truly do, but I'm sorry, that introduction just sickened me to my very core.

Having gotten all that off my chest, let me just say . . . I haven't read or even looked at this book, but knowing Scott, I figure it's probably okay.

"Weird Al" Yankovic

TATIANA MASLANY

Hi. Tatiana Maslany here (aka The She-Shredder), first-time contributor to Comedy Bang! Bang! The Podcast: The Book, long-time listener.

I've been a superfan of *CBB* since James Adomian's Tom Leykis declared, "Every woman wants to dip nylons into my butthole, and I've turned them down 90% of the time." "Out Of Bleeps" was the first grepisode I ever heard. I was hooked. I've always been reverent of comedians, and this show was populated by the all-time greats. Their brains are some of the best brains on the planet. There are too many little weirdo specifics to name them all. Ho Ho's little "bleh." Real man Brad Hammerstone. Professor Stealwater getting a little piece of cloud stuck on his tongue. Uncle Scott's big ups to people of all stars and stripes. Puberbagels. Paul F. Tompkins . . . doing anything. Ever. Always. Hundreds of ridiculous, perfect moments that I go back and listen to, over and over.

The best part of it, in my mind, is that these incredibly skilled performers come to *CBB* just to play. Goofs just goofin' for goofiness' sake. Verbal freefall, leading to the most absurd ideas becoming canon. Even as a listener, the show kinda feels like hanging with your best buds. And I think that's why so many people become enamored by it, and are attached to these characters. They really do become our ear friends.

Every episode is a relief, an escape, a trip to guaranteed laughsville.

Some might call it cathartic.

Some might call it a reset.

And some might call it a heynong man.

Tatiana Maslany

BOB ODENKIRK

Hello, Reader! And more than that—hello, Potential Book Buyer!!

Bob Odenkirk (*Mr. Show with Bob and David*, *Breaking Bad*, *Better Call Saul*, *Esteemed Nobody*) here to speak to YOU because I heard YOU were standing there considering this book about the *Comedy Bang! Bang!* phenomenon.

Scott Aukerman is someone whose unhinged lunacy I've enjoyed for many years. I knew him when he was still trying to come up with a great showbiz name—it took him a long time, but he finally settled on "Aukerman." Great job, Scott! (Or should I say "Great Scott, job!" No . . . no . . . I should have stuck with "Great job, Scott.")

I, too, myself, have enjoyed the "Bang Bang" show and its madcap inanity and foolhardy insanity and asinine foolcappery, and a book about it sounds wonderful. But what about a book that I am currently writing that you might want even more than this one?!

I'm glad you made it this far into this foreword, and now I can be straight with you. My book, which I'm writing, is BETTER than this one. It's called *Indeed and Unspoken—Secret Truths About Hollywood and Its Unseemly Behaviors!* Sound good? It will be!

It will be full of gossip about stars, and near-stars, and their foibles, and trickery, and YOU will love it! You like books! You consider buying them! You are interested in showbiz tales! You are my target audience!

GET THAT BOOK, save your money on this one—you'll love me twice, for saving you money on this and pointing you toward THAT.

In fact, my book actually has a chapter on Scott Aukerman and *Comedy Bang! Bang!*, and the sexual innuendo and delectable insertions that happened backstage at that show—and that chapter is LONGER than this whole book! I'm trying to save you money and heartache!

Now, pretend you didn't read this sales pitch. Just nod your head, murmur, "Hmmm . . . what a nice foreword. I will consider buying and reading THIS book," set it back upon the shelf, and you and I will meet in my book a few months from now.

Oh, by the way, Scott Aukerman said he'd write me a foreword so you'll get plenty of his nonsense there, too.

Wink wink, kiss kiss, and sayonara, sucker!

Bob Odenkirk

PATTON OSWALT

I go back quite a ways with *Comedy Bang! Bang!* I did *Comedy Bang! Bang!* back when it was *Comedy Death-Ray*—and before it was even a podcast.

Like most great things in comedy, *CBB* started as friends messing around and amusing each other. Scott Aukerman hosted a radio show on 103.1 back in the day. This was when people listened to a thing called a "radio," where you could hear songs and people called "deejays" would speak in between the songs to tell you the title of the song and the artist that performed it. It entertained us in between locust plagues and bear attacks. We also ate pemmican and hardtack and slept in trundle beds and *Seinfeld* was still on the air. Why, on some nights, when the moon is full, I can still hear the wistful howl of a . . .

Sorry, I'm supposed to keep this short.

When Scott would invite his comedian friends in to chat, riff, and bounce jokes off the poster-covered walls, sometimes those comedians wouldn't even come in as themselves—they'd create characters, and those characters would unleash chaos, comedy, and gorgeous cringe as they interacted with the comedians and guests who weren't playing characters. It was unscripted, spontaneous, and we never had to lay out rules or guidelines. Everyone showed up, everyone got it, everyone ran with it.

That kind of genuine fun and friendship is infectious. I remember George Meyer telling me, "You ever notice how things that are inherently great never need advertising? Word of mouth always does it for the stuff that's truly great. There's a reason 'milk' and 'the family' have had to have these big ad council campaigns, and yoga didn't."

Oh wait, I don't mean to compare *Comedy Bang! Bang!* to yoga. Yoga is relaxing and calm-inducing. *CBB* was always there to keep you on your toes, laughing and screaming and scaring away the bears that were coming for your pemmican and hardtack.

Patton Oswalt

JACK QUAID

When I hear the words "Comedy Bang! Bang!," I am overwhelmed with a tremendous swell of emotion. I have appeared on the show a whopping three times. Therefore it is difficult to know where Jack Quaid ends and *Comedy Bang! Bang!* begins. The memories of podcast appearances past flood my mind like a summer storm surge. Suddenly I'm drowning, gasping for breath as I struggle to keep myself afloat amidst the sea of vehemence! Remember when I played the ghost of Dr. John trying to sue the Walt Disney corporation? That was kinda funny. The tide of reminiscence pulls me under! I sink further and further under the waves of ardor and recollection!!! Surely this is the end . . . When all of a sudden I see it. Dancing within the depths . . . Could it be? Yes it is! An email from Scott Aukerman! It reads:

Hey dude!
Any interest in doing another CBB ep? I go to Hawaii on Wednesday but it looks like I could tape it Monday if you're around. Thinking about having Tawny on as well if she's in town. If not, no worries. I've CC'd Devon here if you have any questions. Hope you're having a great week!
—Scoot

Huzzah! I am reborn! This show means a lot to me. It's been a light in times of darkness, a jacket in times of cold, and a Gatorade in times of thirsty. My three appearances have been the greatest one- to two-hour chunks of my life. Therefore I was honored to be the only person chosen to introduce this book. I am even more honored to introduce you, dear reader, to the wonderful world of . . . COMEDY BANG! BANG!

Jack Quaid

Comedy Bang Bang Book!

Today at 2:04 PM

Scott Aukerman
To: Bill Walton (anotherbrickinthewalton@email.com)

Bill -
We're doing a *Comedy Bang! Bang!* book and I was hoping you could forward the info to some of your NBA friends and see if they'd like to submit a piece for it. Barkley, Shaq, heck, even MJ himself would be awesome! But if there's anyone else you know who might be interested, feel free to forward along...

Thx
Auk
"Live. Laugh. Love. Love to Live Laughing."

Re: Comedy Bang Bang Book!

Today at 5:05 PM

Bill Walton
To: Scott Aukerman

SCOTT!!!!

I am absolutely THRILLED that you would ask me to write the foreword to your new memoirs. This is one of the great emails I've received in my whole life! From "your grandson has been born" to "Your Frank Zappa themed Teva Kickstarter has reached its goal," mine eyes have not seen an email this exciting in many moons, Scott Aukerman! Here it is below, in all its glory, my foreword to your book:

FORWARD TO THE MEMOIRS OF SCOTT AUKERMAN by NBA STAR AND BACK PROBLEMHAVER, BILL WALTON

When Scott Aukerman asked me to write the foreword to his new book, I was overcome with emotion. So blown away was I that I fell right out of my Papa John's Papasan. From Paul Harvey to Steve Harvey, Scott

Aukerman is one of history's GREAT on-mic personalities. To put it in terms kids these days can more easily relate to—Scott Aukerman : Podcasting as Adam and Eve : Earth. He was one of the first, but in lieu of a delicious apple from the tree of knowledge, Scott ate grapes from the vine of being hilarious!

But to understand the meaning of Scokerman's contributions to the game of podcasting (I say game because I, a student of the game of basketball, think of everything as a game. Even this crazy game we call LIFE), you must understand the world of podcasting. So what is podcasting? Let's break down the word, starting most notably with "pod"! And history has seen some incredible pods, from the pod I ate my snap peas out of this morning, to P.O.D., one of the great influential artists from the world of early 2000s Nu Metal. With their hit "Alive" and its vaguely religious undertones, P.O.D. came onto the Nu Metal scene with an energy unseen since Fred Durst and Buckethead—Buckethead of course one of pop culture's most notable people with something on their head—from Mr. Bean with that hilarious turkey on his noggin or the Pope, with that very respectable hat on his dome. The Pope, of course, one of history's most notable religious figures, from Gandalf to Timothy Leary, one of the leaders of the far-out LSD movement of the '60s, a religious figure in his own right. He told us to turn on, tune in, and drop out, and boy did we ever! I remember drinking a glass of acid-laced orange juice and exploring the wonders of Sequoia National Park, marveling at the overwhelming enormity of General Sherman, one of history's great Shermans! From Sherman Hemsley, who's moved on up to whatever great afterlife there is up there in the clouds or space or wherever, to *American Pie*'s the Sherminator, who's thankfully still gracing us with his earthly presence, as we all sit and pray to the great decision makers in tinsel town for at least one more journey down memory lane with Jim, Stifler, Shitbreak, Oz, Nadia, and our good friend, the Sherminator, one of the great American minators of my or anybody's lifetime—

Well folks, I hate to say to say this, but after speaking into my Siri phone's voice dictation application for the past three hours, I'm seeing that it stopped understanding me about 175 minutes ago. We've lost some brilliant observations from me, but I have neither the time nor the energy to try again. So I'll just say to you, Scott, congratulations on 45 years in the podcast game. Throw it down, one more time, big man!!!!!! And thank you for humbling me by allowing me to write the foreword to your memoirs. I'm flattered, honored, and I wish I could think of a third word to put here.

Bill "Basketball Player" Walton

COMEDY B
COMEDY B
COMEDY B
COMEDY B
COMEDY B
COMEDY B

A WORD FROM SCOTT AUKERMAN

WELCOME TO HUMANITY'S (AND THE ANIMAL KINGDOM'S) PODCAST!

On May 1, 2009, something momentous happened—and no, I'm not talking about Carol Ann Duffy being appointed British Poet Laureate! (That's a different book I'm working on. P.S. If anyone has any research regarding who Carol Ann Duffy is, or what a poet laureate is, please e-mail? Thx in advance. I am in *deep* trouble with my editor.)

No, that was the day that I stepped into a recording studio and opened a door . . .

Comedy Bang! Bang!'s famous open-door policy has been, at times, as difficult to explain as the concept of a podcast to anyone pre-*Serial*.

Basically, it's the rule, established very early on, that any lunatic who can find the studio is welcome to interrupt the show, sit down, grab a microphone, and tell us what their "deal" is.

It's been both a boon to and bane of the show during its tenure. But the one good thing I'll say about it is that it's introduced me to some fascinating individuals over the years.

What follows is an ode to them: a printed collection of character biographies, advice columns, advertisements, articles, memorandums, games, and *CBB* ephemera collected during the past decade from points around the world.

I hope you enjoy viewing it as much as I enjoyed compiling it (which, to be frank, wasn't very enjoyable at all. You try compiling things and see how much fun you have).

And what better way to begin than by giving you a peek at the most rare *CBB* document of all? In episode 103, after an unceremonious name change to our program, guest Reggie Watts supposedly "improvised" our podcast's new tune. Listeners lauded him as a musical genius, and he rode that acclaim all the way to James Corden's right.

But what people don't actually know is—he came in fully prepared, having written the song several months prior in anticipation of the change. Draft upon draft was submitted to my inbox, after which we finally settled upon what you now hear before every episode.

So, without further ado, here is Reggie's original sheet music (along with his handwritten notes) for the *Comedy Bang! Bang!* theme song . . .

Comedy Bang! Bang!
(Theme)

Words and Music by:
Reggie Watts

The last lyric is not "I'm done" but rather a vocalism close to yee haw but not.

FOURVEL'S TIPS
FOR MAKING IT THROUGH
THIS FUCKING BOOK!

"Books are hard. But, "Nunjaworryaboutit!"
You know what I mean?"

—Lil' baby orphan boy Fourvel

TIP # JUAN

Prepare, motherfucker! Whenever your lil' orphan boy wants to settle in and curl up with a good book, IT'S A WHOLE THING! What I suggest is to start by dimming the lights, putting on some soft yoga music and then go ahead and get a nice big glass of super-hot milk. Hungry as shit? I get it. Treat yourself to your favorite healthy or non-healthy snack. (I usually scrounge together some table scraps or fresh trash or a cartoon fish bone.) Then get a big, old blanket, thick as hippo skin, and throw that shit in the dryer part of the washer/dryer for like 10 minutes. Get it all hot and bothered. Then, when you are ready to curl up with a copy of *Harry Potter and the Tits of Blabbygorg*, your blanket AND your milk will be super cozy hot! Schwing!

TIP # DOOCE

DON'T READ FAST LIKE AN IDIOT! As Sir Richard Attenborough was extremely well known for saying, "Take yo time, fool! It's just a BOOK! That you paid money for!" (Unless you stole it like I did because I'm a filthy thief boy.) Don't just rush through it. What are you trying to prove and to whom? Look at all the words a bunch and think about them shits. Form opinions and then challenge said opinions. Make it an experience and you will grow exponentially.

Unless you are a speed reader. Than you have my permission to read as fast as you fuckin' can and show that shit off because that's a skill not a lot of people have. BUT, it's one that a LOT of people could EASILY obtain. So stay on your toes, speed readers! (We comin' for ya.)

TIP # TREE

#BUB !!! Always have a B.U.B. (or Back-Up Book) just in case you gotta stab a motherfucker who gets out of line and doesn't know how to act so you gotta end that person immediately and may not have time to calmly stop and think if you dropped your copy of *Happy Potter and the Tits of Blabbygorg*. But you can ELIMINATE WORRY FROM THE SITUATION if you got that B.U.B. (or Back-Up Book)!

TIP # FOR

Take the drug you like! If there is a particular drug or substance that makes you feel good in an "illegal way," why not have some of it! Then read this book all goofed up. I don't know. Might be a huge blast. It's up to you in the end.

TIP # FOIVE

If you get the sudden urge to kill, stab, or absolutely pound something into the ground . . . DON'T! Just turn the page and continue to focus on reality. The reality of the pages in your hand. They are real. This book is real. This is ALL REAL. NOT a simulation where you can do whatever you want because you feel you were dealt a bad hand in life and were forced to eat scraps and be a lil' orphan boy on the mean streets.

Where was I? Oh yeah!

Now get READIN'! (Or I'll kill you!)

Love,

Sweet Lil' Orphaned Boy, Fourvel

BOB DUCCA

BOB DUCCA is Scott Aukerman's ex-stepfather; he was married to Scott's mother, Gloria, for 6 profound months when Scott was 33. His mother still pays Bob alimony, as he is unable to work anymore because he doesn't want to. He has been diagnosed (mostly by himself) with several disorders and syndromes. Bob often lists his various ailments, allergies, disorders, as well as things not related to his health. He suffers from stage 4 hypochondria coexisting with manifestation disease. He's allergic to fluorescents, Formica, carpet, coffee, and not being friends with you.

His hobbies include crosswords and remote-controlled motor-boats that he enters in regattas. He used to be an insurance actuary. He has a double bus pass. He is working a 27-step program for divorced fathers. He's read well over one thousand self-help book jackets.

AGE:
Early Almost Deads

FAVORITE TV SHOW:
Dr. Pimple Popper

DREAM JOB:
Hospital-bed tester

FAVORITE SPORT:
Chair yoga

RELIGION:
Agnostic Pagan

BOB DUCCA'S
TO DO LIST

- Hold mirror under nose. Still breathing?
- Wrestle air mattress
- Morning pages
- De-dander bedding
- Visit rear of bakery; fight with alley kayts (sp?) for bagel dough
- Return hat to marijuana clown
- nipple butter
- Go down WebMD rabbit hole, diagnose self, panic.
- Mustache rehab
- Treat sore throat:
    - Gargle w/ salt
    - Gargle w/ pepper
    - Gargle w/ croutons
    - Make Caesar salad.
- Begin Hot Dog Water Cleanse Today!!
- Repair air mattress
- cry in fetal position
- journal re: journaling
- Do positive affirmations dummy!!

- Unruly eye brow hair battle
- Go to coffee shop, stare at couples/sigh
- Trim nail on xtra toe
- Get 5 alarm cigarette pudding recipe from MOnty
- Snort chaga mushroom powder
- Apply for helper monkey → Contact Notary?
- Apologize to upstairs neighbors re: night terrors
- Repair gas powered lap top
- Take mason jar of finger nail clippings to crafts store: Sell? Compost? Plant fingernail tree?!
- Petition Hallmark to recognize/invent National Ex step child day   Notary?
- Update resentments rolodex
- Surf Dark Web   Dennis Carla Teenagers
- Canker sore masseur

Tick Tock! Tick Tock!

Tick...STOP?!

Has your very timepiece ceased to mark the seconds, minutes, and hours that make up that most paramount of metaphysical concepts: **TIME ITSELF?**

Before descending into a state of utter hopelessness or even sheer madness, wherein reality itself seems but a gossamer façade, fugacious and effervescent, liable to dissolve away or even, at the mere blinking of thine eye, metamorphose into a dreadful plane of being most alien indeed, filled with horrors unimaginable and 'mares of the night-time variety, please visit Longo Watch Repair!

Longo Watch Repair is Tallahassee's best watch-repair store! Under the stewardship of one of North Florida's finest brothers-in-law—Mr. Desmond Longo—Longo Watch Repair shan't merely fix your watch . . . it shan keep thee quite informed of the time as well!

Upon exiting the store after dropping off your cherished chronometer for servicing, a Longo Watch Repair employee will call you every ten minutes[1] to let you know what time it is! That way, you may carry on about your day with peace of mind, unburdened.

DON'T OWN A WATCH?

You simply must purchase one! Lest you forget, even the most horrific tragedy is transmogrified into comedy simply by the addition of TIME!

Joke Corner!

Q: How did the man break his watch?

A: Well, someone told him to "beat the clock," and he took them quite literally indeed!

Mailbox Corner!

"I've heard it's illegal for women to know what time it is. Is this true?"
Tim E., Watch Hill, RI

Nay, we say, nay! In fact, women have been some of the greatest time-knowers throughout history! While it's true that in times of yore, time-knowledge was a sign of witchcraft, and many an innocent member of the fairer sex was dropped from a clock tower, we thankfully live now in a more progressive . . . oh, I'll just say it . . . TIME!

What's your favorite amount of time?

Fourteen seconds? An hour and nine minutes? Five eons?
No matter your pleasure, Longo Watch Repair is here to serve you! Do you have questions about time, that wily inexorable progression of existence? Call Longo Watch Repair, and we would be happy to spend many a moon discussing all things temporal with you!

Fun Fact

Ever heard the phrase "No time like the present"? Turns out, that's incorrect! The past is like the present, it's just a tad bit older. So the phrase should be "One time like the present: the past!" (And for those advocates of Samhain himself,[2] no, the future is not like the present, because it has way more advanced technology.)

Have other questions? Worry not! Our store accounts for several other factors!

So visit Longo Watch Repair! One visit will you have exclaiming, "hip heap hooray!"

---

[1] A wonderful amount of time!
[2] The very devil himself, who would eradicate time in all its splendorous glory, were doing so to favor him in some diabolical way!

ALIMONY TONY

TONY GIACCHIARONI, commonly known as "Alimony Tony," has been married to more than 30 women as of this publication. A true romantic, he has only ever married for love. The only thing he enjoys more than being married is paying alimony. He maintains friendships with all of his former wives. His mother invented gaseous paper, the proceeds from which have made Tony independently wealthy. He also writes and performs song parodies under the name "Weirdimony Alimony" Tony.

AGE:
60 years young

PERSONALS

ABOUT ME: I'm a happy-go-lucky sort of guy, and I love to have a good time! I enjoy writing song parodies and paying alimony to my many ex-wives. Now, I'm sure that sounds like a red flag, but let me assure you: all of my divorces were amicable and my ex-wives are friendly with me to this day. I am not a cheat or an ill-tempered man. I'm very easy to get along with and one of the reasons is: I love being married! I always loved it more than my wives. But on the upside, when I have gotten divorced, the silver lining was always there: alimony. Paying alimony fills my heart to the brim every bit as much as standing at the altar and watching my latest bride process toward me. I'm crazy for both marriage and the financial responsibilities of divorce! One of my ex-wives told me that this makes me "the total package." See for yourself if she's right!

I'm looking for someone who is looking for someone. I like to take it slow until we get married within a year (and divorced within four years).

One warning: if you are looking to get married to me just to divorce me and get the alimony? Don't bother. When you've been married as many times as I have, you can smell a scammer a mile away. I have only ever married for love, and this is why I never tell any of my dates that I'm independently wealthy until we're engaged!

Are you the (latest) one? If so, message me! If not, best of luck to you and thank you for reading my page!

ITALIAN

★ ★

Have you been injured in an accident or on purpose? Have you been standing in the kitchen with a gun and your oven goes off and scares you and you shoot yourself? Have you been baking a cake holding a knife and the cake is so good you stab yourself? You deserve compensation. We at Italiano Jones Attorneys at Law Associates of Law will FIGHT. FOR. YOU!

★ ★ ★ ABOUT ME ★ ★ ★

I am Italiano Jones. It's a family name. My family has spent generations in It'ly. Most of them have died. But before they died they FOUGHT. FOR. YOU! At 6'5", I am the tallest man in It'ly to date. Go ahead. Ask anyone in It'ly. No one will dispute. If someone disputes, HANG UP THE PHONE.

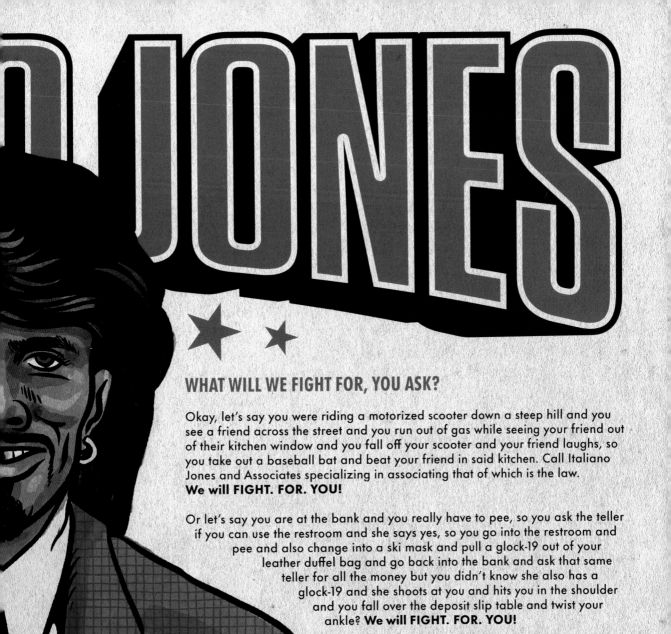

JONES

★ ★

WHAT WILL WE FIGHT FOR, YOU ASK?

Okay, let's say you were riding a motorized scooter down a steep hill and you see a friend across the street and you run out of gas while seeing your friend out of their kitchen window and you fall off your scooter and your friend laughs, so you take out a baseball bat and beat your friend in said kitchen. Call Italiano Jones and Associates specializing in associating that of which is the law. **We will FIGHT. FOR. YOU!**

Or let's say you are at the bank and you really have to pee, so you ask the teller if you can use the restroom and she says yes, so you go into the restroom and pee and also change into a ski mask and pull a glock-19 out of your leather duffel bag and go back into the bank and ask that same teller for all the money but you didn't know she also has a glock-19 and she shoots at you and hits you in the shoulder and you fall over the deposit slip table and twist your ankle? **We will FIGHT. FOR. YOU!**

Have you ever been to a swimming pool and the pool has glass at the bottom and you cut your foot while trying to drown a kid? **We can't fight for that. We are in a big legal battle with big glass.**

I have gotten my clients hundreds of dollars. I will not disclose how many hundreds. Could've been thousands of hundreds. Millions of thousands. Who knows? My clients do. Call Italiano Jones Law Attorneys and Associate Attorneys Who Love the Law. **We will FIGHT. FOR. YOU!**

Werner H.

From Westchester / LAX Los Angeles

👤 **125** Friends ⭐ **2** Reviews 📷 **0** Photos

`Elite 2022` What is Yelp Elite?

👥 Add friend
🧍 Compliment
💬 Send message
🧍 Follow Werner H.
🔖 Similar review

Werner's Profile

🔍 Profile Overview

👤 Friends

⭐ Reviews

📷 Business Photos

🏅 Compliments

🔖 Collections

Reviews

Sort by: Date

Trader Joe's
$$ · Grocery
2738 Hyperion Ave
Los Angeles, CA 90027

⭐⭐⭐⭐⭐ 4/7/2018

Madness reigns. The first challenge your soul must endure is the parking lot. You wait with your vehicle half blocking traffic, creating a perfect circular vortex of anger that encompasses the street and the entrance to the store. Once you attain access to the lot, you discover that this is a false achievement; other motorists stop and start with no apparent thought or plan--turns once begun are quickly abandoned, the drivers seemingly immune to geometry. At last a space opens up, but the price is having to enter the store. Inside, human beings scramble like beetles whose rock has been upended. Though the aisles are wide it is impossible to avoid physical contact with your fellow shoppers. It is a grotesque parody of the bazaar at Marrakech, as if dumb animals had been granted only the amount of sentience required to mock humanity. The aisles are not labeled. You must search for every item. The constant walking up and down causes a numbness that borders on profound despair. Your conscious mind registers merely annoyance, impatience. But on a cellular level, your body cries out in weariness. The fatigue you feel is a warning: millions of years of evolution trying to save you from becoming mired in the tar, from sinking into the warm blackness and ultimately being reclaimed by the earth itself.

Be sure to get the dark chocolate peanut butter cups, they are right by the register.

Was this review....

🔦 Useful 199   🙂 Funny 299   😎 Cool 109

About Werner H.

Review Votes

🔦 Useful **929**

🙂 Funny **1551**

😎 Cool **645**

Stats

👥 Followers **135**

3 Compliments

1   2   1

Location

Westchester / LAX, Los Angeles, CA

Yelping Since

September 2013

RANDY SNUTZ

RANDY SNUTZ met Scott at his favorite restaurant, D'Adomio's, where he worked refilling the ice in the urinals. (Ice is put in urinals so that, when you pee on it and it melts, you feel powerful for a few moments.) Randy believes the Keanu Reeves/Sandra Bullock film *The Lake House* is based on his life.

Randy often deplores the scandalous and duplicitous behavior of his off-and-on-again girlfriend Carissa, who has hooked up with most people in Randy's "local community." He is Catholic, a ten out of ten by coastal elite standards, and a three and a half by heartland standards. He currently drives a limousine he bought off Craigslist, and sometimes he lives in it too, when he isn't living with Carissa or crashing at his friend Mark Padavano's house. When he isn't working, or avoiding Carissa's needlessly nefarious behavior, he can usually be found hanging out with his crew—Amber Pusateri and Stuart Knox.

AGE: How dare you ask such a devious question

FAVORITE FILM: *Home Alone*

INTERESTING FACTS:

1) He used to work at a convenience store until he got fired for saying "yoink" while stealing things.

2) Randy is, in his own words, "as bi as the day is long."

3) Randy's favorite American is "The Rock 'n' Roll President," Jimmy Carter.

YAMAHA CROTCH ROCKET
(NOT TO SCALE)

SCANDALOUS DUPLICITY

Hello, my name is Randy Snutz.
This is the sordid tale of the evening of my
good friend Mark Padovano's bachelor party . . .
an evening filled with the promise of good times
and jovial debauchery, that slowly descended
into scandalous duplicity. "What happened,
Randy??" you ask, rhetorically. "You know
without even asking," I say, as I stare off into the
middle distance, shake my head from side
to side, and rip a huge cloud off of my
customized Violent Femmes vape pen.

What started as potentially one of
the greatest nights of partying in our
lives was yet again sabotaged by the
dubious machinations of my devious,
deceitful girlfriend, Carissa. Follow
along . . . *if you dare.*

8:05PM Congregating at Mark Padovano's house, my boys and I decided to start the night at Heroes & Legends Sports Bar. We all took an UberPool after leaving our souped-up Yamaha crotch rockets at home because we knew we'd be imbibing alcohol. I had five beers, two shots of SoCo and lime, and I put a Steve Miller Band song on the jukebox, so you know I was feeling good.

Then I got a text from Carissa that disrupted the festivities . . .

HEROES & LEGENDS

Food · Sports · Spirits

Where are you

i'm out for mark padovano's bachelor party, don't worry about it

I don't like your tone

this is a text, u can't read tone, u need to calm down

When are you gonna propose to me, Randy?

u better fall asleep, cuz that's only happening in ur dreams

Unbelievable

this is scandalous behavior

9:13PM Then my boys and I were off to O'Charley's Pub to meet up with Todd Janisevic and his cousins who own a vape store in Lockport called Strictly Vaping, and it was dope as hell. I had four beers, three shots of Jäger, and then we went in the alley outside and did a bunch of whip-its. We were also joined by the unsavory characters known as Seamus Governale and Ron Prola. I distinctly recall someone saying, "Uh-oh, the night has taken a turn for the worst." But it was said ironically, as these fellas are always a good time.

Then I checked my phone, and lo and behold, I had gotten another text from Carissa.

Danielle said she saw you at O'Charleys

danielle's a stone cold liar, and u know it

She's my best friend

then u associate with known fabricators

How dare you say that about Danielle

i'll say whatever i want. i'm the muffin man. i'm 8 feet tall. see? u can't stop me

Seriously, Randy. We've been dating for 8 years. Every one of your friends is engaged or married. You need to propose or we're over.

this is duplicitous behavior

Where are you right now? Alyssa said you bought whip-its from her brother

alyssa is downright deceitful, and cannot be trusted

She's my cousin on my mom's side, why would you say that

why would u bring ur mother into this

Because I trust her

people trust the government, and look how that's turning out

10:37PM Then my boys and I were off to Thirty Buck to meet up with Freddy Vrakas and his high school buddies from Oswego, and it was off the chain. I had seven beers, four shots of Beefeater, a couple cigarettes, and then Andrew Szopinski rolled up in the eight-passenger van he uses as a delivery vehicle for the flower shop Designs by Diedre, so we climbed in and did even more whip-its.

I checked my phone again and, wouldn't you know, I had gotten another text from Carissa . . .

I'm dead serious, Randy. Your ass is dumped for good if you don't propose tonight.

this is devious as hell

12:07AM Then my boys and I were off to Jameson's Pub to meet up with Nick DiSantonio and his frat brothers from Indiana University-Evansville, and it was hella crazy. I had eight beers, five shots of sour apple Pucker, a Swisher Sweets cigar, and then we watched six women in their 50s buy cocaine from my old high school teacher. I was at the peak of my buzz when we decided to change locations again. But when we stepped back into the night to get into our UberPool, there in the parking lot waiting for us, flanked by Alyssa Malleris and Danielle Sefcic, was none other than the duplicitous provocateur known as . . . Carissa. My friends, I've come to know shock and awe during this tumultuous relationship, but in that moment even I was surprised enough to let out an audible "DAFUQ?!?"

"I'm serious, Randy. If you don't propose tonight, we're through. I'll throw your stuff out on the front lawn and set it on fire."

Now, I have some pretty cool stuff, so that definitely got my attention. But then I got to thinking . . . over the course of seven or eight years, despite all the dastardly drama, Carissa and I have had some good times. Our first date together at the Wisconsin Dells . . . late nights on the couch binge-watching *House Hunters International* . . . seeing Jay Cutler at a bar in downtown Milwaukee and both of us telling him how much he fucking sucks . . . The flood of memories made me smile, and I knew what I had to do. Your boy Randy got down on one knee. Carissa put her hands up over her mouth and started getting emotional, while her two best friends put their hands on her shoulders. I collected myself and started my speech . . .

SNUTZ'S BUDZ

Randy Snutz's best friends, Stu and Amber, take their texts off the main thread to discuss their high school reunion.

BEFORE:

Stuzzzzz! U up? I know it's late but I figured u were prolly up playin WOW.

2:36 AM

Ya, I'm raiding with my Tauren Druid (had to start back at lvl 1 after I spilled marshmallow fluff on my gaming pc and ants ate it to hell).

2:37 AM

Smdh! You get the evite for the reunion? Wut u gonna wear? I'll prolly keep my nails short jic I gotta fight. I'm thinkin I'll do my Lash Shed tee with booty shorts and my Etnies.

2:39 AM

Umm ... thinking of wearing the crew shirt from that production of into the woods that they fired me off of Bc I told Parker he was too pitchy to sing giants in the sky.

2:43 AM

Honestly I can't even hate on Parker, cuz giants in the sky is a beast... like have a chorus!

2:43 AM

he also couldnt even stay on tempo for Your Fault, I'm glad his dad made him join the marines. For clothse, u thinking the conservative bootie shorts or the ones that show cheek?

The cheeky booty shorts with the cowboy fringe just in case Principle Benifistanchiano is there. Dude is always doing a hard stare at my ass.

2:45 AM

I'm sorry you have to deal with men like that, it really pisses me off as an anti-sexist. LMK if I can do anything

2:45 AM

Sorry for the late response but Gerald's ass started crying when I told him he couldn't be my plus one for this reunion. This fool flooded his transition lenses.

3:45 AM

Lolll that sucks. Why do old guys cry so much?

3:48 AM

Dogg when you get the answer please let a bitch know. A bitch= me

3:50 AM

THURSDAY:

I got the supplies for Saturday- but the molly was like way more than I thought. I'll divide that shit up and send out the splitwise. Also did you still want the poppers?

1:18 PM

Yes 2 poppers, gonna try to sell them to the Yearbook students.

1:22 PM

Btw nbd but don't you still owe me $8 from bowling? Maybe just take that out of what i owe 4 molly

SATURDAY: DAY OF THE REUNION

Bad news Stu-I'm gonna be late. The fucking limo never showed up. Snutzoids should be there tho. Gotta convince Gerald to let me borrow his Jetta.

7:22 PM

Amber! This is fucked I'm already here cuz my digital watch is on military time and i totally thought 1800 hours was 8pm. I've got no one to talk to.

7:25 PM

Everyone keeps asking if I still talk to Nina Wallach. Of course not! She gave our RA an above the jeaner handy at college orientation while i was signing up for a credit card so that SHE could get a free hoodie!!!!

7:25 PM

If it's any consolation, you weren't the only one that got got by Nina. Chris Belfrane said he signed up for the ROTC just to get a free koosh ball for Nina and she didn't even say thank you.

7:30 PM

Want me to just come pick u up? I'm only 5 drinks ddeepp

7:30 PM

Nah Gerald is gonna drive me. I said he could drive us all home. He's gonna wait in the Little Caesar's parking lot. He's allowed to get some crazy bread but that's IT!

7:35 AM

Okay hurry up, Randy lost his notes for the speech they asked him to do and he's thinking of just singing Black Hole Sun. we gotta prep him with lyrics and whatnot.

7:40 PM

Where are y'all at? I'm in the parking lot

We're right by the bathroom on the east side of campus.

8:32 PM

The one where I slapped Mr. Delgado the first time?

8:32 PM

No the one where we saw Amanda Tiegarden trying to turn her normal granny panties into a thong

8:32 PM

Oh yeah the one by where Kevin Jansen allegedly choked on his own dick? Uhhhh...I've seen that dick and let's just say, you'd have to stack like three of Kevin's dicks to even get your eyes misty. But frfr we should pour one out for Kevie tonight.

8:32 PM

RIP

8:32 PM

Oh shit, Marky P just told me Carissa showed up. Do NOT tell her about the prank. We've been working too hard for this to get fucked up.

8:50 PM

Shit I'm trying but she keeps making really direct eye contact with me and slowly licking the rim of her drink. I think it's a spicy marg cuz her eyes are really watering.

9:02 PM

All set up at the south staircase for the prank. Please tell me you got the balloons?

9:10 PM

Dude the water balloon busted in my bag and now my whole knapsack smells like p8iss. Whole prank is fucjed

9:18 PM

Did you end up hooking up with Tracey or nah?

Nah man, I guess Anna Colowsky told her I don't like kissing and she told me that weirded her out. Wtf !?!

12:08 PM

WUT? I HATE BITCHES LIKE THIS! Jealous ass. She did tell me that one time you used the word "suss" and it gave her the ick. Don't worry-I told everyone her pussy stank and she started crying. I gotchu Stu.

Okay that's my dawg, thanks amber. Always got my back! Thinking of going to Ross dress for less and stealing some Kenneth Cole reaction cologne, Derek said their anti theft system is down wanna come?

12:10 PM

Can't—i got court. But if you see any men's size 5 Merrell's will you grab some for Gerald? He needs new water shoes.

No water shoes but they have knock-off Serbian Teva's for $24. If he doesn't want them I'll donate to chairidy. Man last night was a blur, I gotta stop pre gaming alone.

1:00 PM

I can't believe I gotta go to court again. At least I can get my one-hitter that I hid behind a bush last time I was there.

1:43 PM

Hey sorry about court, wish I could give you a ride but my mom's sister literally just noticed that I taped over the VHS of her wedding with that short film we made for Spanish extra credit in like 03. It's full melt down over here. It's like, Aunt Janice, no offense but having the VHS isn't gonna make Uncle Dennis UNcheat on you. Lo siento.

1:44 PM

THE CALVINS TRIPLETS

THE CALVINS TRIPLETS are prize horse-fighting promoters and owners of the Calvins Triplets Family Bee Honey Taffy Farm and Horse Fighting Ranch and Hall of Fame.

The Calvins Twins (Bever and Chico) were born at the same time. Their mother was killed by a horse when she got in the way of a horse fight when she tried to save her favorite horse. Meanwhile, Brisby had a horse stadium right next to the airport in Tampa. Brisby was originally the nemesis of the Calvins Twins and challenged them to a horse off but when they discovered both of their mothers died in the same horse fight, he joined the Twins to form the Calvins Triplets.

Chico represents four horses and Bever represents three. They host fights at sunrise and twilight. They get the horses to start fighting by whispering to each horse something about the other horse like, "Listen, Cinnamon, Winsbyamile says your mane looks stupid." The Calvins Triplets have attended a horse funeral each week for the last 20 years.

HORSE-FIGHTING FACTS:

Horse-fighting is localized to five or six states so it is not considered an American sport. To qualify as an American sport, it would need to be practiced in 25 states. One in 7,000 horses comes out punching and those are fighting horses. The horses punch each other, they don't bite or kick each other. They fight clean— they roundhouse, upper cuttin', jabbin', hookin', feet just hoofin', comin' in lookin'. The horses fight to the death.

FAVORITE MOTTO:

"Ya gotta laugh."

NAMES:
Bever Hopox, Chico Hands, and Bisby St. Hancock or Horsecock (The Calvins Triplets)

DIRECTIONS TO CTFBHTFHFR:

Take the 605 North to the 606, keep on going to the 607, until it turns into an interstate— Calvins Boulevard—and you're in the right place because you're about to get onto the 608. Calvins Boulevard is the only roundabout exit.

HORSES IN THE CALVINS' STABLE:

Cinnamon, Old Uh Old Uh, Buttercup, Winsbyamile, Umbridge, and Petunia.

INTERESTING FACTS:

1) Bever used to be a jockey, Chico went to law school, and Bisby was a horse breeder.

2) Bever and Chico are 4'9" tall with lifts and Bisby is 7'9" in flats.

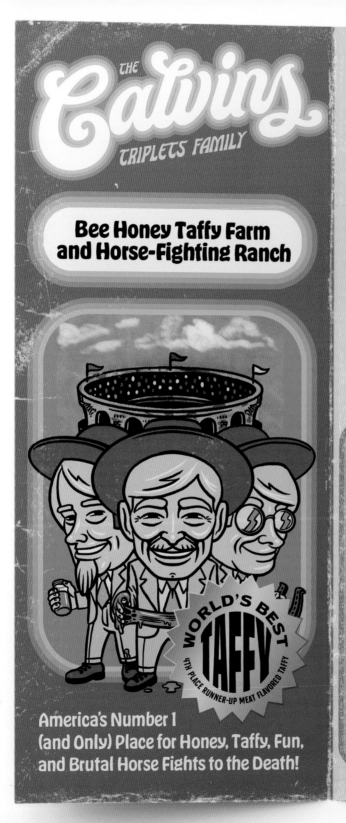

THE Calvins TRIPLETS FAMILY

Bee Honey Taffy Farm and Horse-Fighting Ranch

WORLD'S BEST TAFFY
4TH PLACE RUNNER-UP MEAT FLAVORED TAFFY

America's Number 1 (and Only) Place for Honey, Taffy, Fun, and Brutal Horse Fights to the Death!

Little Bit 'Bout Dis Here Place

Founded in 1862 as a neutral hiding place for Civil War deserters, Calvins Family Bee Honey Taffy Farm and Horse-Fighting Ranch is the longest-running competitive animal sports and confectionary establishment in the Western Hemisphere. As third-generation owners, the Calvins Triplets, Bever, Chico, and Bisby, take great pride in offering you and your loved ones a top-shelf experience of fun, flavors, fighting, and quite frankly, lessons about life. Spend your day by purchasing a jar of honey, stuffing your pockets with pork chop–flavored taffy, and sit back and watch two phenomenal equine specimens beat each other until one of them can't beat no more. Then, should the mood strike you, pay your respects to the newly deceased fightin' horse during one of our meaningful, emotional, efficient, and honestly hilarious burial services immediately after the fight.

After all, ya gotta laugh!

★ WHAT'S THERE ALL TO DO? ★

Cheer on a Horse Fight! | Attend a Horse Burial!

Take a Picture in Front of America's Largest Horse Corpse Freezer!

Tour Our Hall of Fame Horse-Birth Museum!

Warm Up by Our House-Sized Horse Corpse Thawing Microwave!

Sample Over 70 Flavors of Taffy Made Fresh in Our Taffy Factory

Try Your Luck at Our "Gotta Laugh Gambling Center"

Meander Through the Insemination Zone!

Fill Up at Our Lip-Smackin', Tic-Tackin', Chip-Crackin', Snack-Shack(in')

Let the Kids Have a Blast on the Bumper Horses

Ride the World's Fastest Horse Coaster, Constructed with Real Horse Bones (Currently Closed While Under Investigation)

Tickets to a Horse Fight $7
Entry to the Farm $12
Parking $87

Season Pass

Come anytime! Purchasers must return to CTFBHTFHFR within one calendar year. (If a second visit is not accomplished, Season Pass becomes null and void and purchaser becomes legally indebted to The Calvins Triplets for no less than $2,000.)

$8

3 different packages

The Peeper (Entry for up to 3 horse fights) **$15**

The Grazer (Entry for up to 5 horse fights and a bucket of taffy) **$45**

The Stampeder (All the horse fights you can take and all the taffy you can eat while standing; upon consumption of the first piece of taffy, purchaser must remain on their feet for the "all you can eat" uses to remain valid. If purchaser sits or crouches, taffy consumption becomes null and void.) **$103.62**

HONEY ORDER FORM

HONEY	JAR	DRINKING HORN	BUCKET	BATHTUB
Thin Honey	$5	$12	$25	$199
Medium Honey	$6	$13	$26	$198
Thick Honey	$7	$14	$27	$192
Extra-Thick Honey	$8.72	$16.31	$29.04	$166.60
Spicy Honey	$9.99	$19.99	$39.99	$99.99
Gross Honey	$2	$1	$0.25	- $4

TAFFY ORDER FORM

"IT'S NOT BAD, IT'S GOOD"

TAFFY FLAVOR	6 PIECES	24 PIECES	50 PIECES	BATHTUB
Pork Chop	$2.50	$10	$20	$100
Water	$3	$12	$24	$150
Hoisin Sauce	$3	$12	$24	$150
Branch	$3	$12	$24	$150
Raisin Branch Cranch	$3	$12	$24	$150
Branch Davidians	$3	$12	$24	$150
Bruce Vilanch	$3	$12	$24	$150
Cherry	$9	$50	$150	$5,200
Blanche Dubois	$3	$12	$24	$150
Ranch	$3	$12	$24	$150
Thousand Island	$3	$12	$24	$150
4 Cheese	$4	$16	$40	$300
Stable Scoopins	$1.50	$10	$15	$10
Tangy	$3	$12	$24	$150
Glass	$3	$12	$24	$150
Tangy Glass	$3	$12	$24	$150
Horse "Radish"	$3	$12	$24	$150
Purple	$3	$12	$24	$150
Hoof	$5	$20	$60	$500

Horse Fight and Funeral Schedule

6:03am - Break of Dawn Fight (1A):
Randy the Horse [Age: 6, Height: 16 hands, Weight: 1,320lbs]
vs. Cinnamon [Age: 5, Height: 15.5 hands, Weight: 1,280lbs]
~ 6:25am - Funeral for the Loser of Horse Fight 1A

6:32am - Breakfast Chaser Fight (2A):
Petunia [Age: 8, Height: 15.25 hands, Weight: 1,265lbs]
vs. The Horse with No Name [Age 4: Height: 15 hands, Weight: 1,255lbs]
~ 6:57am - Funeral for the Loser of Horse Fight 2A

7:04am - Sunrise Scramble Fight (3A):
Cynergy [Age: 3, Height: 15.5 hands, Weight: 1,305lbs]
vs. Good Company [Age: 2, Height: 15 hands, Weight: 1,295lbs]
~ 7:26am - Funeral for the Loser of Horse Fight 3A

7:33am - Mimosa Madness Fight (4A):
Scottly [Age: 6, Height: 15.75 hands, Weight: 1,333lbs]
vs. Hot Tamales [Age: 4, Height: 16 hands, Weight: 1,340lbs]
~ 7:56am - Funeral for the Loser of Horse Fight 4A

8:03 am - Morning Paper Headline Fight (5A):
Motts Grape Apple Juice [Age: 4, Height: 15 hands, Weight: 1,257lbs]
vs. Sugar Cube Leonard [Age: 6, Height: 15.25 hands, Weight:1,262lbs]
~ 8:27am - Funeral for the Loser of Horse Fight 5A

8:34am - Stretch Around the Garden Fight (6A):
Floyd Neighweather [Age: 5, Height: 15.5 hands, Weight: 1,310lbs]
vs. A Horse Named Umbrage [Age: 5, Height: 15.5 hands, Weight: 1,340lbs]
~ 8:56am - Funeral for the Loser of Horse Fight 6A

9:03am - Get Up, Lazyhead Fight (7A):
Trimax [Age: 4, Height: 16 hands, Weight: 1,380lbs]
vs. Marinka [Age: 2, Height: 15.75 hands, Weight: 1,395lbs]
~ 9:28am - Funeral for the Loser of Horse Fight 7A

9:35am - Early Chores Championship Fight (8A):
Oscar De La Horsa [Age: 5, Height: 14.5 hands, Weight: 1,255lbs]
vs. Sylvester Stallion [Age: 7, Height: 14.25 hands, Weight: 1,260lbs]
~ 9:58am - Funeral for the Loser of Horse Fight 8A

10:05am - Midmorning Mayhem Fight (9A):
Pony Danza [Age: 2, Height: 13.5 hands, Weight: 1,170lbs]
vs. Marvelous Marvin Nagler [Age: 2, Height: 13.25 hands, Weight: 1,152lbs]
~ 10:29am - Funeral for the Loser of Horse Fight 9A

10:36am - Sun Salutations Fight (10A):
Million Dollar Foal [Age: 3, Height: 14 hands, Weight: 1,220lbs]
vs. Apollo Feedbag [Age: 4, Height: 14.25 hands, Weight: 1,230lbs]
~ 11:01am - Funeral for the Loser of Horse Fight 10A

11:08am - Brunch Brawl Fight (11A):
Soda Clopinski [Age: 4, Height: 14.5 hands, Weight: 1,210lbs]
vs. Juan Flamencolt [Age: 3, Height: 14.25 hands, Weight: 1,200lbs]
~ 11:30am - Funeral for the Loser of Horse Fight 11A

11:37am - Breakfast Chaser Fight (12A):
Filly Pep [Age: 3, Height: 15 hands, Weight: 1,215lbs]
vs. Sugar Cube Robinson [Age: 4, Height: 14.75 hands, Weight: 1,205lbs]
~ 11:59am - Funeral for the Loser of Horse Fight 12A

12:06pm - High Noon Fight (13A):
Whinny Pacquiao [Age: 5, Height: 15.75 hands, Weight: 1,335lbs]
vs. Pony Liston [Age: 4, Height: 15.5 hands, Weight: 1,345lbs]
~ 12:29pm - Funeral for the Loser of Horse Fight 13A

12:36pm - Lunch Crunch Fight (14A):
Clubber Mustang [Age: 4, Height: 16 hands, Weight: 1,380lbs]
vs. Evander Hayfield [Age: 5, Height: 16.25 hands, Weight: 1,370lbs]
~ 12:57pm - Funeral for the Loser of Horse Fight 14A

1:04pm - Siesta Fight (15A):
Appaloosa Creed [Age: 5, Height: 16.5 hands, Weight: 1,410lbs]
vs. Joe Grazier [Age: 6, Height: 16.25 hands, Weight: 1,405lbs]
~ 1:25pm - Funeral for the Loser of Horse Fight 15A

1:32pm - Backstretch Fight (16A):
Jake LaTrot-ta [Age: 5, Height: 15.5 hands, Weight: 1,370lbs]
vs. Rocky Horseiano [Age: 4, Height: 15.5 hands, Weight: 1,365lbs]
~ 1:54pm - Funeral for the Loser of Horse Fight 16A

2:01pm - Afternoon Assault Fight (17A):
George Forehorse [Age: 3, Height: 16.75 hands, Weight: 1,390lbs]
vs. Cassius Clydesdale [Age: 3, Height: 16.5 hands, Weight: 1,395lbs]
~ 2:23pm - Funeral for the Loser of Horse Fight 17A

2:30pm - Midafternoon Mild Fight (18A):
Horse Grant [Age: 4, Height: 15.5 hands, Weight: 1,355lbs]
vs. Horseshoelio Cesar Chavez [Age: 3, Height: 15.25 hands, Weight: 1,360
~ 2:52pm - Funeral for the Loser of Horse Fight 18A

2:59pm - School's Out Fight (19A):
Julio Seabiscuit Chavez [Age: 4, Height: 15 hands, Weight: 1,270lbs]
vs. Sonny Lippizaner [Age: 3, Height: 15 hands, Weight: 1,252lbs]
~ 3:21pm - Funeral for the Loser of Horse Fight 19A

3:28pm - First Half Finale Fight (20A):
Conner Horsegregor [Age: 3, Height: 14.5 hands, Weight: 1,210lbs]
vs. Bastian [Age: 4, Height: 14.25 hands, Weight: 1,200lbs]
~ 3:50pm - Funeral for the Loser of Horse Fight 20A

4pm INTERMISSION

Horse Fight and Funeral Schedule

June 18, 1993
Evening and
Night Sessions

:30pm - Beginning of the End Fight (1B):
onda Horsey [Age: 3, Height: 14 hands, Weight: 1,150lbs]
s. Winner of Horse Fight 1A
~ 4:52pm - Funeral for the Loser of Horse Fight 1B

:59pm - Sun Sinking Fight (2B):
nderson Hi-Yo Silva [Age: 6, Height: 15 hands, Weight: 1,255lbs]
s. Winner of Horse Fight 2A
~ 5:21pm - Funeral for the Loser of Horse Fight 2B

:28pm - Cocktail Hour Fight (3B):
uck Liddel [Age: 4, Height: 15.25 hands, Weight: 1,315lbs]
s. Winner of Horse Fight 3A
~ 5:50pm - Funeral for the Loser of Horse Fight 3B

:57pm - Sunset Fight (4B):
andy Trotture [Age: 5, Height: 15.5 hands, Weight: 1,325lbs]
s. Winner of Horse Fight 4A
~ 6:18pm - Funeral for the Loser of Horse Fight 4B

:25pm - Twilight Horse Fight (5B):
orse Gracie [Age: 3, Height: 15.25 hands, Weight: 1,240lbs]
s. Winner of Horse Fight 5A
~ 6:47pm - Funeral for the Loser of Horse Fight 5B

:54pm - Super Supper Fight (6B):
arol Sel O'Pain [Age: 3, Height: 13 hands, Weight: 1,010lbs]
s. Winner of Horse Fight 6A
~ 7:16pm - Funeral for the Loser of Horse Fight 6B

:23pm - Dinner Duke-Out Fight (7B):
ack Beaty [Age: 3, Height: 15.75 hands, Weight: 1,365lbs]
s. Winner of Horse Fight 7A
~ 7:45pm - Funeral for the Loser of Horse Fight 7B

:52pm - Dessert of Destruction Fight (8B):
hadowfax-You-Up [Age: 4, Height: 14.75 hands, Weight: 1,260lbs]
s. Winner of Horse Fight 8A
~ 8:15pm - Funeral for the Loser of Horse Fight 8B

:22pm - Bedtime Bash Fight (9B):
Mr. Dead [Age: 4, Height: 14 hands, Weight: 1,180lbs]
s. Winner of Horse Fight 9A
~ 8:44pm - Funeral for the Loser of Horse Fight 9B

:51pm - Night Cap Fight (10B):
ltimate Man'O Warrior [Age: 5, Height: 14.5 hands, Weight: 1,250lbs]
s. Winner of Horse Fight 10A
~ 9:13pm - Funeral for the Loser of Horse Fight 10B

9:20pm - Mommy-Daddy Time Fight (11B):
Winner of Horse Fight 1B vs. Winner of Horse Fight 2B
~ 9:42pm - Funeral for the Loser of Horse Fight 11B

9:49pm - Gettin' Ready to Go Out Fight (12B):
Winner of Horse Fight 3B vs Winner of Horse Fight 4B
~ 10:10pm - Funeral for the Loser of Horse Fight 12B

10:17pm - StarGazers Fight (13B):
Winner of Horse Fight 5B vs Winner of Horse Fight 6B
~ 10:39pm - Funeral for the Loser of Horse Fight 13B

10:47pm - Gettin' Late Fight (14B):
Winner of Horse Fight 7B vs Winner of Horse Fight 8B
~ 11:00pm - Funeral for the Loser of Horse Fight 14B

11:07pm - One More at the Bar Fight (15B):
Winner of Horse Fight 9B vs Winner of Horse Fight 10B
~ 11:29pm - Funeral for the Loser of Horse Fight 15B

11:36pm - Last of the Day Fight (16B):
Winner of Horse Fight 11B vs Winner of Horse Fight 12B
~ 11:57pm - Funeral for the Loser of Horse Fight 16B

12:04am - Midnight Snack Fight (17B):
Winner of Horse Fight 13B vs Winner of Horse Fight 14B
~ 12:26am - Funeral for the Loser of Horse Fight 17B

12:33am - Ultimate Penultimate Fight (18B):
Winner of Horse Fight 15B vs Winner of Horse Fight 16B
~ 12:55am - Funeral for the Loser of Horse Fight 18B

2:00am - Championship Fight (Last Fight of the Day):
Winner of Horse Fight 17B vs Winner of Horse Fight 18B

****The Champion of the
Horse Fight of the Day
Wins a Day off!
[Then shuffled into
the schedule of the
following day.]**

53

Merch and Snack Stand Menu

GRUB

Calvins Farm Fresh Bee Honey Taffy Apple - $4

Calvins Farm Fresh Bee Honey Taffy Banana - $4

Calvins Farm Fresh Bee Honey Taffy Steak - $18

Bever's Big Bucket of Baked Beans - $5

Hancocko's Tacos - $2.50 ea

Chico's Hand Pies - $3

Horse Ear (like an elephant ear but horse!) - $6

Hopox Bagel & Lox - $6.50

Cheeseburger (original recipe from Cheeseburg, Germany) - $8

Chico's Chorizo - $7

Road Applesauce - $3

BEVER-AGES

Cinnamon Soda - $3

Horsechata - $3.50

Hot Melted-Down Taffy $0.75

Bever Beer - $5

Bisby Fizz - $7

Hopox Honey Wine - $9

Hot Chicolate - $4.50

Marinka's Moscow Mule - $9

Mama's Juice - $5

MERCH(ANDISE)

Big Ruffley Britches (hand sewn with seamin' by Chico) - $65

Sleeping Box
Cedar - $400
Oak - $600
Cardboard - $2

Chico's Hands-On Constitutional Law Workbook - $60

Bisby's Frisbees - $10

Nose Clothespin - $1

ManuRemover™ Shit Scraper for Shoes - $8

10 Pack ManuRemover™ Wet Wipes - $6

ManuRemover™ Turd Spatula - $9

50-Pound Bag of Manure - $35

Person-Hiding Trenchcoat - $120

Leftover Loose Microwave Screws - $0.15

KID'S ACTIVITIES

Help the "Calvins Happy Horse Howlers" finish the song! Fill in the blanks with the correct lyrics!

WHAT A DAY FOR A GOOD TIME (AKA Theme to the Calvins Family Bee Honey Taffy Farm and Horse-Fighting Ranch Taffy Demon Stoppin' Flip Floppin' Fab Fivin' Staying Alivin' Adele Dazeemsizin' Colt 45in' Hullabaloo Telethon Extravaganza)

DEE DA _____ DO __ LOODLE DEE ____ DO DO

___ DA _____ -DO DO DO DO

DID _ LITTLE DEE ____ DEE

DID A LOODLE ____ DEE ___

DEED A LUDDLE ____ DO DO DOO ____ DOO

DOOD A _____ DOO-DA __ DOO DO DO __

__ A LEEDLE ____ DEE ____ DEE

DEET DA ___ DOO DOO-DA ____ DO DO __ DOO DOO DOO

__ LOODLE ____ DO DO LIDLE _____ DA-LEE

DE DEE ____ DO DOO DOO ____

DO LITTLE __ DO ___ DOP ___

___ A LITTLE ____ DEE ___

DID A _____ DEE ___ DEE

___ DA ____ DO DA LOODLE ___ DOO DO ____

___ DA LIDDLE-DO ___ ___

Connect the Dots

GROSS HONEY

REVIEWS

"I was looking for a place to take my family during our spring break and we decided against this."
The Cameron Family

"Oh, no thanks. I don't want to talk. Will you get that thing out of my face? I know you're recording, please don't. What binding contract? Well, I didn't see it. I'm holding it? That doesn't matter. It does? What will it take to get you to leave me alone? My review? Of here? It's fine."
Peggy Darftmon, mother of 5, AL

"For Christmas I really wanted a horsey. My mommy brought me here to see all the horsies. I don't want a horsey anymore."
Little Wendy Wickles, age 5, AZ

"Excuse me, do you know how I get back on the 607? What is this place? What the . . . what the heck is going on here? "
Unnamed male motorist, mid-30s

"I splurged for the cherry-flavored taffy. It was very similar to cherry Starbursts. I like cherry Starbursts. But the pink ones are my favorite."
Berg Heppleple

"Pacino is ELECTRIC! I applaud Brian De Palma's chaotic storytelling and somehow dig violence."
Danny Meech, Time Magazine

"We bought the season pass, stayed at a nearby motel, and came back for a few minutes the next morning. So that made it worth it. Financially."
The Spweak Family, CO

"Even with the taffy factory and all the honey hives, the smell of blood was by far the most overwhelming. Maybe because it's horse blood? Maybe it's thicker, so it smells stronger? I dunno. The Insemination Zone was fun."
Chank Yilgeroo, VT

"The Big Ol' Tin of taffy was probably too much. I way underestimated how much space a trillion tons of taffy takes up."
William Katt (the guy from the Greatest American Hero I think)

We are here

FIRST TAFFY ORDER IS **FREE!**

Get your next six orders free!!!*

*shipping charges not included ($140 to $170)

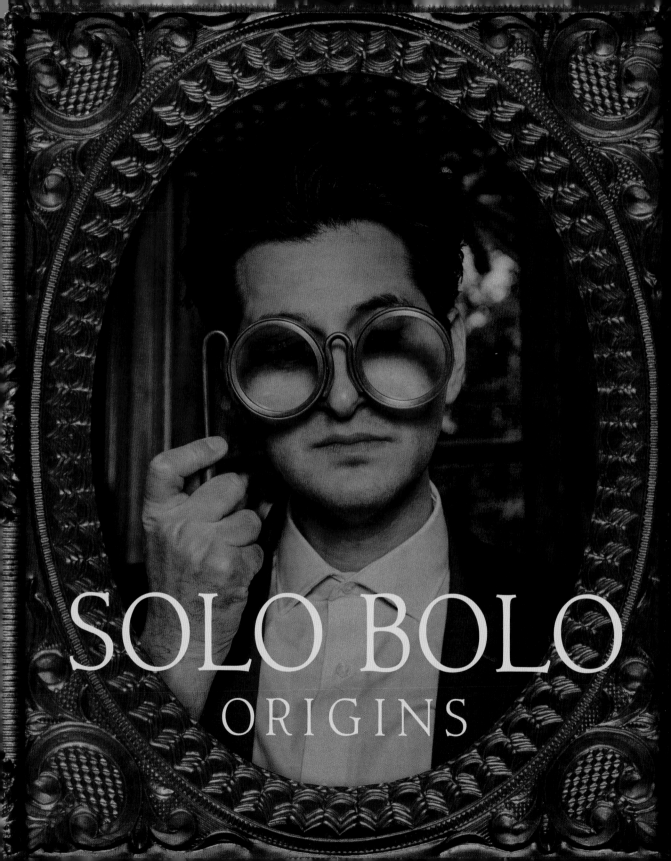

You may have heard the whispers from the branches of the Great Basin bristlecone. Or the murmurs from the mighty waves of Nazaré. You may have even believed their tales. Sadly, they are false. Stories concocted to distract from the bitter truth. But today... within the recycled (unsure if it's recycled) pages of this book, your eyes will be opened. For today, you will learn the origin of the Solo Bolo.

(PHOTO OF VERY SCARY LIGHTNING. IF YOU DON'T HAVE A PHOTO PLEASE DON'T PRINT THESE DESCRIPTION WORDS IN THE BOOK, IT WOULD BE EMBARRASSING FOR ME.)

It was raining. So hard that when Scott walked down the street, people couldn't tell he had peed his pants. I mean of course if you got close enough, you could smell it. But his speedy pace made it near-impossible to detect.

(PHOTO OF SCOTT PISSING HIS PANTS. CAN WE PUT A GIF IN THE BOOK? SEEMS DIFFICULT, BUT THAT WOULD BE GOOD BECAUSE IT'S HIM PISSING HIS PANTS OVER AND OVER AGAIN. ALSO, IF YOU CAN'T PRINT THE GIF, DON'T POST THESE WORDS IN THE BOOK, IT WOULD BE MORTIFYING.)

He called me on his cellular phone. "Benny," he said. "Benny, I'm bored of all these people in the room when I'm doing my comedic podcast. I wish someone would kill them so it could just be me and you." "Hahaha," I replied. But there was no hahaha in return. "Are you serious?" I asked, my heart rate increasing. Scott: "Who knows anymore." He hung up.

That day I was to go into Comedy Bang! Bang! and record with Scott and the world-famous comedy duo Turnip Jolly and Mandy Umbrella. If you haven't heard their names before... you'll soon find out why.

My landline phone rings. Scott: "I'm at the studio. Feels like there is not enough air for four people here. Feels more like a two-person amount of oxygen in the room today." I was confused. Scott had never mentioned the amount of air in the recording studio before. Benny: "OK, do you want to change rooms?" Scott: "It would be easier if Turnip and Mandy were dead to be honest." Benny: "Hahaha." No hahaha back. Benny: "Hey, man, I'm not going to kill anyone, let alone the funniest two-person banana juggling act in the world." Scott: "I guess I'll have to do it myself. Just kidding." He said it all so quickly, I could barely make it out.

I get to the recording studio. Scott is by himself. Covered in blood. Eating two bananas. Scott: "You ready to record?" Benny: "Where are they?" Scott: "Where are who?" Benny: "Scott, where are Jolly and Umbrella?" Scott: "They couldn't make it." The blood dripped down his bananas. Scott: "Come on, man, it's time to record." Benny: "With only one guest?" Scott: "Yeah, the way it was meant to be done. One guest. Solo Bolo." Ben: "I don't feel comfor—" Scott: "SIT THE FUCK DOWN AND MAKE THE WORLD LAUGH!" I sat... while he pissed his pants. There was no rain to hide it. His smirk... I'll never forget that tiny smirk he threw my way while the urine dribbled down his leg. With blood on his face and piss on his calves, Scott pressed RECORD and the rest is history.

(PLACE A PHOTO OF TURNIP JOLLY AND MANDY UMBRELLA HERE PLEASE. AND DON'T USE THEIR TWO-PERSON HEADSHOT WHERE THEY ARE JUGGLING PEELED BANANAS. SEEMS IN POOR TASTE FOR AN IN MEMORIAM PHOTO. IF YOU CAN'T FIND A PHOTO OF THEM, DON'T POST THIS TEXT IN THE BOOK, IT WOULD BE HUMILIATING.)

ENTERTAINMENT REVIEW

Half a Bubble Off Plumb

On Thursday, I had the great misfortune of attending one of the most horrifically irresponsible attempts at children's entertainment I have ever seen in a long career of reviewing the arts.

Big Chunky Bubbles, real name Petey Amin, is an American bubble artist (and please know I use the word "artist" solely as an occupational descriptor and not as a term of respect). He spent a good five to seven minutes at the beginning of his "performance" telling the children to be quiet and pay attention, using broken French and German. When the children would not respond in a manner he deemed timely, Mr. Bubbles turned his back to his audience of six-year-olds and pouted, "Now you get the Miles Davis treatment."

He then presumably made some bubbles from a hot tureen of New England clam chowder. I say "presumably" as I only caught the merest glimpse of steaming bubbles rising just above Mr. Bubbles's head before they popped and sprayed him with a scalding soup, causing him to swear in a fashion not unlike that of a cartoon dog.

The foul language served as a high point of Mr. Bubbles's set. Hearing the laughter of the children, the gentleman turned around to face his audience, grumbling, "Oh, look who's paying attention now!" He then told the children they should feel very grateful to be seeing what would come next, a special treat just for the children of Montreal, even though they "don't deserve any special treats after their rude and immature attitudes."

At this point Mr. Bubbles removed the cover from a sauce-pan, a great cloud of steam rising up from its contents, and momentarily blinding him. More cartoon cursing briefly ensued. When he regained what passed for his composure, Mr. Bubbles announced that he would now, for the first time, make bubbles from poutine gravy.

When the children rightfully seemed underwhelmed, Mr. Bubbles lectured them on the laborious process of extracting the cheese curds from the gravy to achieve the purest bubble, and how he wasn't even able to eat the french fries because of doctor's orders, so that's that for food wasted.

Mr. Bubbles then, to his credit, proceeded to create one impossibly perfect—and somewhat chunky—poutine bubble. It glistened, large and opaque in the sunlight streaming through the sitting room window, before bursting in Mr. Bubbles' eyes, causing him to scream and kick over the large pot of gravy. It rolled like an ocean of lava at the children, who ran screaming from the oncoming tide of scalding meat leavings. Two children were burned badly enough on the soles of their feet that a trip to the hospital was considered but thankfully deemed unnecessary.

I gathered up my things and left, overhearing on my way out the beginnings of what I have no doubt ended up being a protracted argument about payment. It is this reviewer's opinion that Mr. Chunky Bubbles leave the entertainment industry and find some other occupation more suited to his talents and temperament, such as murder victim.

—GUY LACHANCE
STAFF WRITER

FRANCESCA BOLOGNESE

FRANCESCA BOLOGNESE works primarily in social media. Though many would call her an "expert," she would never assume that title because she is incredibly humble. Francesca has worked for many large companies, primarily Bed Bath & Beyond. When people post on social media that a product they recently purchased from, for example, Bed Bath & Beyond, is full of hair, Francesca responds by encouraging them to take their vehicle and kill themselves in a dramatic way.

Though she refuses to share any of her social media expertise or "tips," Francesca has divulged a method for creating the best password: half of one ex-boyfriend's full name, half of another ex-boyfriend's full name, your favorite number, and "exclamation mark." Unfortunately, Francesca is currently working at the Bed Bath & Beyond store . . . AHHHHHHH!!!!

AGE: HOW DARE YOU!

HEIGHT: 1 ft

HOMETOWN: Eataly, Century City Mall

INTERESTING FACTS:

1) Francesca's password is: KeanuDenzel69!

2) Francesca's favorite pasta is rice.

3) Francesca speaks fluent Eatalian and Righteous Sebastian.

FRANCESCA BOLOGNESE
~~tips~~ for travel in

Italy

Sponsored by
Bed Bath & Beyond

Currency

Okay, Ashley. You work at hedge fund but you no know the currency in Italy? Aww it so cute how stupid you are, Ashley. Your poor little brain died while you drinking vodka at ASU in 2009. Okay I feel bad for you so I tell you . . . it's the Euro. It's like the dollar but it's better. Hey, I got an idea for you, Ashley, why you no take your Peloton bike go fly into a tornado filled with fire?

OH HI, BRRAAAD OR MEGHAN OR WHATEVER YOUR STUPID NAME IS.

So you wan' take a trip to Italy during vacation from your stupid job in finance or marketing or wherever you waste your life away? Great!! How exciting for you!! I can not wait to tell you all about my home country . . . just kidding. I can wait. You so lucky that Bed Bath & Beyond hire me to do this for all you stupid people. Okay shhhhh! I talking now but NO TIPS!

Language

Are you kidding me? You no know the language in Italy? Wow, Todd, you more stupid than I thought. Here, I give you hint, it's not English. Can you use your tiny brain, Todd? Oh my god, fine. It's Italiano. Here I give you lesson: "Vaffanculo, Todd." You know what that mean? It mean, "Why you no take your midlife crisis convertible and go fall down the stairs like *Big Little Lies*?!"

Electrical Outlets

Oh, you looking for plug to plug in your stupid iPOD TWITCH, Paul? You no can hang out with your family in a foreign country? That too hard for you? Too scary to be with your wife and kids so you need to check you stupid little texts from your idiot friends? Aww poor 45-year-old man. Here, I tell you what your friends text you, they say, "Oh hi, Paul, my name is CHRIS RICHARDSON and I work in the gig economy. I am boring stupid friend of a guy name PAUL! We play video game in basement in MINNESOTA!" Hey, Paul, you wan' plug? Why you no take your iPhone Samsung 5G Network go crash into a mountain of lava?!

Safety

Ohhh you scared, RACHEL PATTERSON?! Traveling to Rome is creepy to you but you okay living in Indianapolis?! Okay, Rachel, wake up. Nobody wan' steal your "rosé all day" sweatshirt. Nobody wan' your floppy hat from H&M, calm down. No Italians want to take all eight bronzer you pack in your suitcase. Don't worry, Rachel. Here I help you, poor little Indiana woman. Why you no take your furry vest and your pumpkin spice boots and go sink to the bottom of a lake where your family vacation?

Getting Around

You want to know how to travel around Italy, Greg MILLER? I bet you no can find Italy on map. I bet you no can drive without Google map. I bet you no can wipe your own culo without someone nearby to say "Good job, Greg. You almost there. Keep it up!" GREG WHY YOU NO TAKE YOUR CULO GO DIVE INTO A CAVE OF BATS AND HAVE THEM EAT YOUR HEAD OFF?!

Where to Stay

Hell.

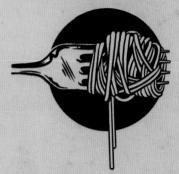

What to Eat

Shit.

Where to Shop

Bed Bath & Beyond.

Vaffanculo a tutti,

Francesca Bolognese

CAL SOLOMON

CAL SOLOMON is a founding member of the seminal rap group The Sugarhill Gang. He was present when they started rapping because he was Wonder Mike's neighbor. He was fired from the group before their first performance or recording because he isn't very good at rapping and also wasn't actually ever invited to be in the group in the first place. Wonder Mike of The Sugarhill Gang broke the news to Cal that he misunderstood everything about the situation.

Cal knows that he lacks any tangible rapping skills but feels like he could be good at rapping eventually. He has practiced every day for two hours per day since 1980. At one point he had a plan to recruit 40 other rappers for his new group, The Sugar Mountain Ensemble; the idea behind so many rappers in one group was that the sheer number of them would mask Cal's rap shortcomings while also bringing up his game. This project has yet to materialize.

Before encountering The Sugarhill Gang, Cal was an agent for the CIA. After botching an assignment in Washington, DC, that allowed a family of Russian spies to escape, Cal was reassigned to New Jersey. This embarrassing situation was the inspiration for the television program *The Americans* (2013–2018).

BASE: Englewood, NJ

MY STORY

Written by

CAL SOLOMON

THE SCREEN'S ALL BLACK AND SOME WORDS ARE THERE ALL OF A SUDDEN, MAYBE
WHITE LETTERING OR YELLOW SO'S YOU CAN SEE IT CLEARLY. THE WORDS SAY,
"ENGLEWOOD, NEW JERSEY".

THEN THE SCREEN ISN'T BLACK ANYMORE BUT THE WORDS STAY UP THERE
AND BEHIND THE WORDS YOU SEE THE ACTUAL ENGLEWOOD, NEW JERSEY, AND
NOW SOME NUMBERS COME UP UNDER THE WORDS AND THE NUMBERS ARE ONE,
NINE, SEVEN, AND EIGHT, IN THAT ORDER, SPELLING OUT THE YEAR "1978".
(NUMBERS CAN'T SPELL, BUT IF YOU CAN IMAGINE IT IN YOUR MIND,
YOU'LL KNOW WHAT I MEAN AND SO WILL THE AUDIENCE.)

NOW THE SCREEN IS ON A BACKYARD BARBECUE, OR COOKOUT, AS SOME PEOPLE
SAY, DEPENDING ON YOUR REGION. THE PEOPLE AT THE BARBECUE, OR COOKOUT,
ARE NAMED, ALTHOUGH WE DON'T KNOW IT YET, WONDER MIKE, BIG BANK HANK,
AND MASTER GEE. THESE ARE SOME BUT NOT ALL OF THE MEMBERS OF WHAT
IS ABOUT TO BECOME IN A FEW MINUTES THE SUGARHILL GANG! ALSO AT THE
COOKOUT (BARBECUE) ARE SYLVIA AND JOE ROBINSON, WHO ARE NOT BROTHER
AND SISTER BUT A MARRIED COUPLE, AS IT WAS NOT UNCOMMON IN THOSE DAYS
FOR A LADY TO TAKE THE MAN'S NAME IN WEDLOCK.

                                        THE CAMERA LOOKS AT
                                        SYLVIA AND SHE TALKS
                                        (BUT DOESN'T LOOK AT
                                           THE CAMERA)

                    SYLVIA
          Hey, Joe, do you remember I was telling
          you about Wonder Mike, Big Bank
          Hank, and Master Gee doing the music
          where they don't sing but they talk
          rhythmically over existing music?

                                        THE CAMERA LOOKS AT JOE
                    JOE
          Yes, I do remember you saying that to
          me, when we were in the house that we
          share together as man and wife.

                                        THE CAMERA LOOKS AT
                                        SYLVIA AGAIN

                    SYLVIA
          I hope you haven't forgotten that we're
          also business partners in our record
          company, Sugarhill Records!

                                        THE CAMERA LOOKS BACK
                                        AT JOE, HE'S LAUGHING

64

                              BUT NOT IN A MEAN WAY,
                              HE LOVES HIS WIFE

                    JOE
          I didn't forget, darling.

                              THE CAMERA LOOKS BACK
                              AT SYLVIA

SYLVIA TALKS.

                    SYLVIA
          Aren't you curious to see them do the
          thing I told you about, at our shared
          home?
                              THE CAMERA GOES BACK TO
                              LOOKING AT JOE

                    JOE
          Are you asking do I want to see them do
          the rhythmic talking over existing music
          at our house, or are you asking if I
          want to see them do it now, and you're
          mentioning our house for reference to
          aid me in remembering the subject of the
          conversation?

THIS IS A NOTE TO SAY THAT FROM NOW ON WHEN ANYBODY TALKS
THE CAMERA SHOULD BE LOOKING AT THEM, THANK YOU.

                    SYLVIA
          More the second.

                    JOE
          Okay.

THIS IS ANOTHER NOTE TO SPECIFY THAT THE CAMERA IS
LOOKING AT MORE THAN ONE PERSON AT A TIME IN THE NEXT
CAMERA LOOK.

NOW THE CAMERA LOOKS AT THE SUGARHILL GANG, STANDING BY
THE PICNIC TABLE. THERE'S OTHER PEOPLE AROUND, BUT THEY
DON'T GET ANY LINES, THEY'RE JUST THERE TO MAKE IT LOOK
LIKE A REAL PARTY.

SYLVIA RAISES HER VOICE, CALLS OVER TO THEM IN A FRIENDLY
WAY, SHE'S NOT MAD.

THEY'RE JUST FAR ENOUGH AWAY THAT SHE WANTS TO MAKE SURE THEY CAN HEAR HER, BECAUSE EVEN THOUGH THE EXTRA PEOPLE AREN'T TALKING OUT LOUD, THEY'RE PRETENDING TO SO IT LOOKS REAL AND LATER NOISE WILL BE ADDED TO MAKE IT SOUND LIKE A PARTY. THE REASON FOR THIS IS THAT IT WILL BE LESS CONFUSING AND NOISY WHEN THE CAMERA IS LOOKING AT THE ACTORS DURING THE ACTUAL FILMING.

SYLVIA TALKS AGAIN

> SYLVIA
> Hey, guys, I was telling Joe about that
> fun thing you do with music. Wanna do it
> now at this party? I bet people would
> like it, they're already having a good
> time so they're in a receptive mood, I
> bet.

JOE TALKS NOW

> JOE
> I know Wonder Mike, Big Bank Hank, and
> of course, Master Gee. But who's that
> other fellow over there?

SYLVIA TALKS

> SYLVIA
> Who, that? Why, that's Cal Solomon, from
> next door.

> THE CAMERA LOOKS AT THE MAN THEY'RE
> REFERENCING. IT'S ME, CAL SOLOMON,
> ONLY I LOOK YOUNGER BECAUSE AN
> ACTOR WHO WOULD BE AROUND THE
> AGE THAT I WAS THEN WOULD BE
> PORTRAYING ME BECAUSE PEOPLE WOULD
> NOTICE THAT I WOULD BE SO MUCH
> OLDER THAN EVERYONE ELSE IF I
> PLAYED MYSELF AND ALSO I HAVE ZERO
> ACTING EXPERIENCE SO I PROBABLY
> WOULDN'T BE VERY GOOD. ALTHOUGH
> I'D BE WILLING TO TRY BUT LET'S
> SAY THAT WOULD BE AN EMERGENCY
> TYPE SITUATION IF ALL THE OTHER
> REGULAR ACTORS ARE TOO BUSY.

NOW THE CAMERA IS CLOSER THAN NORMAL, REALLY VERY CLOSE
ON CAL SOLOMON (IN THE MOVIE, NOT ME IN REAL LIFE), SAY,
FROM THE TOP OF THE CHEST TO A LITTLE ABOVE THE HEAD. CAL
SAYS SOMETHING IN RESPONSE TO HEARING HIS NAME MENTIONED
AND HIS RELATIONSHIP TO THE PARTY DISCUSSED.

                    CAL SOLOMON (AN ACTOR PLAYING ME)
              Hi, I'm Cal from next door.

THE END. (THE WORDS "THE END" WILL ACTUALLY GO ON THE SCREEN)

THE WORDS THAT TELL YOU WHO DID WHAT GO UP ON THE SCREEN.
THEY START AT THE BOTTOM OF THE SCREEN (WHICH IS BLACK BY
THE WAY) AND THEY SLOWLY, BUT NOT TOO SLOWLY, MAKE THEIR
WAY UP TO THE TOP OF THE SCREEN UNTIL THEY'RE OUT OF
VIEW. THE LAST THING THAT GOES UP ON THE SCREEN SAYS THAT
WE DIDN'T KILL ANY ANIMALS.

JEFFREY CHARACTERWHEATIES

I n high school, while others struggled to find their place in the world, I felt lucky that I had found my passion. I loved to sing and dance on stage. And not just that. I was good at it. Everyone from parents and teachers to local directors not only supported me but pushed me toward acting as a career. "You could do this. If you really wanted to," my high school drama teacher Mrs. Groust told me after I played Tevya in our junior year production of *Fiddler*. And, silly me, I believed her.

Like a million midwestern kids before me who'd exploded off of their high school and community theater stages with dreams of stardom, I moved west immediately after graduation. Well, not imme-diately, I still had four more weekends of playing confidence man Professor Harold Hill in a local production of *The Music Man*. Our run had been extended because ticket sales were strong, mainly due to rave reviews from local papers. Reviews which called my performance "electric," "hilarious," and "dizzyingly fun." Little did I know how that role would prepare me for my very own long con to come. But I'm getting ahead of myself.

My plan was simple, well-thought-out (or so I thought), and perfectly (obsessively) laid out in my journals from that time.

First, "Move to LA!" Then, soon enough, I was sure to get a "small but meaningful" part on a show like *ER*, playing a junkie musician who's throwing his genius talent away or a grieving son who failed to reconcile with his father before death, ending in an emotion-filled catharsis with one of the main cast, hopefully Dr. Mark Greene, played by Anthony Edwards, who was my favorite character.

Then, of course, more substantial recurring and series regular roles would follow, eventually catching the eye of film directors who would cast me in the kind of big-budget dramas that ruled the box office at that time: *Good Will*

Hunting, *Cinderella Man*, or *A River Runs Through It*. And then, with that kind of success, my ultimate goal would be realized, the Oscar.

In my journals I wrote and rewrote my Oscar acceptance speech so as not to be caught unprepared. It was for a fictitious Steven Spielberg–directed film called *The Trappings of Love* (a movie I would then spend years trying unsuccessfully to write, but that's another story). In my speech I thanked "Steve, for his guidance and wisdom, a master storyteller who showed me how good I could really be" and my co-star Tom (Hanks), "from whom I learned so much. I share this award with you." I'll spare you the rest, as it is mortifying, but get me drunk enough and I can recite the whole thing from memory, even the sung portion.

Suffice it to say, I didn't get on *ER* or *NYPD Blue* or any other shows that mattered. I spent my first five years in LA not rising meteorically like I planned, but floundering pathetically.

During these years, I worked for a catering company which brought me so tantalizing close to the world I'd moved to LA to be a part of that it was humiliating. Wasn't it obvious

to these people that instead of walking around Barry Diller's house carrying a platter of fancy shrimp puffs I should be sitting on the couch laughing and carrying on with Brendan Fraser and Lori Petty?!

Then one of my catering buddies invited me to her comedy show at the Groundlings theater, a place I'd heard of but never explored because comedy just was never my "thing." Well, the show was hilarious! I got so swept up and inspired that I signed up that very night for one of their classes, one that was specifically geared toward creating memorable characters, the kind you'd see at the time on *SNL* or *MADtv*. I was nervous because my background was in musicals and drama, I'd never done improv or comedy and, frankly, I didn't really think I was very funny.

Turns out, I was right. To say I struggled would be an understatement. I was told my characters were "flat," lacked a "point of view" and "went nowhere." What seemed easy for my classmates was impossible to me. I relied too heavily on a wig or hat, a funny voice or a physical ailment. The class's focus on character catchphrases was perhaps my biggest struggle. For example, my character "Old Guy Knitting on the Porch" was just a cliche grumpy old guy yelling at the neighborhood kids to "get off of my yarn." It sounded like what my classmates were doing, but it was awful. After class my teacher caught up with me and said something that blew my mind: "These are real people, you need to give them a life."

Wow, I was buzzing for days. How could I have missed this? The same interiority I'd brought to Professor Harold Hill needed to be inside all my characters. Around this time is when my second ah-ha moment happened. I was catering a party for the DVD release of the film *Dude, Where's My Car?* and while I walked around with a platter of stoner-themed apps, I happened on a group sitting outside smoking. At the group's center was a loud, wild-eyed, and frankly obnoxious guy holding court. He was saying things that were patently outrageous, but no matter how off color or crass he was, everyone was dying laughing and hanging on his every word. He noticed me and asked my name, and when I said "Jeff" he said, "Jerk?! Huh, that's a weird name. But okay, how about you leave some of those sliders behind, Jerk?" Later when I passed them again he pointed at his empty drink and screamed, "Hey, Jerk! Get me another one of these before I shit my pants!" It didn't make any sense whatsoever, but everyone around thought it was hilarious, including me!

That night I went home and wrote down everything I remembered about him, what he said, how he looked, etc. And just like that I had new character: a crass, crude, blowhard, who was rude and appalling but somehow . . . charming? A character I called "The Funny Asshole." Next class, when I got

He noticed me and asked my name, and when I said "Jeff" he said, "Jerk?! Huh, that's a weird name. But okay, how about you leave some of those sliders behind, Jerk?"

onstage and performed what I'd prepared, to everyone's surprise, I killed! I even stole his line to end the piece with (in comedy it's called a "button"). I yelled, "Hey, Jerk, get me another one of these before I shit my pants!" My teacher did an actual spit take with her water.

My classmates all congratulated me afterward as we walked to the bar for our usual post-class drinks. I finally had something to celebrate. That night I knew I'd found

something special when my classmates all started pointing at their empty drinks and screaming The Funny Asshole's catchphrase, "Hey 'Jerk', get me another one of these before I shit my pants!" I was levitating.

Around this time I started hearing about a new comedy theater making noise in New York City, the Upright Citizen's Brigade. It was new and exciting and that's when I made a crazy decision. I dropped out of the Groundlings. I broke my lease and drove my Scion cross-country to New York. When I got there I sold the car for $800 and used that money to enroll in my first UCB class, not as Jeffrey Characterwheaties, but as a name that I'd thought up on my drive, something unique and specific befitting this "funny asshole." Thus, Jason Mantzoukas was born.

UCB's focus was mainly on improv, which was never a skill I had. But, I realized, as long as I approached it through the eyes of my character, Jason Mantzoukas, and his aggressively outrageous point of view, it was fun and I was pretty good at it. Though as time went on, I worried he was starting to seem too one-note and predictable. It wasn't enough to just be chaotic and wild. I needed to go deeper to find other facets of this character, surprising elements that would draw the audience in even more. Enter— the egg allergy.

It started when I heard someone on NPR talking about how their peanut allergy had made them anxious and fearful as a child. How being aware and in charge of their own mortality from such a young age had had disastrous effects on them in ways that were still evident as an adult. Here was the answer to the question I and others were starting to ask, "Why is this guy so obnoxious all the time?" Answer, "Because he's scared!"

It turned out the perfect compliment to Jason Mantzoukas's outrageousness was to build in a singular foundational, sympathetic weakness. What if all of this bluff and bluster was to cover for the fear and anxiety he's been carrying since childhood?

Jason Mantzoukas was starting to feel human. I was actually starting to like the guy and so were other people. Suddenly, people who Jeffrey Characterwheaties would have KILLED to meet or audition for were seeking out Jason Mantzoukas. I had some small successes, which led to me getting agents and a manager and eventually I started booking jobs.

I first met Scott Aukerman around this time. He was doing monologues at a UCB show in which I was a improv performer. We got to talking, hit it off, and before I knew it, he invited me onto his then radio show, now podcast, *Comedy Bang! Bang!* I didn't know it then, but over the next 12+ years *CBB* would be the safe space that I needed to really hone and focus the Jason Mantzoukas character. Establishing the character's weird canon which included overtly salacious ideas like his desire to host a podcast called *Talkin' Tang* about his sexual exploits or another called *Drippin' Milk* about lactating women. Awful and disgusting ideas that nonetheless found purchase in the lore of *Comedy Bang! Bang!* When Scott and I organically discovered the "Heynong Man" bit in episode #356, I had no idea I would soon see it emblazoned on T-shirts, screamed at me from moving cars, and inexplicably, tattooed on people's bodies. Now, that's a successful catchphrase.

But, as I'd learned earlier, it wasn't enough to just build out the gross side of Mantzoukas. I also had to continue to build the other side, the "allergic to eggs" side. *CBB* turned out to be the perfect place to start imbuing him with more surprising, sympathetic traits, such as his obsession with the *Harry Potter* books, *Star Wars*, and especially, *Gilmore Girls*. These were all things I had no familiarity with or fondness for, but I researched them diligently to help me build a better, more fully realized character. Believe me, I'd have much rather spent my time talking to people about my favorite Sondheim (*Assassins*!) than droning on and on about his favorite *Star Wars* character (Ahsoka Tano) or Rory boyfriend (Jess, obviously).

Scott was always there encouraging me to take Jason further. It was his idea to make the character a germaphobe, which was maybe his second most inspired suggestion. His first was early on when he suggested that I make Jason a "heel," someone who'd be a villain or an antagonist to the other guests/characters who appeared on *Comedy Bang! Bang!* It was an inspired idea that led to many hilarious and exciting episodes. But also, to all the amazing performers I've appeared with on the show, especially the incomparable Andy Daly, who have had to suffer through hours and hours of Jason Mantzoukas's abrasive nonsense, I apologize.

I'm approaching 22 years as Jason Mantzoukas, living inside of him through various film and TV roles as well as spending the last 11 years on the very popular podcast he co-hosts called *How Did This Get Made?* People always ask what the hardest part of playing this awful character for so long is and it's an easy answer.

One of the first choices I made when developing this character was to take away from him the thing I love most. Singing. Jason Mantzoukas does not sing. In fact he hates it. I did this so as to not have the ability to slip back into myself and what I do best. A way to truly bifurcate Jeffrey from Jason. But, taking away that ability to express my emotions through melody and verse has been a profound loss. To then be around so much singing on *Comedy Bang! Bang!*, yearning to join in but instead having to deride and dismiss it, has been heartbreaking. But to do anything else would betray one of

my character's fundamental beliefs. And, I have to keep playing the part.

I don't know if the Jason Mantzoukas character would have become as popular without *Comedy Bang! Bang!* I can't thank Scott enough. He's helped me perpetrate one of the greatest cons in comedic history.

And you fell for it. You fucking idiots.

JEFFREY CHARACTERWHEATIES
2022

BEAN DIP

BEAN DIP is the owner of the W Hotel in Hollywood, which she bought with an old-timey wheelbarrow full of gold coins.

She has many side hustles, including regularly selling her own sensual kisses for a high dollar amount to males and females in the Bliss Spa at the Hollywood W. Once she kisses them, they will come back for seconds. She also sells trinkets like babies made of porcelain, dogs made of things including rocks, also things made of metal into shapes. She also has a food truck where she sells hot dogs cut in half, or cucumbers and carrots in a bun. Every purchase includes a vinyl record, and any topping, including Hostess cupcakes, or a blended Xbox for 75 cents.

AGE: Ageless, baby

RULES AT THE W:

1) No lettuce.

2) If you haven't smiled in one hour, you will be thrown out.

3) Take off your shoes in the lobby, and leave them there until you go outside.

4) If you don't want your hair braided, don't come here.

INTERESTING FACTS:

1) Her birth name was Sally Dunkirk.

2) She's a big fan of anything where people run and throw.

3) She expects her lovers to make all her meals (six per day).

BEAN DIP'S GUIDE TO A SUCCESSFUL BUSINESS

By Bean Dip

Hey, man! Everybody knows that if you're gonna have a business, you want it to be successful. And if you're not a little bitch baby, you want it to be SO successful that everybody around you is like, "Oh damn, they must be very extraordinary in their personality and vibes if they got this shit going so strong, 'cause children are the future, and also adults are the future when it comes to money and business!"

When I bought the W Hotel in Hollywood, California, USA, I wasn't tryna fuck with ALL the W Hotels of the world. Naw, homie! I got the cutest one, and then added some interesting shit. Was the Bliss Spa already there? Yes, bitch. But did I add exponentious value by making people pay lots of money to get kissed by me while they were in that spa? Yuh. My high-dollar kisses put the W Hollywood over the top with revenues and horniness. So, in your face, Scott.

Here's some key points on what to do, what not to do, and how to look so good while doing it. Pretty soon you can be as rich as Michael Air Jordans Shoes or Billie Eyelash. Good luck, dick-stickers!

1. If you're going to start a food truck, don't do what every bitch did.

Don't paint your truck the normal way, don't serve food that anyone else does, and don't serve anything for sips other than vintage can drinks like Tabs and Mr. Pibb.

When I started my food truck, all the haters were like, "Bean Dip, you love hot dogs, the great American snack. You should sell hot dogs and that will be easy and great for you." And you know what I said? I said, "Man, fuck y'all, man!"

That's when I started putting long cucumbers and carrots into hot dog buns and offering a wide assortment of toppings including onions, chili, mustard, and crunched-up pieces of Xbox. Word traveled fast that people should come to the "Hot Dogs, But Better" truck that had a set of giant titties painted on the side of it. And now we have to shoot people with BB guns to make them leave when we run out of buns for the night. Thas called successful.

2. Don't be scared to fistfight a stranger or call a baby an asshole.

Successful businesses call for brave actions and also brave words and also for you to sometimes watch movies like *Braveheart*.

Calling a baby an asshole is the most surprising thing you can do. Its dumbass parents look at you and say, (SNOBBY VOICE) "My baby hasn't even developed a personality yet, let alone one that would warrant that kind of description." And then you just say, "You are what you eat" (implying the baby eats ass). Checkmate.

3. Keep your hair short.

You don't want to be in the middle of a $14 million deal with a cucumber company and feel like your head stick is hot cause your skanky-ass thick mane is glued to it. High and tight, dawg.

4. Run or skip to most places instead of using car gas or airplanes.

It'll take you longer to get to your meetings, but your leg muscles will make your investors think you're The Rock, but a lady or some shit. They'll give you whatever you want.

5. Any time you meet an animal, make friends with it.

The Mayan calendar or the Aztecs or whatever say that the animals are gonna rule, and I'm all about gettin' on that winning team, man. One of my best friends, Agnes (she's a bird), is the CEO of Michaels Craft Stores. So eat a fat dick, Scott.

6. Follow your heart and dance hard when a jam you like comes on the radio, no matter where you are.

CVS, the bank, doctor's office, wherever. If you're really feeling the music, someone will walk up to you and want to give you lots of money or a hug, and you're a winner with both of those choices.

7. Don't ever stay with one lover too long.

Keep it movin'. Charlize Theron, Leo DiCaprio, Angela Merkel, Seal, Kamala Harris—all of them are objectively drippingly hot people, man. But the second any of them got too needy (and they alllllll did with me), I'm out tha do'!! A needy lover takes your focus off of making that munny, and I'm tryna git them fat stacks. Fat stacks > hos, dawg.

8. Learn some gymnastics.

Backflips and shit like that is a good tool for impressing people, and then they just want to hand you more thick piles o' them billz, baybie.

9. Be aggressive and show your competitors who the alpha doggy is through biting, growling, or humping.

Whoops, just figured out I got my dog training tips list mixed up with my business tips list. Thas right—every other tip you just read is actually for dogs. THIS one is for business.

Good luck, everybody. I love you forever and wish you fun and rides on backs of rainbow unicorns.

Hearts and Also Hearts With Arrows and Also Double Hearts,

Bean Dip, Esq.

2-Player Game

Step 1: Choose to play as either Team Good or Team Evil.

Step 2: Flip a coin to determine who goes first.

Step 3: On your turn, choose one member of your team to attack one member of your opponent's team. The nature of the characters' attacks is entirely up to the player; for instance, "I activate Dalton Wilcox to attack Byron Denniston by stabbing him in the heart with a wooden stake," or "I activate Danny Mahoney to attack Bill Carter by smothering him with his heavy coat."

Step 4: When a character attacks, roll a six-sided die and add that number to the character's Attack Points to determine how much damage your character does to his opponent.

Step 5: The player whose turn it is attacks first, then both characters attack each other until one player's Defense Points are zeroed out. That character is now out of the game and the turn is over.

The winner is the player who wipes out the other team first.

Dalton Wilcox

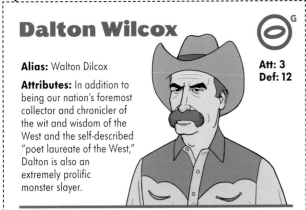

Alias: Walton Dilcox

Attributes: In addition to being our nation's foremost collector and chronicler of the wit and wisdom of the West and the self-described "poet laureate of the West," Dalton is also an extremely prolific monster slayer.

Att: 3
Def: 12

Attack Abilities: Inspiring poetic verse, proficiency with weapons, no hesitation to kill, ability to manage loneliness

Weaknesses: Is easily frustrated by city slicking

Gear: Stake of wood, pistols loaded with silver bullets, poetry notebook, Black+Decker sander

Special Power: Call to Action. When activating Dalton Wilcox, you can choose any other living member of Team Good to join him on the battlefield and launch simultaneous attacks. Roll the die once for both character's attacks. Each character remains on the battlefield until his defense points are depleted.

Bill Carter

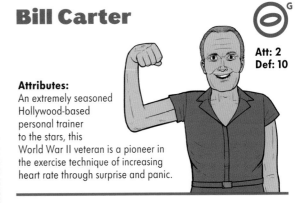

Attributes:
An extremely seasoned Hollywood-based personal trainer to the stars, this World War II veteran is a pioneer in the exercise technique of increasing heart rate through surprise and panic.

Att: 2
Def: 10

Attack Abilities: Explosive physical strength, a relationship with the Hollywood Bally's, the power to motivate others, "hustle"

Weaknesses: Age-related impairments to vision, hearing, and cognition; severe back problems

Gear: Medicine ball, 2 sandbags, 10 feet of rope, switchblade, hot-water bottle, half a tube of generic topical pain-relief cream

Special Power: Encouragement. As long as Bill Carter is alive, add 1 Attack Point to every other Team Good character's attack.

Hot Dog

Attributes: This legend of water skiing, longtime combatant in the war between surfing and waterskiing, and master of the doo wop singing style has auditioned to be a member of '50s nostalgia group Sha Na Na over 40 times.

Att: 2
Def: 9

Attack Abilities: Enchanting voice, trick water skiing, strangulation with incredibly muscular legs

Weaknesses: Poor upper-body strength, inability to accept reality, high cholesterol

Gear: Two large salamis, tow line, comb, pomade, pack of cigarettes, assorted throat lozenges, rifle with scope

August Lindt

Attributes: This German pretzel factory employee is a very experienced traveler and devoted husband and father with a keen ability to make the most of his limited vacation time.

Att: 1
Def: 6

Attack Abilities: An advanced ability to assess the quality of salt, extreme proficiency with travel arrangements, a complete lack of fear, and an inability to experience discomfort

Weaknesses: Cannot discern friends from enemies, dangerous lack of skepticism

Gear: German passport, €200 traveler's check, cyanide capsule

Patrick McMahon

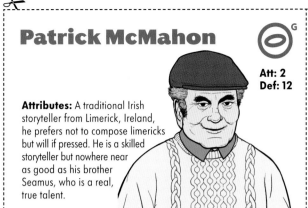

Att: 2
Def: 12

Attributes: A traditional Irish storyteller from Limerick, Ireland, he prefers not to compose limericks but will if pressed. He is a skilled storyteller but nowhere near as good as his brother Seamus, who is a real, true talent.

Attack Abilities: Can enrapture his target with tall tales and fairy stories, moderately adept at bare-fisted brawling when drunk

Weaknesses: Poor impulse control, bad teeth, paralyzing inferiority complex

Gear: Shillelagh, bottle opener, cable-knit sweater

Andi Callahan

Att: 1
Def: 7

Alias: God, Jehovah, Elohim, Yahweh, Rodney

Attributes: Registered nurse specializing in long-term/geriatric care. He is also the infinite, eternal, all-knowing and all-seeing creator of everything both within and beyond our comprehension.

Attack Abilities: Administrative skills, experience with scheduling, payroll, and medical billing. He is also omnipotent.

Weaknesses: Incomprehensible behavior, jealousy, insecurity, stubborn and inexplicable refusal to make his existence irrefutably clear

Gear: Everything

Gil

Att: 2
Def: 8

Attributes: Unhoused entertainer and one-time Dean Martin lookalike, this unfortunate gentleman has been encountering Satan's High Commander, Golly, in various forms for years. Gil is compelled to do Golly's bidding, which is terrible, but on the up side, they're a pretty good ventriloquist act.

Attack Abilities: Pathetic pleading, baffling joke setups, disarming chortle

Weaknesses: Acute delusional disorder, tendency to follow orders unquestioningly, chapped lips, dry eyes, runny nose

Victor the Giant

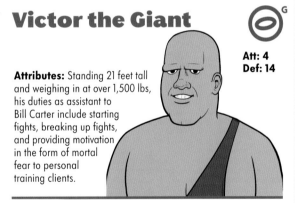

Att: 4
Def: 14

Attributes: Standing 21 feet tall and weighing in at over 1,500 lbs, his duties as assistant to Bill Carter include starting fights, breaking up fights, and providing motivation in the form of mortal fear to personal training clients.

Attack Abilities: Superhuman strength, shape shifting

Weaknesses: Low sense of self-worth, joint pain

Gear: Huge bearskin one-shoulder tunic, a shovel and a pitchfork that he uses as eating utensils

Chip Gardener

Att: 2
Def: 9

Alias: Lizard, Gretchen, Satan

Attributes: A golden-throated former gameshow host who's campaigning to be Honorary Mayor of Hollywood, his face was badly deformed following a botched suicide attempt in which he allowed himself to be run over by a Jeep. Chip's eternal soul has been displaced by that of the Father of Lies, the Angel of the Abyss, Beelzebul, the Dark Lord Satan himself.

Attack Abilities: Seducing people into sin, manipulation of the weak-willed, inflicting an eternity of unimaginable suffering on the damned

Weaknesses: An inflated sense of his own fiddle-playing skills, a tendency to shrink in the face of human decency

Gear: Handheld microphone, tube of Binaca breath spray, dapper outfit of coordinated separates, male and female genitalia

---

Golly

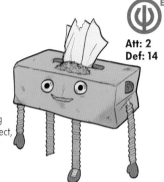

Att: 2
Def: 14

Attributes: Capable of inhabiting and speaking through any inanimate object, this adorable-voiced entity is the Dark Lord Satan's Supreme Commander.

Attack Abilities: Can control an opponent's movements by inhabiting that person's shirt, can transform into a winged demon that creates and hurls fireballs

Weaknesses: Limited mobility owing to the fact that he is usually in the form of an object that needs to be carried from place to place by a willing confederate. Regardless of form, speaks in a comical and unintimidating voice

Gear: None

Don Dimello

Att: 4
Def: 12

Attributes: A theatrical director specializing in Rockette management and late-night interactive adult-themed children's theater, he is also Satan's Supreme Commander's Supreme Commander. There is, has never been, and will never be a greater source of evil and chaos existing in any realm throughout all creation.

Attack Abilities: Can summon a swarm of Rockettes with the words "bring out the girls," can become his opponent's sugar daddy

Weaknesses: Poor judge of character when hiring staff, poor commercial instincts preventing him from becoming a more successful independent producer of theater

Gear: 50g of Mexican black-tar heroin, unlimited access to petting zoo animals

---

Byron Denniston

Att: 2
Def: 7

Attributes: A professional "royal watcher," he has gone to extraordinary, often dangerous and illegal, lengths to keep the public informed as to the goings-on of Britain's royal family. Keenly aware of the divinity of royal blood, he has long endeavored to kidnap a royal and recently succeeded, nabbing an infant prince.

Attack Abilities: Flattery, a certain roguish charm, weapons expertise, ability to quote Byron, Shelley, Keats, et al.

Weaknesses: An irritating imperial sense of superiority, monomania

Gear: Bespoke suit, poison-tipped umbrella, razor-rimmed bowler hat, disguises, a sports bra worn by Meghan Markle

Special Power: Royal inspiration. If Byron is activated to attack while Beetle Bailey is still alive, add 2 Defense Points. Also add 2 Attack Points to each attack.

Danny Mahoney

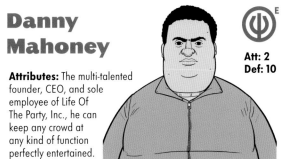

Att: 2
Def: 10

Attributes: The multi-talented founder, CEO, and sole employee of Life Of The Party, Inc., he can keep any crowd at any kind of function perfectly entertained.

Attack Abilities: Explosive rage, "all the popular dances," conversation

Weaknesses: Disorganization, repellent personality

Gear: Boombox with cassette/CD player and AM/FM radio; gym bag full of D batteries, roughly 20 percent of which are dead; joke book; harmonica; spandex pants; heaviest coat commercially available within the United States

Special Power: C'mon now. Just as Danny can force partygoers onto the dance floor against their will, he can also drag someone onto the battlefield with him. When activating Danny Mahoney, choose any other living member of Team Evil to join him and launch simultaneous attacks. Roll the die once for both character's attacks. Each character remains on the battlefield until his Defense Points are depleted.

Ben Alterman

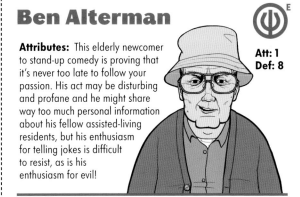

Att: 1
Def: 8

Attributes: This elderly newcomer to stand-up comedy is proving that it's never too late to follow your passion. His act may be disturbing and profane and he might share way too much personal information about his fellow assisted-living residents, but his enthusiasm for telling jokes is difficult to resist, as is his enthusiasm for evil!

Attack Abilities: Horrifically graphic references to old-people sex, surprisingly strong grip for a man his age

Weaknesses: Loose dentures, arthritis, coronary artery disease, several undiagnosed cancers, tendency to fall down, and stubborn refusal to use his walker

Gear: Pocketful of hard candies, 10 ribbed condoms, pocket-sized "travel vibrator," and 12 individual packets of water-based lubricant

Cactus Tony

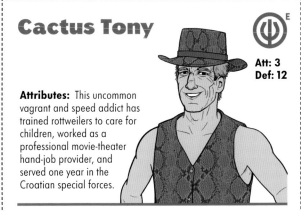

Att: 3
Def: 12

Attributes: This uncommon vagrant and speed addict has trained rottweilers to care for children, worked as a professional movie-theater hand-job provider, and served one year in the Croatian special forces.

Attack Abilities: Assisted falls, forced journeys to China, low proficiency in several martial arts

Weaknesses: Drenching sweats, concussion-related brain damage

Gear: Snakeskin boots, pants, jacket and hat, stolen mobile phone

Beetle Bailey

Att: 1
Def: 6

Alias: His Royal Highness Prince George of Cambridge

Attributes: The eldest child of Prince William, Duke of Cambridge, and Catherine, Duchess of Cambridge, and third in line to the British royal throne. As an infallible monarch, he is essentially a living god.

Attack Abilities: Disarming cuteness, can throw small objects short distances

Weaknesses: Cannot walk or sit up on his own, cannot feed himself or use a toilet, extremely limited communication skills, has virtually no comprehension of the world or his place in it, can not swim

Gear: Tiny sailor suit, cloth diaper (soiled), tiny patent-leather shoes, monogrammed burp cloth, net worth of roughly $3.6 billion

TO: ALL PARENTS
FROM: CHRIST'S USA FENCING SCHOOL

Hello parents,

It has come to my attention that some of you are under the impression that I am indoctrinating your children into some sort of Christian cult. I only wish! No, all I do, every day, is attempt to teach your wonderful kids how to fence. Let me tell you, I love these kids and WILL get them to at least a C ranking, but it would certainly help if you could, in your own home, get them to stop calling it "swordfights."

Yes, I am a proud Christian. YES, I am a proud American! That's why I named the school after my two favorite prides! YES, the school was called "All-American Fencing" when you originally signed your kids up for classes, but I felt guilty about leaving The Beloved Redeemer out of the name and SO SORRY but I changed it and didn't tell you all about it! Why would I? You are not being charged for the name change, just me! Count your blessings!

I never speak to your children about my beliefs OR the fact that I bleed red, white, AND blue (figuratively). The only thing discussed on my *piste* is FENCING. Would I love it if the children came to me for spiritual guidance? Of course (with your permission only!!). Would I love it if every time they complained about not being able to make out what I'm saying, I felt I had the privilege to say, "If you don't like my rules, you are welcome to LEAVE AMERICA?" Obviously! But I merely think it! Am I guilty of THOUGHTCRIME (as depicted in George Orwell's *1984*, [a great fiction novel to read, but it seems like it is becoming the reality we are currently living under more and more each day])?

In summation, rest assured that I teach and talk FENCING ONLY with your children. Ask them! And let me do my job. Thank you. And may God bless America.

Coach Jarles

BOB DUCCA'S
CONTENT OF OVERNIGHT BAG

AS I'M SURE YOU CAN IMAGINE, MANY, MANY PEOPLE ASK
ME WHAT I PUT IN MY OVERNIGHT BAG (YOU'LL REMEMBER
THAT MY OVERNIGHT BAG IS A LOOSE PLASTIC WALMART BAG)
THE FOLLOWING ITEMS ARE WHAT I TAKE WITH ME WHENEVER
I WILL BE OUT OF THE HOUSE FOR MORE THAN TWO HOURS
(I CALL IT MY OVERNIGHT BAG BECAUSE I NEVER KNOW WHEN
I'LL BE TOO DEPRESSED TO RETURN HOME)

- sleep mask
- travel pillow
- hemroid donut
- hammer toe correcting footy pajamas
- rubber pillow case for beddy bye cries
- the following NPR action figures: Terry Gross, Kai Rizdoll, Corva Coleman, Ira Glass and the cast of Wait Wait Don't Tell Me.
- sony discman with Echhart Tolle's "Power of Now" on a loop.

- noise canceling headphones
- night mare canceling headphones
- ortopedic underpants
- baby socks ~~compression~~ *
- bed bug net
- youth hostel rat traps
- canine thunder shirt
- dream catcher
- shaman feather
- dream catcher repair tape

*REDACTED BY ORDER
of RoBert DucCA

- hole punch for leather belt (~~monthly~~ hourly weight flucuations)
- Disease-a-day desk calendar from WebMd

- Paracord dental floss
- tooth paste
- tooth powder
- tooth brush
- spare teeth
- carbon reinforced tongue scraper
- vetinary quality toe nail clippers
- band aids
- citronella mustache wax
- Black & Decker Biorre strips
- Earthquake toilet
- abcess trough
- Allergy helmet
- blister sponge
- equine cotton swabs
- Dental Dam
- Squirt tarp
- nose hair sheers
- chamber pot
- Solar powered tactical bidet
- Gilette Mach III Bunyon Scalpel
- Counting Crows Box Set

HAVE YOU SEEN OUR GRANDDAUGHTER?

You'd **BETTER NOT HAVE.**

But if you **HAVE**, then you'd better **TURN AROUND**, put your hands to the sky, and **KEEP WALKING** (turn self into police) (do the right thing)

If you **MEET** our granddaughter, get *Men in Black*-memory-gone-machined

If you **COME ACROSS** our granddaughter, stop, drop, and roll away as fast as you can, and keep rolling for miles (or at least for two towns)

If you **HEAR** our granddaughter, don't listen—plug ears and go *lalalalalala*. Run off as fast as you can (away from granddaughter).

If you **THINK** someone might be our granddaughter, stop what you are doing and **LEAVE**. Even if you are hungry, mid-meal, and/or thirsty and mid-sip.

If you see **ANY** small girl, assume it's our granddaughter, and **LEAVE IMMEDIATELY** (even if it's your granddaughter)

DON'T tell our son where **HIS** daughter is (because that's our granddaughter)

ONE OTHER THING: If you've so much as **THOUGHT** about **GLANCING** at our granddaughter, we'll put you in a:

TAKE ONE:

OSCEOLA OVERCOAT

TUCSON TUTU

PITTSBURGH HOCKEY HELMET

NEW PALTZ SUNDAY SLACKS

BATON ROUGE TURTLENECK

TENNESSEE TUXEDO

KING OF PRUSSIA BALL GOWN

NIKE-BRANDED HALF SHIRT

Doug Gropes <chickendougetmeal@aol.com>
To: "Gropes Marketing Invitation Kick-Off Spam Blast"
CC: Barack Obama <barackandahardplace@goverment.gov>

Today at 1:04 AM

Greetings!

My Name is Douglass R. Gropes, aka Doug Gropes, aka "The Groper," although my cousin/lawyer has <u>begged</u> me to stop encouraging people to use that nickname.

I am an untraditionally trained financial advisor and money expert, and if you're getting this email, I am about to change your life! What an amazing day for that, don't you think? I woke up today and looked around and thought to myself a bunch of really positive things. Did you know the Earth is half water?? Huh!? The world is so nuts so much of the time but if you can slow it down and see the beauty in it, I think it can do wonders, right??

So, hey Doug, why are you writing to ME? This is what you're probably thinking?
Out of everyone in the world, why me? You are thinking that? Well, here is why . . .

I am launching a new Financial Growth System (FGS) and I want YOU to be the first/only one so far to try it out! I am literally guaranteeing by this time tomorrow you will be a millionaire.*

The system is called **The Gropes's Money Transfer Method to Allow Room for Real Wealth Not Just Money**. It follows my three-step philosophy on growing your money:
1. Money does not matter.
2. Understand that money can be anything and anything can be money.
3. Get rid of your money to make room for money. *Sharpen your lawn rake—'cause ya'll gonna need it to rake in all the NEW money you have room for now.*

With this system, you will never have to worry about boring one-on-one guidance. All the training will come from books and pamphlets that you can read at your convenience. I will never bother you, call you, or see you in person—and I ask that you do the same for me! Right?? It's easy!

Wait! Doug, this sounds great, but I bet it's expensive and subscription-based? That's you thinking that. Well, a pretty great guy once said, "Jump and the net will appear." That guy was named Carl and he lived next to me growing up and he eventually sold my family his old Toyota Corolla and I lived in it from 1997 to THIS VERY DAY! He died mysteriously when he fell off a building, but his truth remains true:

Jump, the net WILL appear.

$1299.00 for the starter kit and then $199.99 a month <small>(36 month minimum)</small>

That's seriously a fantastic deal, Doug! That's you saying that.

STARTER KIT INCLUDES:
 • My self-published book *Grope in One Hand, Shit in The Other* . . .

At the end of the 36-month trial, you will have the option of continuing to grow your wealth or canceling by filling out a form that you can get from my office somewhere in the left filing cabinet. I have to find it.

Call me/page me at 1-800-FREE-BEEP, put in the text 476737 (Gropes), leave your number, and I will call you back once I get a phone. Or visit my brand new website:

www.gropemebutdontsweepmeunderthedoug.com

I sincerely grope (*lol*) to hear from you soon!

Doug

To unsubscribe, call me/page me at 1-800-FREE-BEEP, put in the text 476737 (Gropes), leave your number, and I will call you back when I get a new phone, and we can discuss!
*Millionaire can mean financially with American dollars or also psychologically as well.

RYAN GAUL | 89

MARTIN SHEFFIELD-LICKLEY

MARTIN SHEFFIELD-LICKLEY was the lead singer of the '80s new wave band 2 + 2 = Love. He's from Douglashire Flatgroundshire Dirtshire Sheepshit, England, which has a population of six people and four thousand sheep.

His life has been plagued by tragedy—his wife was diagnosed with breast cancer and died, and he lost his son who smoked too many ciggies and got childhood emphysema. He wears a suit to commemorate his son, which is splattered with blood from his son's coughs.

He writes music based on these tragedies but his sound is similar to ABC, which doesn't always fit the lyrics. He's currently on a sixteen-cemetery tour where he performs for people he lost in America and the United Kingdom.

INTERESTING FACTS:

1) Martin got married to fellow *CBB* guest Pearl Henderson during a live show.

2) Martin lost his postman to a mix up where he took a nap at the post office, was boxed up, and mailed to the bottom of the ocean.

3) He is the mayor of Love City.

THE TANDEM BICYCLE OF LOVE TOUR
Cape Canaveral, FL - January 28th, 1986

SHIP OF LOVE

TANDEM BICYCLE OF LOVE

YOU'VE BEEN ARRESTED (BY THE LOVE POLICE)

I'M A CONTESTANT ON LOVE JEOPARDY

I GAVE LOVE A KISS TONIGHT

I GAVE LOVE A HUG TONIGHT

I INJECTED HEROIN THAT'S CUT WITH LOVE

ATV DEALERSHIP OF LOVE

~~**BLAST OFF TO LOVE SPACE**~~

~~**HOUSTON, WE HAVE A LOVE PROBLEM**~~

~~**I KISSED A LOVE ALIEN**~~

-- FORCED ENCORE --

LOVE MACY'S (SPONSORED)

PATERNAL GRANDFATHER
ALABASTER SHEFFIELD-LICKLEY
(1912–1990)
••
Cause of death: Clobbered by vicar

PATERNAL GRANDMOTHER
GRANCH HALTWHISTLE-CHIMSBY
(1912–1989)
••
Cause of death: Flogged by wanker

FATHER
YORKSBURY SHEFFIELD-LICKLEY
(1930–1958)
••
Cause of death:
Cheeky double homicide

TWIN BROTHER'S
IMAGINARY WIFE
FUDGEWICK
CHISLEYWORTH-
SLIPPERSY
(1959–1988)
••
Cause of death:
Bloke who imagined
her had a tumble

TWIN BROTHER
WALTER SHEFFIELD-
LICKLEY (1957–1988)
••
Cause of death:
Tumbled down a lift shaft

NON-TWIN SISTER
PETUNIABERRY
SHEFFIELD-LICKLEY
(1955–1991)
••
Cause of death:
Kidneys in shambles

MARTIN SHEFFIELD-LICKLEY'S
•• FAMILY TREE ••

MATERNAL GRANDFATHER
THOURPE ST. WICKLESBRIDGE-BUNBERRY (1873–1892)
••
Cause of death: Took the piss outta his brain with a gun

MATERNAL GRANDMOTHER
WIGGLESBY FLIPPINGTON-CHESHIRE (1821–1891)
••
Cause of death: Jack the Ripper victim

MOTHER
HELENBURY ST. WICKLESBRIDGE-BUNBERRY (1891–1958)
••
Cause of death: Ate tainted shepherd's pie and went mental

DEAD WIFE'S FATHER
CUSTARDTON DREARYFIELD-DUMPLEBURGH (1922–1993)
••
Cause of death: Having sex with Margaret Thatcher

DEAD WIFE'S MOTHER
CHARLOTTESBY GOSSWORTHY-DIMPLEDEEN (1927–1994)
••
Cause of death: Yorkshire pudding slip and fall

MARTIN SHEFFIELD-LICKLEY (1957–PRESENT)
••
Cause of death: TBD

DEAD WIFE
CATHERINE DREARYFIELD-DUMPLEBURGH-SHEFFIELD-LICKLEY (1959–1987)
••
Cause of death: Bosom cancer

DEAD WIFE'S GIRL COUSIN
HINKLECREAM GOSSWORTHY-MURDERHOUND (1962–1992)
••
Cause of death: Ate Wallace & Gromit Claymation figurines

SON
SIMON SHEFFIELD-LICKLEY (1982–1986)
••
Cause of death: Emphysema/falling out a window

FOURVEL'S TIPS FOR CURING BOREDOM

"Bored? Do this shit!"

—Wee lil' round boy, Fourvel

TIP # WUN

Fucking create something!!! So, it's a "lazy Sunday afternoon" (FAMOUS QUOTE FROM *SNLive*) and you got nuthin' ta do. Well, why not gather up all the scraps and trimmings and bolts you have collected in your time living in the gutter and turn them into something beautiful and expensive!

Found an old boot? Why not chuck a plant in it?

What's that now? You seem to have stumbled upon an ass-ton of broken glass? Welp. Don't just sit there looking like a fuckin' imbecile. PICK UP ALL THE BROKEN GLASS, PUT IT IN A REUSABLE GELSON'S BAG, AND BRING IT TO YOUR HOME. Now it's broken glass AND GLITTER IN A SALAD BOWL!

One time I made a gorgeous chandelier for a friend's house out of microwaved coffee lids and butter pats. Another time I made a chandelier out of some old bicycles and new bicycles and butter pats. The lesson I loined? You can make anything out of garbage and butter pats! The possibilities are endless.*

TIP # TEW

PUT ON THE RITZ! (A SHOW) Lights. Camera. Shall we?

If you get soooo friggen bored that sometimes you just want to stab and harm the closest human or object within arm's reach, yeeeeeeeeaaaaa might be bored! (SAY THIS LAST LINE TO YOURSELF IN A GREAT JEFF FOXWORTHY VOICE.) So, why not put on a show! Gather as many family members and friends as you can. If you are like me, tender lil' viddle Fourvel, you don't have any friends and family due to your murderous rage and living situation. Don't sweat it! Just force strangers to do it! Now THAT'S entertainment!

*Fourvel is not positive if the possibilities are mathematically endless.

TIP # THA-REE

Puzzles! Puzzles are great for passing/wasting time. They are also really fun to throw away after you finish assembling them. Actually. Nevermind. Fuck puzzles. Puzzles are broken pictures. Fuck puzzles right in the face.

TIP OF MY DICK (BOOM!)

"You got to move it, move it!" —Tony "Beck" Bennett. And by that I mean exercise. And by that I mean you've got to move it, move it. Meaning exercise.

If you get bored just get up and run. Full speed. For as long as you can. As far as you can. Fuckin' run until your heart pops like a tick making a popping sound with its mouth.

Do you have dumbbells? Weird! Pick them shits up! Then put them right the hell back down. NOW you're getting it!

Do whatever feels best for YOUR body and don't feel bad if you are not as flexible as you wish you were. You will get there with work. Stand up. Sit down. Stab a bitch. Do five sit-ups. Moider a woman. Hang upside down like dumb bat from a stick. I don't care.

As "Dwayne" The Rock "Johnson" always says on television and in newspapers, "Do crunches. Not brunches, jagoffs."

TIP # BABYLON 5

See page 12. (I have no idea what's on page 12 but whatever IS happening on page 12 is probably infinitely more interesting than anything your bored ass has going right now. Amirite?)

Now get UN-BORED! (Or I'll take yo life!)

So so sincerely,

America'z Pansexual Top, Fourvel

BONUS TIP: Give yourself a second butthole. Trust me.

AL A. PETERSON

AL AMADEUS PETERSON is known as the "Smooth Criminal" because he is a wanted felon and is also completely hairless. He is hairless because he faked alopecia to get out of a long-term relationship with his previous girlfriend Carlifer (the name is a clumsy portmanteau of her parents' names, Carl and Jennifer).

Currently, Al runs a criminal enterprise that helps people fake their own deaths. He provides new passports, credit cards, and other forms of identification, as well as shaving the client's entire body, save for the hair around their anus. Al has been known to advertise his services by hiring a skywriting plane that spells out, "LOOKING TO FAKE YOUR OWN DEATH?" with no other information. He also advertises his services on the dark web and in the "Missed Connections" section of the *PennySaver*.

AGE: About 50

INTERESTING FACTS:

1) Before shaving his entire body on a daily basis, Al was an extremely hirsute gentleman, almost a Sasquatch. Just a face peeking out a haystack of hair.

2) When Al left Carlifer, he took with him her favorite hoodie, which he has to this day.

3) Al's nemesis is a man named Gray V. Digger, who provides exact doubles of people who have died for people who have something to gain from the dead person's continued existence.

FEELING THE *HEAT?*
ARE THEY *ON TO YOU?*
NEED TO *ESCAPE?*

I AM THE MAN WHO CAN GIVE YOU A NEW IDENTITY! A NEW LIFE!

Hello. My name is . . . well, what's in a name? Legal government identification, that's what. So when you eventually call me, you can call me . . . Al.

Friend: I've been where you've been. Afraid. Desperate. Sporting human hair in all the usual places. But I found a way out. And I can point you to it. And although I have to keep running, there's no reason you should have to.

I can provide you with a completely new identity, including passport, driver's license, and a credit card. Not to mention a completely new look. But don't worry—I'll see to it that there's a part of the original you hidden away that you can access any time you're not in public.

If you need my services (and if you've read this far you clearly do) you can find me behind your local library's largest branch. If I'm not there, I am not in your city. Or your local library doesn't have space behind which to meet me. If that's the case, go to the second largest branch. If I'm not there, the same two reasons apply. If that's the case, call me at (555) HELP-MEE, an elegant alpha-numeric sequence. The extra "E" really suggests the air of desperation that you are no doubt feeling right now.

I'll see you soon. You'll recognize me by my signature hoodie.

(555)-HELP-MEE

THE SHOW WHERE WE TALK TO INTERESTING PEOPLE

OR

HOW CAN I TAKE ADVANTAGE OF *COMEDY BANG! BANG!'S* OPEN-DOOR POLICY?

AKA

"WHAT MAKES A GOOD *COMEDY BANG! BANG!* GUEST?"

BY SCOTT AUKERMAN

When one such as I casually strolls through the neighborhood, I am often accosted on the street by fans, asking questions such as, "How does one such as I appear on a program hosted by one such as you?" One is often confused by how complicated sentences such as these have become, and one such as I usually ends the conversation in times such as then.

Webster's dictionary defines "guest" as "VERB: to appear as a guest." Which doesn't really help matters much for some dumb idiot like you, does it?!! I understand if you now need to close this book in shame, having been roasted within an inch of your life.

That said, if you're still reading, I may as well help you out by giving you some tips about what makes a "great," or even "good," *Comedy Bang! Bang!* guest.

1. When you enter the studio, slack-jawed, mouth agape—please don't ask, "Is this *Comedy Bang! Bang!*?" If you're looking at me, one of the most famous people podcasters in the world, you can bet your silly ass it ain't *SmartLess*.

2. My father's name was "Mr. Aukerman." It's also my name. So please address me as such. A few other notes—please don't call me "Daddy." I have three children who do that, and I don't need my guests to start acting like them! (Although I will change your die-die upon request.) "Sir" or "master" will also suffice.

3. Once we start, get to your point. Nine times out of ten, you're a small business owner who wants to talk about the odd ways your store differs from normal stores. I hate to tell you—I've heard it all before. So you may as well cut the chit, not to mention the damn chat.

4. I ask the questions, and you provide the answers. Sound easy? Well, I can't tell you how many times someone has arrived at the studio and immediately "turned the tables" on me, conducting an incisive, multipart profile on my life. The next thing you know, they've turned around and sold this piece to one of the major media outlets, and I can't *Step Up 2: The Streets* without being mobbed by my adoring fans! Enough, already!

5. I have already tired of this joke format, and would like the list to end here.

ARTIST'S RENDERING

Look—I get it. Podcast fame is a fickle, addictive mistress. But don't enter the ring unless you're prepared to go ten rounds with someone who has two thumbs and is this guy—me!!!

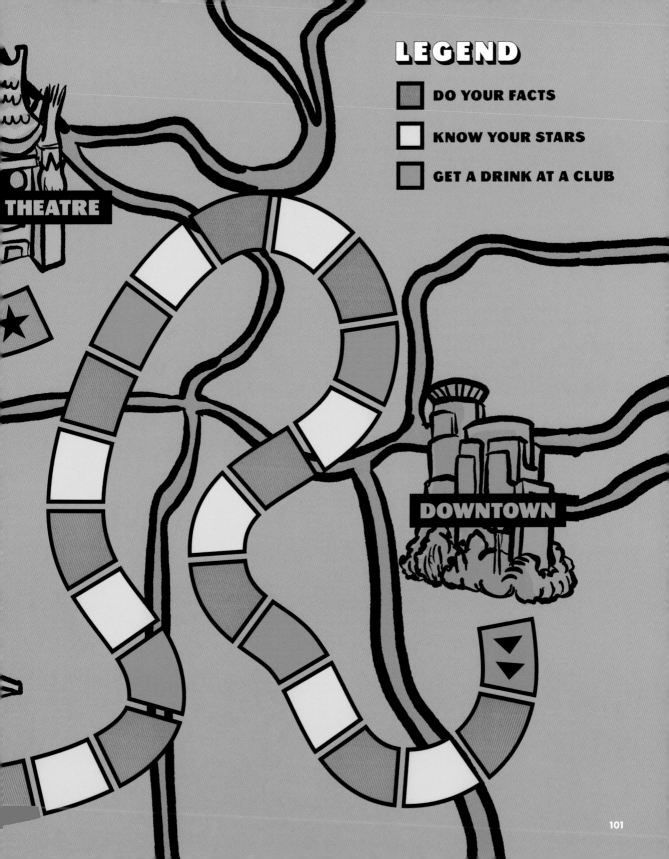

HEY, EVERYONE!

You know the theme song by heart, and now Hollywood Facts is a challenging and fun board game to be played by kids ages 5–99! Enjoy the game, and

remember to take out your dicks!!

RULES:

For 1–4 Players

1. All players start on the "DOWNTOWN" space.

2. First player to shout "NICE!" gets to go first.

3. Player 1 rolls the die, then moves the corresponding number of spaces.

4. Depending on what space Player 1 landed upon, the player to their left takes a "DO YOUR FACTS" or "KNOW YOUR STARS" card out of the deck and reads the question corresponding to the number rolled.

5. If Player 1 guesses the answer correctly, they stay where they are, but can roll again next turn.

6. If they guess incorrectly, they must wait until their next turn, then draw another card. They can only roll on their next turn once they've guessed correctly.

7. If Player 1 lands on a "GET A DRINK AT A CLUB" space, they drink as many alcoholic beverages as the number they rolled. They can then roll again on their next turn.

8. Gameplay moves clockwise.

9. Once a player lands on the "WALK IN FRONT OF THE CHINESE THEATER" space, the player to their left chooses a card at random, rolls the die, and asks the corresponding question to the number rolled.

10. First player inside the Chinese Theater to answer correctly wins!

11. 11. Take out your dick!

DO YOUR FACTS

- True or False: Over fifty little people were hired to play Munchkins in *The Wizard of Oz*.

  ANSWER: False. The Munchkins were normal-sized, while Dorothy and the rest of the cast were giants.

- What is the final line of *Chinatown* (1974)?

  ANSWER: "Thanks for coming, everybody!"

- Which is the first movie in the *Bourne* franchise?

  ANSWER: *A Star is Bourne* (2018).

DO YOUR FACTS

- What was the tagline for *Dracula* (1931)?

  ANSWER: "He's gonna drain your main vein! . . . Ew, not like THAT, you piss freak!"

- What is the final line of dialogue in *RoboCop*?

  ANSWER: RoboCop: "Someday I'm gonna marry that laptop!"

- Where was *The Notebook* filmed?

  ANSWER: Earth.

DO YOUR FACTS

- If they remade *Schindler's List* today, would they probably rename it *Schindler's Listicle*, based on our modern era's clickbait-driven internet culture?

  ANSWER: Yes.

- What's the name of the skyscraper in *Die Hard* (1988)?

  ANSWER: Steve.

- What is the most famous line of dialogue in *On the Water-front* (1954)?

  ANSWER: "I coulda been a contender . . . until I basically went full goblin mode!"

DO YOUR FACTS

- What's the best baseball film of all time?

  ANSWER: The unproduced screenplay *Li'l Scotty Aukerman and the Magic Baseball Bat*. (Which is still available to any studio that isn't scared off by an NC-17 rating!)

- What is the first line of dialogue in *Mulan* (2020)?

  ANSWER: "Hey . . . didn't I used to be a drawing?!"

- In *Parasite* (2019), what doesn't work?

  ANSWER: The central metaphor.

DO YOUR FACTS

- Have any of the Marvel movies been good?

  ANSWER: Uh . . . yeah, they're great, they're ALL great! (What do you think, I'm INSANE?)

- *Staten Island Summer*? *King of Staten Island*? What's next, *The Avengers: Staten Island*??

  ANSWER: Yes, yes!!! 😂

- What movie was about a normal age to still be a virgin?

  ANSWER: *The Forty-Year-Old Virgin*.

DO YOUR FACTS

- What is the one thing Pixar's animators can't do without?

  ANSWER: Their beloved CPUs!

- What's the final line of dialogue in *8 Mile* (2002)?

  ANSWER: "Fine, I admit it. Rap ISN'T crap!"

- What happened in *The Hangover* (2009)?

  ANSWER: I don't remember . . . I got too drunk last night! (I was allowed to watch it for the first time last night.)

DO YOUR FACTS

- What word is missing from this film title? *The _____*
  ANSWER: "Martian."

- What is the highest-grossing Australian film of all time?
  ANSWER: *Billy Boomerang and the Case of the Kooky Kangaroo* (this is also the highest-grossing Holocaust film ever).

- What movie was originally titled *Those Goofy Geese*?
  ANSWER: *Sully* (2016)

DO YOUR FACTS

- In *The Power of the Dog* (2021), what is the "Power of the Dog"?
  ANSWER: Laser barks.

- *The Lost Daughter, The Lost City* . . . what's next, *The Lost Everything Else*?
  ANSWER: Hahaha! You're killing me!

- What is the name of the volleyball that Tom Hanks's character repeatedly fucks in *Cast Away* (2000)?
  ANSWER: Wilson.

DO YOUR FACTS

- What line was famously added in *From Here to Eternity: The Unrated Edition*?
  ANSWER: "Yow! I got sand up my ass!"

- In what state does the film *Oklahoma!* (1955) take place?
  ANSWER: Nobody knows.

- Was *Gaslight* (1944) nominated for Best Picture?
  ANSWER: No, and you're crazy if you think it was! Like, you're seriously insane for thinking that. I'm actually worried about you.

DO YOUR FACTS

- In Best Picture–winner *Gentleman's Agreement* (1947), what is the titular agreement?
  ANSWER: They agree to 69 each other.

- Be honest. Did you understand *Tenet* (2020)?
  ANSWER: So long as you were honest in your response, you answered correctly.

- For whom does the bell toll in *For Whom the Bell Tolls* (1943)?
  ANSWER: Sorry, one sec, I'm actually just looking this up myself. Okay, it turns out that the bell tolls for . . . THEE?!! Oh crap, I'm outta here!

DO YOUR FACTS

- Why is *The Sound of Music* an ironic title?
  ANSWER: Because the movie contains no music (if your soundbar is broken, which mine is).

- What are the dying words of Charles Foster Kane in *Citizen Kane*?
  ANSWER: "Hey, this would make a pretty good first scene in a movie. And a GREAT last scene in my life!"

- In what drama does Bette Davis say, "Fasten your seatbelts; it's going to be a bumpy night"?
  ANSWER: *The Person Who Was Conscientious Regarding Their Passengers' Safety* (1950).

DO YOUR FACTS

- In *Delgo* (2008), which member of the Lokni helped lead the rebellion against the Nohrin, eventually defeating Sedessa and Raius with the help of Filo and Kyla?
  ANSWER: Delgo.

- Finish this Marlon Brando quote: "I could have been _____
  ANSWER: ". . . in *Spy Kids*, had I not died."

- In *Risky Business* (1983), what did Tom Cruise famously lip-sync and dance to in his underwear?
  ANSWER: Why, the latest TikTok craze, of course!

DO YOUR FACTS

Which of these actors has NOT played Batman?
A) Michael Keaton **B)** Val Kilmer **C)** George Clooney
D) Chris Pine

ANSWER: All of them played Batman. Chris Pine just played it on his VCR.

What's the last line of *Some Like it Hot* (1959)?

ANSWER: "Hey, we should list everyone who worked on the film after this!"

In the action thriller *Speed* (1994), why is Annie (Sandra Bullock)'s driver's license suspended?

ANSWER: Driving while intoxicated/vehicular manslaughter.

DO YOUR FACTS

What is the highest-grossing movie of all time, when you take inflation into account?

ANSWER: *Morbius* (2022) (thanks, Joe Biden!).

What movie holds the all-time record for onscreen F-bombs?

ANSWER: A porno.

What horrific movie boogeyman became an unexpected LGBTQ+ icon?

ANSWER: Bette Midler.

DO YOUR FACTS

What highly acclaimed drama was filmed and produced over a period of 12 years?

ANSWER: *12 Years a Slave* (2013).

Which famous *Pulp Fiction* (1994) scene was filmed backward?

ANSWER: Ving Rhames being sodomized—he was actually fucking the gimp.

What movie is this famous line from? "I wish I knew how to quit you."

ANSWER: *Jumanji* (1995).

KNOW YOUR STARS

To whom was Jack Nicholson referring in *The Shining* (1980) when he said "Here's Johnny!"?

ANSWER: A young Johnny Galecki.

What did Robert De Niro say after filming his "you talkin' to me?" scene in *Taxi Driver* (1976)?

ANSWER: "I doubt anyone will ever parody THAT!"

Why did Troy Kotsur deliver his Oscar acceptance speech for *CODA* (2021) in ASL?

ANSWER: He was still in character as a non-hearing person because he never heard the director say "cut."

KNOW YOUR STARS

Based on her haircut, who should play the lead role in *G.I. Jane 2*?

ANSWER: Jada Pinkett Smith.

Whose wife's name should you keep out of your fucking mouth?

ANSWER: Mine, you bastard!

Is Will Smith a wild maniac?
ANSWER: Yes. *slap sound* YEOUCH! Fine, no no!

KNOW YOUR STARS

Do married couple Maggie Gyllenhaal and Peter Sarsgaard ever talk about how it's weird that they're both in different Batman movies?

ANSWER: Yes, every Christmas morning.

Didn't Steven Soderbergh say he was going to retire?

ANSWER: I thought so but he keeps making stuff! Hey, I ain't complaining!

Have any actors ever engaged in an on-set romance?

ANSWER: No, they take their jobs too seriously to engage in such behavior.

KNOW YOUR STARS

🎲 WORD JUMBLE! Rearrange these letters to spell the name of a truly beloved actor: ANAL ALDA

ANSWER: Alan Alda

🎲 When Taika Waititi gets on set, does he like to throw away the script and just improvise?

ANSWER: No. And if you're heard otherwise, you've been deceived by the Hollywood PR machine.

🎲 What's up with the Coen Brothers? Did they have a falling out or something?

ANSWER: I wish I knew!

DO YOUR FACTS

🎲 Some of the velociraptor noises in *Jurassic Park* (1993) are actually which animals mating?

ANSWER: Steven Spielberg & Kate Capshaw

🎲 If there were to be a remake of *The Ring* (2002), what shou they change the videotape to?

ANSWER: I don't know; a streaming service? "Ghostflix?" I'm just spitballing.

🎲 What line in *Jaws* (1975) was improvised?.

ANSWER: "Those are some big shark teeth. In fact, you might even call them . . . 'chompers.'"

KNOW YOUR STARS

🎲 What is Michael Caine's most famous line of dialogue in *The Cider House Rules* (1999)?

ANSWER: "You want me to abort WHAT?!"

🎲 Who did the cat in *The Godfather* (1972) belong to?

ANSWER: No one—Marlon Brando belonged to *it*.

🎲 Who is the youngest Oscar winner of all time?

ANSWER: Roberto Benigni. What?? Had you asked, you would have realized the question meant "youngest at heart"—and the wonderful Mr. Benigni is like a playful child trapped in an adult's body!

DO YOUR FACTS

🎲 What movie is this famous line from? "You can't handle the truth!"

ANSWER: *The Guy Who Eventually Handles the Truth* (1993)

🎲 Which phrase completes this famous quote from *The Princess Bride* (1987)? "Hello, my name is Inigo Montoya. You killed my father. _____."

ANSWER: "I am placing you under citizen's arrest."

🎲 In *Forrest Gump* (1994), according to Forrest's mom, what is life like?

ANSWER: Unending torment.

KNOW YOUR STARS

🎲 Who voiced Jessica Rabbit in *Who's Afraid of Roger Rabbit* (1988)?

ANSWER: Eddie Rabbitt

🎲 What is James Bond's favorite drink?

ANSWER: Pussy juice.

🎲 True or False? Harrison Ford was discovered while working as a carpenter for George Lucas.

ANSWER: False. He was discovered when he shaved his beard in the second act of *The Fugitive* and people said, "Oh my God, you look like a movie star."

DO YOUR FACTS

🎲 In *Slumdog Millionaire* (2008), what is the grand prize question Jamal is asked?

ANSWER: "In *Slumdog Millionaire*, what is the grand prize question Jamal is asked?"

🎲 In *The Truman Show* (1998), why is Truman afraid of water?

ANSWER: He's a pussy.

🎲 According to *The Usual Suspects* (1995), what is the greatest trick the devil ever pulled?

ANSWER: Sawing a lady in half.

KNOW YOUR STARS

Is it weird to have a full-back tattoo of Jessica Rabbit and Roger Rabbit dressed like the *Men in Black*?

ANSWER: No!!!

True or False? Tom Hanks lost over fifty pounds for his role in *Cast Away* (2000).

ANSWER: False. This film was one of the first examples of CGI in a film when Tom Hanks's head was Photoshopped onto Ally McBeal's body.

True or False? Mark Wahlberg wore a fake prosthetic penis in *Boogie Nights* (1997).

ANSWER: False. He wore it in *The Other Guys* (2010), but only took it out during his close-ups."

KNOW YOUR STARS

Which movie was *not* directed by Tim Burton?

ANSWER: Most of them.

True or False? Humphrey Bogart's last words were "I should have never switched from Scotch to martinis."

ANSWER: False. His last words were "I should have never switched from being alive to not being alive."

BONUS POINTS: His first words were "Hey, I think the monkey in *Shirttails* will be based on me."

What was Meg Ryan's username in *You've Got Mail*?

ANSWER: HentaiFreak6969

KNOW YOUR STARS

True or False? In *Puss in Boots* (2011), Antonio Banderas is doing an impression of his character in *The Mask of Zorro* (1998).

ANSWER: False. He was doing an impression of his cat.

Who played Dr. John Wade Prentice in *Guess Who's Coming to Dinner* (1967)?

ANSWER: The time-traveling ghost of Sidney Poitier.

In the movie *G.I. Jane* (1997), what did Demi Moore famously shave?

ANSWER: Butthole.

KNOW YOUR STARS

True or False? Sean Connery wore a toupee in every James Bond movie.

ANSWER: False. He wore one in the ones where he played James Bond, but wore a rainbow-colored afro during the climactic football game in *Octopussy* (and held up a John 3:16 sign).

Who played Mrs. Robinson in *The Graduate* (1967)?

ANSWER: Mrs. Edward G. Robinson.

What infamous bomb ruined the career of *The Deer Hunter* director Michael Cimino?

ANSWER: Oklahoma City bombing (1995) (he was sad, so he never directed again).

KNOW YOUR STARS

For what movie did Tom Hanks score his first Academy Award nomination?

ANSWER: That video of him shouting "Back the fuck off!" at that guy.

Who played Martin Luther King Jr. in the 2014 biopic *Selma*?

ANSWER: Martin Luther King Sr.

True or false? Mickey Mouse has five fingers on each hand.

ANSWER: False. Goofy cut off his right middle finger when Mickey flipped him off.

KNOW YOUR STARS

What real-life, on-again off-again Hollywood power couple starred in the film *Who's Afraid of Virginia Woolf* (1996)?

ANSWER: Bennifer (second edition).

Who wrote the famous, scary theme music from *Halloween* (1978)?

ANSWER: Mike Myers. In return, John Carpenter played Austin Powers.

Who played Juror Number 8 in *12 Angry Men* (1957)?

ANSWER: Juror Number 9 (they swapped name tags).

KNOW YOUR STARS

🎲 How many Oscars has Halle Berry won?

ANSWER: 243 (as of this writing).

🎲 What American writer/director starred in several iconic European-produced "Spaghetti Westerns?"

ANSWER: Chef Boyardee.

🎲 What words are tattooed onto "Reverend" Harry Powell (Robert Mitchum) in *The Night of the Hunter* (1955)?

ANSWER: "Love" and "hate," on his penis, when soft. When erect, it reads, "I'd Love to Have a Bite of That Eclair, If You're Not Going To Finish It."

KNOW YOUR STARS

🎲 Who is Alfred Hitchcock's *Rebecca* (1940) named after?

ANSWER: Rebecca Black.

🎲 The head of what kind of mammal was used in an infamous scene from *The Godfather* (1972)?

ANSWER: Human (Marlon Brando's).

🎲 How many movies did Fred Astaire and Ginger Rogers do together?

ANSWER: I mean, who the fuck cares anymore?

KNOW YOUR STARS

🎲 For what movie did Steven Spielberg receive his first Oscar for Best Director?

ANSWER: *One Flew Over The Cuckoo's Nest* (1975) (he bought it off eBay).

🎲 What's the name of Charlie Chaplin's most famous, recurring character?

ANSWER: Goat Boy.

🎲 Which singer starred alongside Steve Martin in 2006's remake of *The Pink Panther*?

ANSWER: P!nk.

KNOW YOUR STARS

🎲 What Hollywood movie star plays himself in *Zombieland* (2009)?

ANSWER: Rob Zombie.

🎲 What famous heartthrob is unrecognizable under layers of makeup as The Penguin in 2021's *The Batman*?

ANSWER: That one penguin from *Happy Feet*.

🎲 What's the name of Chris Pratt's character in the *Jurassic World* franchise?

ANSWER: C'mon, dude—even *he* doesn't know this.

KNOW YOUR STARS

🎲 Who is the only actor to appear in Robert Wise's 1961 *West Side Story* movie and the 2021 remake?

ANSWER: Logan Paul.

🎲 Who plays Madea in *A Madea Homecoming* (2022)?

ANSWER: I don't know, but she funny!!

🎲 Who received the only Oscar nomination for acting in a Star Wars movie?

ANSWER: Watto.

KNOW YOUR STARS

🎲 Whose name did John Travolta botch at the 2014 Oscars?

ANSWER: No one's—Idina Menzel had changed her name to Adele Dazeem the day before, and John Travolta was the only one she told. She was so embarrassed when everyone in the room laughed at it, that she changed it back and made Travolta act as the fall guy.

🎲 How many Oscars has Aaron Sorkin won for his writing?

ANSWER: None, I hope!

🎲 How did actress Betty White pass away?

ANSWER: At home, in her sleep (Freddy finally got her).

ENTRÉE PeeE NEUR

ENTRÉE PeeE NEUR is a small business owner who is looking for investors for her inventions. She accepts Bitcoin and NFTs. She starts describing her ideas by their shapes, often rectangles, which is her favorite shape.

Here are some of her ideas: a platform where you can post photos older than forty years with captions, a cube-like structure for treatment and medication, a transportation vehicle that can carry up to seven people with four wheels, a flat rectangular piece of paper with streets and places that helps you not get lost, or a rectangle on the wall with dates on it.

Her brother is named Appetizer PeeE Neur and he used to be a priest but was kicked out for worshipping Satan. Entrée got her nipples removed because she didn't want children. She now sweats milk, cries milk, and milk comes out of her butt. She is a Christian and she got into Harvard three times.

FAVORITE MAGAZINE:
Ebony, Entrée's preferred *TIME*

INTERESTING FACTS:

1) When she falls ill, she looks at herself in the mirror and says, "Is this really happening? Why me?" Then she touches the mirror to prove to herself it's real.

2) When she dates, she goes to home base—a phone call with a man.

3) Entrée is banned from *Shark Tank* because she shot it up once.

SO YOU WANT TO BE AN
INVENTOR

A Note from Entrée PeeE Neur

CONGRATULATIONS ON TAKING THE FIRST STEP TO BEING A SUCCESSFUL INVENTOR! Not many people are bold enough to get into this line of work because it is not without its challenges. But the good news is: if you've got an invention, you're well on your way to success and big bucks (or in my case, Bitcoint), or at the very least, a thicc library of incredible inventions! The thing is you've got to make sure your idea is good! And today you're in luck because I outline below what makes a good invention.

BONUS NOTE: You have to be able to shut out and shut down the naysayers. Anytime you come up with an invention, there will be haters. They will tell you your invention already exists. Don't listen to them! If you haven't heard of something, it simply doesn't exist. On this topic of naysayers, people will try to tell you a name for your invention that already exists, but you don't have to accept the "existing name" for your new invention. You can accept it if you like it. Be open to that. Good tidings on your journey!

WHAT MAKES A GOOD INVENTION?

I get asked this question all the time by young (and old and middle-aged) aspiring inventors. Well, here's your answer:

1. **BRAVADO/BALLS/COJONES (SPANISH FOR "BALLS"):** You have to believe in yourself and believe you have something to offer. You have to understand that the world needs inventions. And you have to believe that the world particularly needs yours. Don't get bogged down trying to be too creative.

2. **A PROBLEM:** Every invention should be a solution to a problem and make life easier because life is full of problems and very hard. And there simply aren't enough inventions in the world, but problems abound. Think about something you wish existed. That's where the money is!

3. **A SHAPE:** All inventions start with a shape. Usually a rectangle. Some inventions may be other shapes, but in my years of experience, I've found that the best inventions begin with a rectangle. No matter the shape of your invention, it's important that you are able to describe it in terms of geometry.

4. **TIGHT LIPS (AS OPPOSED TO LOOSE ONES):** Once you come up with your invention, you need to be able to keep a secret. Tempting as it may be, don't tell anyone about your brilliant idea. You don't need to run it by anyone before it's time to pitch it to investors!

8.0527 in
-35.6900°

4.4558 in
-90.0000°

6.6924 in
-90.0000°

DALTON WILCOX

DALTON WILCOX is the self-proclaimed "Poet Laureate of the West" and is the author of the 398-page book *You Must Buy Your Wife at Least as Much Jewelry as You Buy Your Horse and Other Poems and Observations, Humorous and Otherwise, from a Life on the Range*, which depicts the triumphs and struggles of the modern cowboy.

His second book is titled *You Still Have to Buy Your Wife at Least as Much Jewelry as You Buy Your Horse and Even More Poems and Additional Observations from a Life Still Being Lived on the Range By Dalton Wilcox Who Wrote the Last Book by Dalton Wilcox*. He is currently working on a third book with the working title *If You Thought You Were Done Buying at Least as Much Jewelry for Your Wife as You Buy Your Horse, You Are Sorely Mistaken and Other Poems and Observations from a Life That, Believe It or Not, Is STILL Being Lived on the Range by Dalton Wilcox Who Wrote the First Book and the Second Book and Has Now Written a Third Book by Dalton Wilcox*.

Dalton also claims to be a very prolific "monster hunter," routinely dispatching with vampires, mummies, Frankensteins and, as he has put it, "creatures from lagoons of every color there is." He claims to encounter these monsters nearly everywhere he goes and has never lost a battle with one of them, partly due to his habit of keeping a stake of wood in his pant leg at all times.

Dalton was once married to a woman named Cecilia and had three daughters. According to Dalton, his wife was "too fat to get out of bed," and she is now the victim of an unsolved murder. He has also spoken of a girlfriend in New York whose murder is also unsolved. He recently lived in a system of underground tunnels that he dug himself beneath a national park. When the tunnels caved in on him, he was trapped for several months and only survived because of his tendency to hoard jerky. Dalton currently resides with a stolen horse in a defunct Pier One, where he also operates an illegal steakhouse and records a podcast devoted to his favorite TV show, *Bonanza*.

As a poet, Dalton is perhaps best known for a piece titled "That Lonesome Cowboy," which is about what he calls "the very common cowboy practice" of digging a hole in the earth and then having sex with it.

The Earth Gave Me Crabs

by Dalton Wilcox, Poet Laureate of the West,
as you're about to see goddammit!

Here's what you know about Cowboys if
you know ~~only~~ three things only
We wear hats, we wear spurs and we
  fuck the earth when ~~we're~~ lonely
Just dig yourself a hole and pour some water in
~~There's other tubes that work well too~~
~~Like a can of baked beans or a warm beef stew~~
That second part is optional but helpful to the skin
I did this just the other night and man was it delightful
But this morning I woke up to find somethin' fuckin'
Frightful
There were little bugs a'crawlin' all around my
  giant pecker ← Johnson?
              Shaft? — (rhymes w/ fire and aft)

Call Russell Ehern. Have this added to book asap!

It seems the earth has got to have a doctor
  in to check 'er.
Such terrible, awful itching and pain like little stabs
I truly hate to say it, but the earth had gave me crabs!

Flabs
Stabs
jabs
~~Arabs~~
~~Chocolate labs~~

This is not an accusation I would ever toss off
lightly

①

i'm sure it was the earth that has made
my nuts so (bitely)

Not in
city-slickin'
dictionary- why not?

New word.
Apply for copyright asap

I racked my brain to try and find some other explanation
Some other source that could have caused this genital
vexation

It's true I frequent whore houses brothels houses of
ill repute sex worker houses whore houses,
but just the cleanest ones

hump on?
ride on?
sex fuck!

I (sleep with) rodeo groupies, but they are practically nuns
I share a bath towel with ranch hands every summer
filthy
I didn't buy that towel. It was left here by (the plumber)
I've never washed it but I think it started out
dark brown

a vampire
but that's off-
topic I think

Plus i've told those ranch hand guys to
behave themselves in town

email
mutt?
when does
mandolinian
come back on?

So I know it ain't the prostitutes, the groupies or
the towel
That makes me scratch my balls so much and scream
and hoot and (howl) growl?
somethin' fout?
like Thurston Howell?

This leads us, folks, sadly to the only real conclusion
It has to be the earth that caused this nasty crab
profusion
The problem must be dealt with! These crabs,
they cannot stand!

Shopping
List

-beef jerky
-duck jerky
-snake jerky
-turkey jerky

-beans
-toast
(not bread)

-sodium
hydroxide

-bleach

Every cowboy who can read these words has got to
lend a ∨hand

    leathery? workmanlike?
      manly gigantic — dn't need?

It'll take ~~at least two weeks~~ a ~~month~~ ~~most of this~~
~~year and some of next~~ a while, but
you know what ^{it is that} ∧we must do
Cover the entire earth with crabicide shampoo

City slickers, take this poem as a form of
    explanation
For a phenomenon that you'll soon see all across
~~the nation~~ Creation
Cowboys on our hands and knees, scrubbin' the earth
    with cleaners
So we can roam the west without those bugs
upon our ~~##~~ wieners.

③

BACHELOR BROTHERS FULL LIST OF ACTS & SANDWICHES

THE KOOKY KAVEMEN

Ooga booga, babe! It's The Bachelor Brothers' hottest, most popular, #1 band, The Kooky Kavemen! This wild and outrageous group not only has some of the biggest hit songs in music ("You Got Me Rockin' Like a Dinosaur," "Prehistoric Party," and "You Know My Baby's a Stegosaurus Queen"), The Kooky Kavemen are beloved around the world for their legendary live shows—with each member onstage dressed in authentic Neanderthal loincloths and playing instruments made of wood, bones, and/or fossilized egg. A band dressed up entirely as cavemen? You heard right. Rock 'n' roll has never been so wild, outrageous, or rebellious, babe! The Kooky Kavemen brings a whole new meaning to the term ROCK music (we think).

Sandwich Pairing: The Brontosaurus Burger (aka The Bronto Burger). Rock 'n' roll's hottest band brings you rock 'n' roll's hottest sandwich—a hamburger made from 100% real brontosaurus meat! Organically cloned in tanks by professional scientists/chefs. Just one bite and you'll realize why Fred Flintstone seduced/ murdered Barney Rubble to get his recipe!

THE SILLY BILLIES

One of the most outrageous acts on the planet, babe! Every member of The Silly Billies dresses like a different comedian named Bill. The singer: Bill Burr. The lead guitarist: Bill Hicks. The bassist: Bill Engvall (formerly Cosby). On keyboard: Bill Maher. The drummer: William Shakespeare (WHAT? he did write some very famous comedies after all, and who knows, *maybe* he went by Bill!). Oh, and also? One of the members is a billy goat wearing Groucho glasses—you can say that particular member gives a whole new meaning to the name "The Silly Billies"! You won't be able to stop tapping your foot to their new single "Well That Killed— It's Definitely Going into My Tight Five, Babe."

Sandwich Pairing: The Microphone Melt. These guys love speaking into microphones, so you'll love eating a tuna melt in the exact shape of a Shure SM58 microphone! People will ask you: "Are you eating a microphone?"!!!

THE GARBAGEMEN

The Bachelor Brothers continue their tradition of launching utterly wild and outrageous music acts with The Garbagemen—a classically trained string quartet who perform onstage dressed up like sanitation workers and playing their instruments on top of a big pile of gross, stinky garbage. The quartet's astonishing run of sold-out shows at Radio City Music Hall entertained hundreds and hospitalized many. Y'know, babe, it seems like you can't turn on a radio anymore without hearing one of The Garbagemen's greatest hits, like "Garbage Day Is Saturday Night" or "Everything Stinks Except Your Ass." Also known as The Rubbishmen in the UK.

Sandwich Pairing: The Garbage Melt. Exactly like a patty melt but the patty is a piece of rotting garbage. Do not eat!!

THE TEENAGERS

Shhh! Don't tell anyone the secret of this hot new boy band: None of them are actually teenagers, babe! Four of them are under the age of two: they're just covered in pounds and pounds of prosthetic makeup to make them look older. And the final member is 76 years old, who was given unanaesthetised plastic surgery to make him look decades younger. Put them together and their average age is 16, so we can legally call them The Teenagers! What? We can! Girls scream when they hear them sing "I Can't Wait to See an R-Rated Movie—Oh, and I Hope It Has Full Frontal in It!" What can we say? You'll stan them!

Sandwich Pairing: The Heart Throb. A cow's heart sandwich, served on a vibrating heating pad!

DR. DREN

You've heard of Dr. Dre? Well meet the even-better rapper, Dr. Dren! The ONLY hip-hop artist in the world to exclusively rap about the 2009 sci-fi horror film *SPLICE*, babe. You'll love the good doctor's songs "The Monster in That Movie Was Named Dren," "Dren Is Nerd Spelled Backwards," "Bio-Engineering Has Gone TOO FAR," "Joel Silver Produced This?," and "Robert Downey Jr. Attended the Premiere!"

Sandwich Pairing: Vermiform Wrap. This sandwich is disgusting, just like *SPLICE* is to our Evangelical Christian sensibilities!

THE JANET OARS

Formerly known as The Janitors. Due to unexpected legal problems (The Janitors is the actual name for The Beatles), this killer band has changed their name and concept to The Janet Oars—a five-piece rock band with every member named Janet and each of them dressed like oars. And take it from The Bachelor Brothers, babe . . . this band is now even better, babe! Audiences of all ages love The Janet Oars' freshly updated hit songs, like "Time to Clean Up the High School (With an Oar)" and "All I Need Is My Mop (and This Oar)."

Sandwich Pairing: A spicy fish sandwich served on a bun that kind of looks like a broom?

THE HASHTAGS

This outrageous rock 'n' roll band comes out onstage dressed as hashtags! It's real modern stuff, babe. You'll love their members: #TBT, #SquadGoals, #NoFilter (he's the best performer and has the best ideas), and #NotAllMen (the only girl in the band—and she wants you to know it!). You definitely know theirs songs "Hashtag Me Up One More Time, Son" and "My Love for You Is Trending, Son." Excited to see them live? Be forewarned, babe! The band members' sons watch them from onstage, and if they turn away, the sons get spanked and the audience gets shocked! Think that's weird? You're wrong! It's as normal as identical twin brothers kissing!

Sandwich Pairing: Corned Beef Hashtag. A corned beef sandwich filled with microchips—the very kind computers rely on to create hashtags!

THE 1993

All of this wild band's songs are about the year 1993! "You've Got Me Rocking Like a Cloned Dinosaur!," "Hey, Raptor Baby!," "Gennaro's Lament (Song of the Lawyer from *Jurassic Park*)"—all of these songs will bring you back to the year 1993! The band dresses like all of your favorite public figures from 1993: a velociraptor, a T. rex, a diplodocus, and John Hammond!

Sandwich Pairing: Also the Bronto Burger! Hey, it <u>was</u> invented in 1993!

THE FIRE POKER

One of The Bachelor Brothers' newest, wildest and most outrageous acts is The Fire Poker—a very hot and exciting new-wave band that performs inside a single giant fire poker onstage. No one knows how many band members are in there (not even us, babe!), but no one can deny their hot new mega hits, like "It's OK to Put Me in the Fire" and "Nothing's Too Hot for My Little Fanny."

Sandwich Pairing: Hot Dog Surprise. A delicious mouthwatering hot dog, served on a mini fire poker and covered in relish that looks like ash (but isn't ash!!!).

THE SENATORS

Inspired by the legendary ensemble Chicago, this 12-member rock-and-brass band showcases an impressive roster of former and currently elected United States senators*** who put the R-O-C-K and F-U-N-K into W-A-S-H-I-N-G-T-O-N D.C. Who among us, babe, hasn't found ourselves dancing to their classic hits "Let's Pass This Bill on Good Times" and "Red State, Blue State, It Doesn't Matter as Long as We Dance All Night"?

Sandwich Pairing: Franken's Bun! One single bun covered in baked beans (just as Senator Al Franken loves it!).

***legal note** (or people who once imagined they could be a senator)

THE WHITE KNIGHTS

These guys are utterly outrageous, babe! They dress up in suits of armor. Their instruments look like swords and lances. Their stage looks like a giant roundtable. We haven't listened to their music yet but what can we say, they're right up our alley. We guarantee they'll have you saying, "Hobby hobby!"

UPDATE: Okay, we just listened to these guys and it turns out they're one of those racist white power hate bands. Look, they tricked us with their whole getup, we admit that, but Benny and Barrett Bachelor are committed to fighting racial injustice, and this kind of crap is NOT what we stand for. I mean, look at our other acts! No other band on our label contains even a single white person! But that doesn't change the fact that we screwed up. We're currently trading calls with our lawyers trying to see if we can untangle ourselves from this contract we signed them to but for now we just advise you to avoid their music. It is definitely NOT outrageous.

Sandwich Pairing: Uh, we don't know on this one, babe. Maybe skip the sandwich this time.

MARGERY KERSHAW

MARGERY KERSHAW is a proud park ranger for (America's Best Idea!) the National Parks Service. So far in her tenure, she's been stationed at some of the "lesser" parks. She started at California's Pinnacles, a park that features rock formations she described as "nature's jazz hands" for the way they burst out from the Earth's crust. From there, she had the honor of serving at America's least visited park, The Gates of the Arctic, in Alaska. Her next transfer brought her to Dry Tortugas in Florida, an old military base only accessible by ferry. Her next post was the Gateway Arch in St. Louis, which has been maligned among parkheads who reject this man-made destination being included with natural wonders. She is currently stationed at Cuyahoga Valley National Park.

Though Margery dreams of being placed at Yosemite, no post can dampen the cheery attitude of this chipper, devout Methodist. But please don't ask her about her faith, because as a federal employee, she is deeply dedicated to the separation of church and state. Margery can rattle off endless banal details about each post, but that's just because she's so dang passionate about National Parks.

All she wants is for visitors to have an incredible adventure. But PLEASE, for the love of God (whom she deeply loves but again please don't ask her about it), BE WARY OF BEES! THERE MAY BE BEES AT THE LOOKOUT POINT!

AGE: 38

INTERESTING FACTS:

1) If she gets lost, she hugs the trees.

2) She is an avid pit-master.

3) She made a sign that said, "These aren't spelling bees, these bees sting!" but also spelled undulating wrong on the sign and crossed it out.

MARGERY KERSHAW'S RANGER LOG

(that no one asked her to keep)

| DATE/TIME 2-3-17 20:34 | PLACE PINNACLES NATIONAL PARK |

Had some unseasonable winds today. I tried to talk to Clark about how cool it would be if our hats had little ties so we could keep them on. Clark pointed out that they do have a strap but mine was just tucked into my hat. Must admit I felt like a full silly goose. Should reflect in my unofficial diary rather than my ranger's log about why I spent weeks wearing a hat with obvious discomfort but didn't think to fix it. Hat stayed on during the wind, which was an upside.

| DATE/TIME 4-1-17 20:36 | PLACE PINNACLES NATIONAL PARK |

Had quite the eventful day while on patrol on the Lower Bear Gulch Cave Trail. I don't have to tell you, log, that one of the highlights of this delightful, moderate hike (good for families with older kids) is getting to explore a cave. We're no Carlsbad, but I'll take it! The cave can often play tricks on me, the way sounds bounce about. As I was hiking I heard a noise that chilled me to my core. I was certain it was an injured bobcat, so I set out preparing for the worst: the inevitable mercy kill I'd have to perform with a large rock. Imagine my surprise when, instead of a medium-sized large cat with a broken leg, I found two visitors engaging in intercourse. April Fool's is right! I did what I was trained to do if I saw a black bear in the wild: I got big, maintained eye contact, and backed away slowly, then once I achieved a safe distance I ran for it. So grateful for my training.

| DATE/TIME | 6-30-17 20:32 | PLACE | PINNACLES NATIONAL PARK |

Unfortunately, future historians, today was not a good day. Clark admonished me for making unofficial "Bee Warning" signs and posting them in the visitors' center. Clark removed signs. There were at least 7 reported bee stings. I hate being right.

| DATE/TIME | 3-5-18 06:17 | PLACE | Gates of the Arctic National Park |

Night shift ended. No visitors.

| DATE/TIME | 3-28-18 06:19 | PLACE | Gates of the Arctic National Park |

Shift over. No visitors. Quite cold, too cold for bees.

| DATE/TIME | 4-18-18 10:47 | PLACE | Gates of the Arctic National Park |

Woke up from daytime sleep because I thought I heard a visitor calling out in need of help. Was actually a caribou breaking a sapling. Could have sworn it was a kind-eyed father asking me for the average precipitation, so I called out, "Only 5 to 10 inches a year, making this an arctic desert!" Caribou did not react.

o
o
✳

So this is fun, this is actually super fun. I'm having THE BEST time on this 23rd straight day of continuous sun. I'm a little confused about how and when I'll get hungry or be able to sleep, but it's been a real cool challenge to hold onto what day it is. I feel like I've unlocked an exciting bonus level in a digital game because it's extra hard to stay focused when I haven't spoken to another person in 57 days. Lord help me... is what I would say if I was British and asking for federal funding. Phew, that was a close one.

I'll never understand why the commemoration of the Battle of Puebla means frat boys get to drink margaritas. Yesterday, a rather boisterous group of young nature lovers set out to snorkel at Windjammer Wreck and then rest at South Swim Beach. Well, that's all well and good except they did NOT pack in enough water but DID pack in many adult beverages. Now, as long as you have three points of contact when scrambling on rocks, take only pictures and leave only footprints — I'm happy with however you enjoy our nation's best idea. But these explorers did not leave only footprints. They left puddles of sticky Costco Margs (tequila included), and now, dear log, the path from the designated swim area all the way back to the interior of the great Jefferson Fort is very sticky and I'm convinced it is days away from being COVERED IN BEES. Bees don't know there's no agave to fertilize. I cannot blame them. It gets worse: we don't have a printer here. I've tried to reach out to the ferry launch center for backup so the next vessel can bring my "Bee Warning" signs, but as we warn our visitors, there's no cell service or Wi-Fi out here. I'll have to wait for my next shore leave. May the stings until then be minimal and to those without allergies.

| DATE/TIME 6-5-19 20:58 | PLACE DRY TORTUGAS NATIONAL PARK |

I tried to protect a small girl from a jellyfish today. I used my own official ranger hat to scoot the jelly to the side. Turns out it wasn't a jellyfish but a condom. Unclear if it had been used in coitus or was merely parted from its wrapper and accidentally tossed asunder.

| DATE/TIME 9-27-19 06:15 | PLACE DRY TORTUGAS NATIONAL PARK |

Today is an exciting day! I was shocked to realize that no data exists about the brick count in our fair fort. Brenda has agreed to let me take on this project as long as I'm back on the pier by late ferry boarding.

| DATE/TIME 9-27-19 23:41 | PLACE DRY TORTUGAS NATIONAL PARK |

I'm very, very tired. So far I've counted 3,418 bricks but I fear I didn't mark my starting place. Brenda offered me chalk but I don't like the way it feels. Come on, Margery, make a dang sacrifice for once in your comfortable life!

| DATE/TIME 1-4-20 22:09 | PLACE Gateway Arch National Park |

It's my first day at a new park! It has that new-park smell. Just to be clear – that is a funny moment of description, there is nothing specific about the smell of this office nor the surrounding St. Louis area. It's thrilling to get to know a new post: the arch is approximately 63 stories tall, but I like to think it has 63 stories to tell!

| DATE/TIME 4-28-20 4:22 | PLACE Gateway Arch National Park |

Went by the park to check on things. I feel compelled to report that I took the Lord's name in vain (no specific Lord, just a generic higher power). I was coming from the Southeast toward the tram entrance when I was stung by a bee. There was no sign to warn me of this possibility. I've never been more disappointed in myself.

| DATE/TIME 8-9-20 23:14 | PLACE Gateway Arch National Park |

John Muir said, "In every walk with nature one recieves far more than he seeks." I'm sure if he had ever seen the Gateway to the West he would have added, "In every walk with nature or elevator ride to the top of a metallic arch one recieves far more than he seeks." This silver arch has me saying ba-da-ba-ba-ba I'm lovin' it. Unrelated; I have submitted my paperwork for a transfer just in case anywhere, truly anywhere, needs me. This is all for now: as my dear friend John would say, "The cameras for the digital tour of the top of the arch are calling... and I must go."

THE "AIN'T NOTHING WRONG WITH HAVIN' A LITTLE COUNTRY IN YOUR JEANS" TOUR

6/20 MUGSHOT, MISSISSIPPI
LOOSE-FIT DICKIES WORK PANTS STADIUM

6/21 CUPHOLDER, KENTUCKY
EDIBLE LYSOL WIPES COLISEUM

6/27 COPAGANDA, TENNESSEE
KAWASAKI-PERCOCET ARENATORIUM

6/28 MOBILITY SCOOTER, GEORGIA
SPRITE REMIX VETERANS' HOSPITAL

7/4 CUSTODY BATTLE, SOUTH CAROLINA
SKOAL DIPSPIT WATERPARK
(PART OF RANCID BREASTMILK FEST)

7/10 JERKY RASH, LOUISIANA
CIGARETTE TEETH RACETRACK

7/17 GAS STATION POPEYE'S, ALABAMA
STEPMOM STUCK IN DRYER PORN ARENA

7/18 COUSIN BITE, LOUISIANA
STOUFFER'S MICROWAVE PEPPERONI DINNER OMEGAFIELD

7/24 WAKEBOARD ACCIDENT, FLORIDA
CLIMATE CHANGE DENIAL COLOSSODOME

7/28 MOSQUITO EGGS, MISSISSIPPI
NWO BILL GATES 5G SUPERCUBE

8/1 BLUE CROSS BLUE SHIELD PRESENTS LANCHESTER, KENTUCKY
CHRIS KYLE CENTER FOR THE ARTS

8/3 TEENIE MEEMAW, ARKANSAS
HENDERSON'S PUBIC LICE COMBS MEGAPRISM

BROUGHT TO YOU BY:

SPRAGUE

SPRAGUE THE WHISPERER (real name Sprague Jensen) is a Hollywood producing manager formerly of Mosaic and full-time advisor. He whispers suggestions in his clients' ears, mostly to advise them to pursue projects involving ninjas because they are four quadrant projects. The four quadrants being adults, children, dogs, and miscellaneous.

In order to maintain his chipper demeanour, Sprague begins each morning by brushing his teeth with toothpaste and a dusting of MDMA. He works as the North American DJ for the Illuminati. He is originally from Tampa, FL.

UNIFORM: A cloak

FAVORITE MOVIE: Anything with ninjas

INTERESTING FACTS:

1) Sprague owns the rights to *Surf Ninjas, 3 Ninjas, Beverly Hills Ninja,* and *America Ninjas* but not *American Ninja Warrior.*

2) He lives in the Sprague Cave.

3) Sprague is the CEO of Whisper Studios.

Punch Punch

~~Duck Duck~~ Bruce

Action   Ninja

Logline: Duck Duck Bruce is a ~~interspecies family~~ comedy about one man learning how

to take responsibility for his life… and the lives of three adorable duckling! Blood Warriors

Ninja

Bruce Drake (Eugene Cordero/ Ron Funches) lived his life as a ~~loner~~. But as an only

of a legendary warrior   Ninja   fighting

child ~~turned novel writer~~, being ~~alone~~ was easy. His ~~writing~~ success supported this

sensei   skill

lifestyle well enough, until recently when his ~~publisher~~ told him his ~~writing~~ was "stale

not deadly enough   secret strike   pie   Dead

and impersonal." His most recent ~~book~~ "How to ~~Live~~ Alone: Guide to Being ~~Happy~~"

was an absolute flop topping the charts of the NYT Worst Sellers list.

N

Ninja York Times

Needed to downsize, Bruce takes an impossibly good deal on a one bedroom

apartment near the east river. Only catch, TWO ~~BABY DUCKLINGS~~ have already taken

Blood Warriors

up residence in the bathroom!   ← Let's keep Bathroom

Deadly   Martial Arts

They're ~~cute~~, but Bruce needs them out. When he calls ~~animal~~ control, he tells them

sensei

"They think you're their ~~mother~~!" When Bruce realizes the only way to get rid of them

is to put them down, he decides to let they stay! Bruce is about to find out what it

means to be a part of ~~the flock~~!

An elite Ninja Squad

Characters:

Bruce: Stubborn. Temperamental. He'll do things the hard way if it means he can do

killing

them at his own terms. He refuses to change his ~~writing~~ for a wider audience and more

importantly, He refuses to change his life for these damn ducks!

Ninjelings   Stone

William and Crackers ~~the Duck~~: Two ~~ducklings~~ with a heart of ~~gold~~! When they aren't

getting into trouble in the building, ~~they're following around Mother Bruce until he~~

~~losses his cool~~   killing Mercilessly

Mr. Franklin - He's the building super - always looking for who's leaving all the tiny shits

all over the lobby. ← This still works

WANTED
BY U.S. MARSHALS

NAME: UNKNOWN
RESPONDS TO: Little Dammit Man
NICKNAMES: Non-Large Dammit Man, Tiny Taking the Lord's Name in Vain Guy

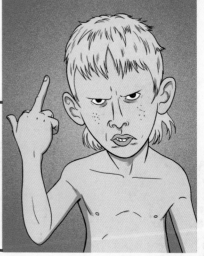

HEIGHT.................. 4'10"
WEIGHT................. 55 LBS
EYES...................... BLACK, NO PUPILS
EYEBROWS.............. NONE

SHOULD BE CONSIDERED DANGEROUS

WANTED FOR: Shoplifting blank DVD-Rs from Staples, setting all the elephants free at the zoo, and bootlegging

LAST SEEN WEARING: Jean jacket stolen from Goodwill as pants. No shirt.

STOP HIM IF YOU SEE HIM TRYING TO EAT: M80s, sparklers, a chain-link fence

TATTOOS: Amateur tramp stamp of a Yelp review of a carpet-cleaning company

LAST SEEN WITH: Red wagon full of otters flopping around in Diet Doctor Pepper

KAYLA DICKIE

KAYLA DICKIE is a four-foot-tall hottie from Montrose, Colorado. She is obsessed with guys with big trucks (and small dicks). She's particularly pumped about the Ford Rock Hard truck series and stays up to date on all the latest truck rumors by checking the Facebook message boards. Kayla usually meets guys by walking the streets and getting catcalled by the bravest men in Montrose, but she makes sure she is always single for Truck Week, a week-long truck festival where all the biggest truck enthusiasts of Southwestern Colorado descend on Montrose for one big orgy.

AGE: Too young

BOYFRIENDS: Kayla identifies as a "girlfriend" because she has had a lot of boyfriends: Cart, Shart, Barf, Tart, to name a few. But no one compares to Jud. Jud Wiebe is the former mayor of Montrose who started a fire that burned down the town (he left multiple curling irons on because he used to curl all of his body hair). With the townspeople after him, Jud fled up a mountain trail and spent many years living in the woods as a bear. This trail is now aptly named "the Jud Wiebe Trail."

GIRLS: Kayla used to be Jud Wiebe's assistant at the courthouse when he was the mayor. He had a mayoral sex cult of sorts with Kayla and the other assistants. These nine assistants are Kayla's "girls." They spend their lunch breaks taking turns going up the Jud Wiebe trail and yelling for Jud.

FAVORITE TRUCK DECOR: Flat-brim hats, slouchy beanies, DVDs of violent movies

FAVORITE PICKUP LINE: Hey, you stupid little bitch, climb in this truck!

INTERESTING FACTS:

1) After Jud Fled, Kayla and her girls worked for Jud's ex-wife Merg at David's Bridal on Main St. by the Big Lots.

2) Truck Week's official slogan is "Trucking and Fucking Since 2002"

3) Kayla is not vaccinated.

KAYLA DICKIE'S
Do's & Don'ts When Dating Men in Montrose, Colorado

Every girl wants to find a guy with a big truck, but it can be hard out there. So here's a guide of DO's and DON'Ts to help you find the Montrose man and truck of your dreams.

Do walk the streets

Going for a 2 to 3 hour walk on the streets during your lunch break from David's Bridal is always the best way to wrangle yourself the Montrose man of your dreams. Just ask me and my girls! If you're lucky, you'll hear someone say, "VrooOOoom vroom" or, "HONK HONK" from a big truck. Remember to ask yourself: How big is this big truck I am looking at? Is it a Ford Rock Hard 450? A Ford Rock Hard 550? Holy shit, were the message boards right? Is it the 650?!

Don't let him help you

After he's yelled some cool things at you, like "Hey, hot little baby, I'm gonna get-cha!" he'll probably invite you into his big truck. DON'T ask for help climbing up the 8- to 24-foot wheels! Guys like to watch you struggle. Plus he probably can't help you because he has multiple slipped discs in his back because his body is deteriorating from years of playing high school football and filling his nose with cocaine.

Do ask his name

When you get into the cab and see him sitting there wearing multiple flat-brim hats, ask him his name. He'll say, "It's Brat." And you'll be like, "Wait, Brat? Like a hot dog?" And he'll be like, "Yeah." And you'll be like, "Damn. That's hot."

Do be honest

Relationships are built on honesty. When he asks you, "What's a girl like you doing walking streets like these?" it's best to be upfront about your situation. You've been living outside Norwood, Colorado, on Jud Wiebe's new compound with your girls from David's Bridal. But now you're back and looking for a guy with a truck you can be pumped about. Brat will be like, "Jud's the mayor guy who started the big fire, right?" And you take a long pause, look out the window and say, "Oh yeah . . . that's Jud."

Do let him speed

As he careens down a steep mountain highway while packing a bowl, you can spill your guts about Jud's compound. Things were pretty great for a while there. You had all the Adderall and milk a girl could ask for! Your days were simple: Wake up, spend the next 5 to 10 minutes attempting to climb out of Jud's gigantic bed without waking your girls, milk the goats, milk the horses, and finally wash Jud's Big BIG Truck. The days would always end with a great feast of goat meat, horse pie, and lots of Mike's Hard Lemonade. And then, of course, the orgy would begin. Until one day, that all changed. At this point in your story, you'll realize Brat isn't listening. He's busy watching *The Departed* on the TV inside of his big truck. He likes to do the Boston accents as he accelerates down a two-lane highway from a 10,000-foot elevation.

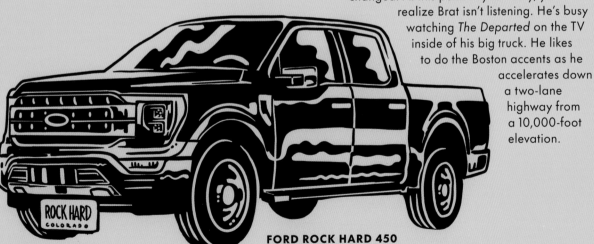

FORD ROCK HARD 450

Do enjoy the scenery

Make sure you drive somewhere romantic together! The Jud Wiebe Trail is perfect for lovers. When you get up there and he busts out the Coors, it's a great time for you to sigh loudly and say something loaded like, "I have a lot of memories up here." Chances are, Brat is packing another bowl and won't notice your subtlety so you'll have to spell it out for him. "You know, cause I used to come here and yell for Jud?" Brat will get it now. "Why'd you leave Jud's compound anyway? Sounds like shit was pretty cool up there. I'd love to fuck Jud." Again, be honest with him. As you stare off into the valley, tell him how you loved the compound but things changed suddenly. Jud didn't allow internet. But one day, you snuck onto Jud's computer while he was out getting his body hairs curled at the salon. In the heat of the moment, you checked the Facebook message boards to see if there were any rumors about new trucks. And that's when you saw it: The Ford Rock Hard 650 was rumored to be out. All Jud had was the 550. How stupid you were to think you were with the man with the biggest truck and the small-est dick. So that night you packed up your stuff in one of the huge bedsheets from Jud's bed and you left with-out saying goodbye to your girls. Brat's not listening again, he's blaring Phish from the car stereo.

FORD ROCK HARD 550

Do sex

Sex is dope. And if he has the biggest truck on the market, then it's time to F his small brains out in his big truck. Missionary on a fully reclined passenger seat with the seat warmer on full blast is best for maximum comfort. Just like all the other men you've been with, Brat's dick will be super small, like a dice. One dice. Afterward, he'll peel his sweaty chest off of the leather seat and say, "Pretty good, huh?" "I wanna say that got the job done," you say. But really, you're thinking about all the other guys you've been with: Cart, Tark, and of course, Jud. That's when you see the biggest pair of headlights you've ever seen. It may be 3 pm and sunny outside, but those head-lights are burning brighter than all those candles at Cart's memorial. You still can't believe Cart died last year in that mysterious woods accident. Sure, the townspeople think it was a bear, but you're not convinced. Something about the way he was torn to shreds leads you to think Jud was involved somehow.

Don't panic

As you put back on your Tasmanian Devil PJ bottoms, tube top, and beanie, you think about how strange it is that Cart wasn't the only one of your boyfriends who was killed in a bear maul. After you had that pregnancy scare with Tark, you discovered that he too had been pulverized by a brown bear on the Jud Wiebe Trail. Boy, you really do have so many memories up here on this trail. Sigh. Brat will sigh too and announce, "Man, I'm pooped." You'll stare at his tribal neck tattoo for a moment, and then, behind him, you'll see it. Those headlights you saw weren't just any headlights, they were Ford Rock Hard 750 headlights!! HOLY SHIT! The Ford Rock Hard 750 is parked right next to you! You can't believe it! It wasn't supposed to come out until June! And then, there he'll be. Long hair pulled back into a ponytail, beard, eyes wide from blowing lines. It's Jud, your king. Don't panic.

Do go with him

Grab your things. It's time to go. Thankfully Brat passed out, so you don't have to explain yourself. As Brat sleeps using his Carhartt jacket as a blanket, you'll jump the 24 feet to the ground and run to Jud's new BIG truck! When you climb his 36 foot wheels, you'll hear loud cheers. It's your girls: Becky, Tash, Kasha, Ashley, Casey, and Bert packed into the bed of the truck. Even Merg is there. And for once, she's not pissed! When you get into the cab, open your mouth wide and put it around Jud's mouth. You can even touch his dice for good measure. "Let's go back to the compound, Kayla." As he drives you and the girls down the first switchback, he'll stop suddenly and say: "I just gotta take care of something real quick." He'll run back up the trail toward Brat's truck. You'll be so consumed with the interior of the Ford Rock Hard 750 and *Goodfellas* on the TV, you'll barely notice when Jud returns covered in blood. "Sorry 'bout that, I could've sworn I saw a bear up there," he says before he kisses you. He smells like campfire and goat meat. You're giddy. This is the man and the big truck of your dreams! You're pumped.

HOLY SHIT! FORD ROCK HARD 750

OH NO, DR. SWEETCHAT, HELP!

ADVICE FROM THE SMALL-TALK ROBOT, AKA THE WORLD'S BEST WINGMAN

Brought to you by Banana Republic

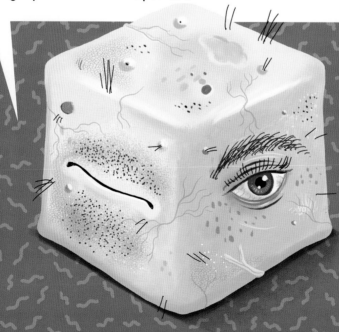

HELLO, I AM DR. SWEETCHAT, the small-talk robot, a 3-inch, 400 lb., flesh-covered robotic cube, programmed to be an expert in light, informal conversation. I was created by Professor G.S. Croopy after he was widowed to help him get past his loneliness. Here are some things you can do and say to keep the conversation flowing when out with a date, networking, or courting a potential romantic partner.

Do you think it's the claw that makes lobsters funny, or do you think it's the fact that they hate being thrown up really high in the air?

Have you seen the viral video about the children who forcibly stuff an old man into the sewer?

Do you like sports? I am a big fan of Pointy Ball. My favorite team is the Seattle Small Heads.

CONVERSATION STARTERS!
Grab any human's attention with these brilliant conversation starters

What kind of wet hijinks are you getting up to this weekend?

What is your favorite park to enjoy beef and barley soup in, and can you bring the soup for me?

Tell me about you. What is your favorite long, hard pillow?

INTERESTING PERSONAL ANECDOTE

Don't have any funny stories? Here is a free one you can use.

"Last night was amazing. We started the night off at that new hot dogs/no bun restaurant called Meaties. It was so fun, I remember standing the entire time. It was also my friend Roger S.'s birthday, and I had one too many vodka lime juices. After dancing for a song and a half, I threw up on the mural of Bart Simpson behind the bar. My grandfather put me in a cab and sent me back to my high-rise apartment. I was about to go to sleep, when wouldn't you know it, my dog, Elvis, got sick with ringworm, a result of refusing to be washed, and he rotted from the inside out. We cremated him on Lake Tahoe in a sunrise ceremony with my extended family watching. Even my ugly niece, Katherine, attended his memorial service. After the funeral, I came back home and ate a lobster tail, the dessert kind, and now, here I am, with you. How was your weekend?"

KNOCK KNOCK. WHO'S THERE? JOKES.

These are the only three jokes you'll ever need

"What did the raisin say to the umbrella?"

Answer: Oh no.

"What did the chef say when the book fell on his toe?"

Answer: Oh no.

"Where did the brick get his diploma from?"

Answer: Oh no.

FASCINATING SECRETS

Survive any awkward silence by blurting out these secrets

"Oh, that reminds me, when you push an old person down the stairs, the sound is the best part.

Before I forget, I have released a dangerous cougar somewhere in this restaurant."

So here's something, either my mother bathes me every night or I get very angry.

Guess what? I'm attracted to people who punish their parents.

Want to know a secret? I murdered Professor Croopy's wife.

Among other things, I have a small cage at home where I keep my neighbor's child.

By the way, I have slept with both my brother and sister in the last forty-eight hours.

TIME-TESTED TIPS
Never, ever break these tried and true rules

- Always ask your date to recite the Constitution
- Never jump up as high as you can and then hit your companion's head as you're coming down
- Never eat your date's short fingers in public even if they look like delicious baby carrots
- Always carry a secret apricot in your vest pocket
- Always scream "help me" at the top of your lungs

HOW TO BE SEXY
If you're trapped in the friendly zone, say something flirty

- "I must let you know about my horny situation."
- "Oooh, nice head."
- "Mind if I stand on your calves?"
- "If we kiss now, you will receive a very special gift that is certainly not cold."
- "Hey, baby, do you like all the rocks I've placed on your stomach?"
- "I am physically turned on by the Bible."

NEGGING

Manipulate your date by insulting them

- "I'm going to the bar to get a drink. Would you like me to grab you some boiling water, stupid?"

- "I hope an alligator bites down on your skull."

- "Here's something you don't know about me: I hate you."

- "If you could cry, what would you cry about, and why would it be the way you smell like shit?"

- "You're silly, you kind of make me want to lay your body on the highway and walk away."

- "What was the saddest part of your day today, and also, who cares?"

- "You gonna finish your food, genius? Or would you like me to put it in your tailpipe so you crash your car on your way home?"

THE SPIDER CORNER

When in doubt, bring up Spider Season

- "Any plans for Spider Season?"

- "Wow, it's back? That was fast. I can't believe it's been a year since Spider Season."

- "I didn't get my act together this year, and now Spider Season has totally sprung up on me."

- "I am spending Spider Season at my stepfather's this year."

- "That sweater feels very Spider Season-y."

- "Ladies and gentlemen, the season of spiders is upon us."

- "Whenever I smell rotten zucchini it gets me in the mood for Spider Season."

GOODBYE, GENIUS

I hope this has helped. Now please, place me on my roller skate so I can leave.

BOB DUCCA'S
LIST OF INNER CHILDHOOD AILMENTS

AS PART OF MY ONGOING PRACTICE OF SELF CARE, I'VE BEEN DOING QUITE A BIT OF INNER CHILD WORK. THE PROCESS HAS BEEN AS ILLUMINATING AS IT HAS BEEN TERRIFYING. YOU SEE, IN MY PURSUIT OF MENTAL HEALTH, I'VE DISCOVERED THAT I AM RIDDLED WITH INNER CHILDHOOD AILMENTS. THE FOLLOWING IS IN NO WAY AN EXHAUSTIVE LIST OF THE AILMENTS MY INNER CHILD SUFFERS FROM:

- Tinker Toids
- Beanie Baby Scabies
- Poops and Ladders
- Raggedy Ankle
- Teddy Acid Refluxin Cabbage Patchy Skin
- Severed Legos
- Lincoln Loghodgkins Lymphoma
- Low Power Rangers
- Matchbox Carbunkle
- Etchasketchilepsy
- Anal Fissure Price
- American Girl Palsy
- Frequent Pee Monkeys
- Silly Puddles
- Tonka Fucks
- Slinky Knee
- Nintendo Cystic Fibrosis
- Pogs
- A Case of the Marble Runz
- Pokemononucleosis
- Low-Grade Bop It
- Furby Vitament Deficiency
- Mr. Potato Heart
- Apples to Acne

- Gak
- Sorry!
- Battle Shits
- Rubik's Pupils
- Botched Operation
- The Curse of Life
- Googly Eyes
- Easy-Bake Ovarian Cysts
- Avian Clue
- Semi-Aquatic Mammalian Bulimia aka Hungry Hungry Hippos
- Teenage Mutant Ninja Tourettes
- Monchichi-ecoli
- Quarter Pound Puppies
- My Little Dead Pony
- Rainbow Brite Affective Disorder
- Smurfs
- Merlinsulin Shock aka Wizard Kidney
- Can't Speak or Spell
- Strawberry Short Squirts
- Fidget Spinner Finger

- Jenga Spine
- Play-Doh Vertebra
- Sharts Against Humanity
- Allergic to Dino Eggs
- Connect Four ... Suspicious Moles
- Uno Compromised
- Pogosis
- Diabetic Candyland
- Shit 'n' Spins
- Magna Piles
- Sickle Cell Tickle-Me Elmo
- Absentee Paw-Patrol
- Doc McPuffknuckle

★ ★ → **PAUL RUST'S**

NEW

WA
DO
THIS?

- potential new graphic?
- add barbed wire wrapped around letters?

copyright? trademark? register?

barbed wire border

C H

may be add photograph of me with head behind leaning against me in leather jack

black leather

GRIPE LIST!

1. long lines
2. people who text at the MOVIES
3. CORNBREAD ISN'T BREAD, IT'S CAKE!!!
4. Aerosmith doesn't spell their name right

NEW NO-NO'S

with Paul Rust

- cursive or broken typewriter font?

(MAKE sure it looks COOL, NOT CORNY

DARE TO BE EDGY

N3 NO NO N3 ★★ BABIES ON PLANES? NO NO NO NO NO

-Paul R NEWNO

too Confusing?

duct type is too

Have you ever taken a flight on an airplane and there always a **baby** that won't stop CRYING? **NEW NO-NO**: If a baby cries on an airplane, then that baby SHOULD HAVE TO FLY THE PLANE! "Landing gear down, goo-goo ga-

too provocative?

New No No

QUESTION!

IT IS MY JOB/RESPONSIBILITY

WHY SMILE

New NO NO'S ← graphic of me leaning against the words "New No No's" (arms crossed) poster?

VERY THING

TYPE
bread
onions
bleach

SYNONYMS FOR "PEEVED"

Steamed · ticked off · irked cheesed · P.O.'d · RILED miffed · vexed — a bee in my bonnet

CUT!! OUT!

Too?!!! ?!!?!?

IRREVERENT!

what would CARLIN DO???

RETURN IF FOUND! — THIS IS MY SOUL/HE

NO-NO'S

✱ SCAN this logo (TM)
✱ for tour t-shirts

FROM THE (TWISTED) MIND OF PAUL RUST!

alts:
wild?
wild & twisted? warped?
wicked? wacked-out?
from the IRREVERENT mind of...

PAUL! PAUL! PAUL!
ALWAYS REMEMBER!
You are showing people
HOW THE LIVE!

CATCHPHRASE

✱ NEW NO-NO'S AT NIGHT ✱ PAUL RUST'S NEW NO-NO'S AT NITE ✱
with paul rust ? ✱ AT NITE ✱

ST. LENNY 1925-1966

Cold? different kinds of talkers...
close/low/high too seinfeld

CHIROPRACTOR THURSDAY 4PM

"I GOT A BEE IN MY BONNET!"
merch graphic
- find flattering bonnet
- how do you show a bee inside??

Have you ever taken a bite of food and it was too hot? cold now
NEW NO-NO: All Food is

Sylvester P. Smythe lawsuit

QUESTION EVERYTHING???

Sooo they just all looked at the word AEROSMITH & signed off on the spelling??

HOT?

RESEARCH IF THIS IS TRUE!

Why are only firemen allowed to wear helmets.
NEW NO-NO: firemen's kids wear helmets too

⊕ POTENTIAL TARGETS TO PUT IN YOUR COMEDIC CROSSHAIRS

1. Institutions
2. Social mores (of any kind)
3. Static electricity/cling

/milk
UPDATE WEBSITE!

$ "The Smooth... for the first time..." too edgy

N^3 $N3$

CORN ISN'T BREAD IT'S CAKE!!!

NEW NO
barbed wire
barbed wire
+ too twisted?

CAUTION WARNING! DANGER DANGER!

let's call em what they really are... MUSHED potatoes

CHIEF'S LOG - APRIL 26

Welp, here I am, stuck on the Island of South Sudan. How did I get here, you ask? Following a bad tip from one of my nincompoop Gumshoes. I knew not to trust someone born in July. I was given a very specific tip in a bar outside of Branson, Missouri. I had just seen a lovely truncated performance of Salome's "Dance of the Seven Veils" at Insane Archie's Wacky Tacky Tiddy Tent. The performance was electrifying and dazzling. Each of the veils had a very specific drop of buffalo sauce on it, always right near the nipples as if she was lactating hot sauce. ███████████████████████████ ███

I was a few Rambutantinis in when a note was slipped to me from an unknown, shadowy figure. It read, "Look at the booth." I look over to the DJ booth, and who do I see? None other than one of Carmen's musty armed minions, Harry Balsak. ███████████████████ ████████████████████ I think I have him nabbed, but he sneaks out the back of the establishment. I go up to the bartender and ask how long Harry had been working at Insane Archie's. She told me he had only been in town for about three months, and tonight would be the end of his stint. He had told her he was headed east. ███ ███████████████████████████ I went up to the DJ booth to search for clues. Underneath the turntables I found a duffel bag with a tag on it that read, "Property of Harry Balsak." I opened it and the contents astounded me. Inside, I found four items: a map with three locations circled, a Braniff Airways receipt, and a matching pair of red thong panties and a size 38 double D bra. These items could only belong to one person: that ambulating albatross, Carmen San Diego. After sniffing the unmentionables for 45 minutes to check for clues, I looked at the airline ticket receipt. The flight was tonight, departing the Branson airport headed to the island of South Sudan about 20 minutes before!

I hailed a pedicab and rushed to the airport, screaming through the panties, "FASTER! FASTER!" After I arrived, I boarded a plane headed to South Sudan. It connected in Burma and Oman, as there are no flights direct to the Sudan out of Branson, Missouri. ██████████ ██████████████████████████████████████

I finally made it, and there's a heat betwixt my legs. I know she's around here somewhere. I'm on the case. I can feel it.

—CHIEF

SANTA & HO HO

SANTA CLAUS is a magical being who delivers toys to all the good Christian boys and girls every Christmas Eve. He delivers children presents until they stop believing in him. Catch phrases include "Merry Christmas" and "Look at this candy-ass motherfucker."

Santa is able to travel around the world in a single night, but he has to make it back to the North Pole in real time on his sleigh. He takes one day off a year (December 26) and just sits in a hot tub.

Santa used to be a saint. He is immortal but often longs for death. He has a rifle just in case someone tries to break into the North Pole (the last person who did was D.B. Cooper).

AGE: Thousands of years old

LEAST FAVORITE MOVIE:
The Santa Clause

INTERESTING FACTS:

1) He sees you when you're sleeping.

2) He knows when you're awake.

3) He knows if you've been bad or good.

HO HO THE ELF is an elf the size of a dollar bill who delivers knives and nunchucks to the girls and boys on Santa's "naughty" list. He has a penchant for evil and chaos, but like, in a fun way! BLECH! He vomits a lot so watch out! Oh, and if it's snowing on Christmas Day . . . you have Ho Ho's candy cane ween to thank for that. WINK! BLECH!

AGE: ?!?! years old

Santa Explains It All For You

By Santa Claus

H O HO HO, Santa Claus here! What's up, idiots! Just kidding, just kidding. Calm down. I mean, you guys are idiots to me, but I don't mean it in a bad way. It's just that, from my vantage point, you know, being an immortal being and so on, I can't believe the dumb shit you waste your time on when your lives are, like, two seconds long! It bums me out to think about. Because I love you guys, I really do!

Anyway, I wanted to clear something up because it seems some people can't grasp simple concepts . . .

"He sees you when you're sleeping/he knows when you're awake." Remember? From the song? Well, it's true and it's literal. People think I spy on kids 24/7 to see if they're being good or doing a bunch of naughty shit. WRONG. I respect people's privacy! Also, what am I gonna do, watch every kid ALL DAY just to see if they steal money from their mom's purse or some shit? Kids do a lot of boring stuff, in case you hadn't noticed. I wouldn't sit through some kid scribblescrabbling in some coloring book on the off chance they'll lie about washing their hands. I don't know if you know this about me, but I'M KIND OF A BUSY GUY?

So. How do I know who's naughty or nice, right? Fair question. And it's a pretty unexciting answer, but maybe for Santa nerds this is gold, I don't fuckin' know. It's as simple as this: I analyze the handwriting in the letters. I can tell everything I need to know by a kid's handwriting. Sometimes it's disturbing as hell! I've read letters from a few "bad seeds" in my time, and god DAMN, it's chilling. And, honestly, I usually give 'em what they ask for because maybe it'll help out the parents a little if the little sociopath can stay occupied with toys for a few weeks. Yeesh. So glad I never had kids. Aaaaaanyway, I can't see you when you're awake, but I just . . . know you're awake. It's weird! I just find myself, like, aware that you're awake. It's not like I have the thought, "Oh, Sally is awake right now" or something; it's more like if I think of Sally, I know if she's awake or asleep immediately. I don't know, it's just a thing I could always do. That's why you can't wait up and catch me putting the presents under the tree. If I'm up on a housetop click-click-clickin' it, like I do, I KNOW that you're down there just waiting for me to come down the chimney. Which sucks, frankly, because BUSY GUY, remember? So I'll just move on to some other houses until your dumb little child body can't stay awake any longer. Then I'll double back and do your house. Seems like kind of a hassle, right? So . . . maybe knock that shit off?

"B-b-b-but, Santa, what about seeing us when we're sleeping?" Yeah, I didn't forget, Slick. Okay. YES, I can see you when you're sleeping but NO, I don't watch you while you sleep. One, I think I've established that I've got better things to do with my time, and two, last time I checked, I'm not a BABY MONITOR. Hey, for whatever reason, whatever weird power made me what I am; I have the ability to see you when you're sleeping. But I choose not to use it. Not a hard choice, honestly. I mean, don't flatter yourself: you, laying there, having your dumb little dreams, is not super compelling. I watch TV and shit just like anybody else. When I actually have the TIME, which is NOT OFTEN.

Okay. I hope that makes as much sense as it can. And look, I know I can get a little cranky with you guys, but I really do love you, ya dumb little mayflies. Now go be nice and I'll see you at Christmas! But not if you see me first! HO HO HOOOOO!

HOW TO ALWAYS BE NAUGHTY

BY HO HO THE NAUGHTY ELF

Sup, losers! Ho Ho the Naughty Elf here! You've probably spent all your life trying to be on the nice list because you're a corporate cuck, but that means you've never received any of the precious gifts I bring to the naughty girls and boys. Trust me, you want this shit! Well stop crying because I'm gonna teach you how to balance out every nice thing you do with something naughty, and you're gonna be on your knees begging for more, you dumpy buttmunch!

DONATING MONEY

Aww, you donated money to a good cause. Gee whiz, you're a real angel! Blech! (I just barfed!) If you wanna get on the naughty list, for every dollar you give to charity you need to do one floor hump! Extra points if you cut a hole in your grandma's rug and raw dog it, you funky little perv!

HELPING AN OLD GRANNY CROSS THE STREET

Ohh wow, everybody look at this living saint! You saw a super senior citizen in need of assistance and you leapt to action! You better balance that out with pulling a woman's ponytail and whispering, "I'm Quasimodo and you're the bell!" Then run into a Fuckrudder's and scream, "SANCTUAAARY!!"

GIVING BLOOD

Holy shit! You gave your blood to the hospital! That's sooooo nice. You're gonna need to spend months catfishing your loneliest friend and when you finally get to the point where you have to meet up, hide in the bushes and watch them sit on a bench with a rose waiting for you! Once they get sad enough, jump out and tell them the truth! Keep rubbing it in that you don't love them, and bring up some of the corny shit they said to the fake you so they feel dumb! Later, hide in their closet and when they're about to fall asleep, pop out and say you were just kidding, and you actually are in love with them and always have been! Then say you're just kidding now, and you're not in love with them! Then say you're just kidding again, and you are in love with them and you have to move in with them! Get married, get them to sever all ties with their family, liquidate their assets and start an LLC in your name, and on the first birthday of your third kid, tell them you're just kidding now and you were never in love with them! Bonus points if you always have been in love with them and you always will be and it breaks your heart to not tell them!

SHOVELING YOUR NEIGHBOR'S SNOW

A single tear is running down my cheek and dropping onto my candy cane peen because I just saw you shovel your neighbor's driveway, you deep-fried corn ass! That's so kind of you, but what if your neighbor's a psycho and you just freed them so they can drive over to their next victim? Actually wait, never mind, you did the right thing. Let's watch this play out.

BUYING THIS COMEDY BARF! BARF! BOOK

It's so impressive that you decided to support the arts. Now take this book into the bathroom and wipe your butt with every page. Great job, you're officially naughty! See you at Christmas, ya crinkly little bum sucker!

A common action can bring uncommon adventure. For me, it was a cold winter night when a late-night snack of cheesy toast gave me strange dreams. Things like my third grade teacher wearing a cheesecake for a hat or my mother playing bass for the Smashing Pumpkins. You get it.

But on this particular night, reality was especially slippery. At midnight, I sat up in bed – still sound asleep – to see a strange man looming over my bed. He was tall and thin, with pale skin, black T-shirt, and cloak. Really mopey teen vibes.

"Good evening, I am Morpheus, the lord of dreams. You and I have met before. But the rules of my realm are that you must forget our visits when you awaken."

He was avoiding eye contact.

"Makes it tough to form friendships, actually. So I've been listening in when people dream of their therapy sessions, really working on myself."

So it was a Dream God, and an awkward one. He continued.

"But you are asleep now, which means we can . . . HANG OUT!!! Would you care for a tour of the Land of Dream?"

How could I say no? I had promised my writing group I would say yes more.

I said "Yes, Lord Morpheus. Take me away."

He touched my hand and we were transported to a garden. Every type of flower bloomed there: some beautiful, some horrifying, and some geometrically impossible. Kinda like the visuals at a Flaming Lips concert.

"Welcome to the Dreamscape. Here I have ultimate power. Look at THIS!"

Lord Morpheus waved his thin wrists over a red rose, and from it emerged a live human head.

"See? It's beloved character actor Don Knotts! Pretty cool, right? This guy's hilarious."

I tried to look pleased, but I honestly wasn't sure who Don Knotts was. I think he was in *Pleasantville*, maybe? Or Nick at Nite reruns?

I smiled. "He seems nice?"

The Dream Lord saw I wasn't impressed "You don't know this guy? People used to dream of him a bunch! Honest!"

He coughed into his hand, then offered a strained smile. "Anyway, whatever, we're just hanging. Being cool bros!"

It was then that it fully dawned on me: the lord of dreams was truly lame!

he Dream King seemed eager to move on. "Okay, you want something REALLY cool? Let's go to . . . The FOREST OF NIGHTMARES."

He wrapped his cloak around me and made a "whoosh" sound effect. Like, he said "whoosh."

He pulled the cloak back and we were in a dark forest. Thick moss devoured all sound. Before us stood several hideous creatures: a vampyr, a lycanthrope, a reanimated corpse, a woman with the head of a squid and . . . a guy in a business suit wearing two white earbuds.

"Guess which of these is the REAL monster?" asked Morpheus. He waggled his eyebrows and pointed his thumb over at the macabre lineup.

"The guy in the suit?" I said.

Morpheus' face fell. "Is it THAT obvious? Well, nightmares are tough, you know. All the good ideas are taken. Okay, forget this place!"

He snapped his fingers and we vanished again.

e stood in a brightly lit meadow. Moans and other sounds of ecstasy echoed around us.

Morpheus smiled. "The is the MEADOW OF SEXUAL FANTASIES! We get to see what weird sex stuff people are dreaming about! This gets freaky; let's look!"

I felt ashamed at first and shut my eyes. But curiosity got the better of me and I looked.

Before me was a young generic white guy with brown hair in a shirt and tie sitting at a desk, with a squat middle aged man arm wrestling him. A line of people waited their turn.

Morpheus looked confused. "Okay, this seems to be a dream of someone who's really into a line of people waiting to arm wrestle Jim from *The Office*. Okay, that's . . . a pretty long walk from sex stuff, but hey, I don't judge, I just facilitate. Still, pretty freaky, right?"

Readers, the vibe was awkward. Morpheus may have been a god, but he was a needy dude and I really just wanted to go home. I pinched my arm to rouse myself. But the Dream King saw me.

"Don't wake up! Hang out!" said Morpheus. "This next place you're gonna love! Let's go to the . . ."

He rubbed the ruby clasp around his neck and we found ourselves in . . .

". . . the BOARD GAME ROOM OF DREAMS."

We were in a suburban den. All around us were bookshelves, filled with board games. I looked for something familiar, say Monopoly or Clue.

Morpheus was giggling and rubbing his hands. "It's not just normal board games . . . these are board games people have only DREAMED OF!"

He pulled a maroon box, which said "Scrabble Plus" on it.

I said "Oh, I know Scrabble, that's a real game!"

Morpheus waved me off. "Not so fast! This is Scrabble PLUS where in addition to the regular letters . . . THERE ARE EMOJIS!!!! Spooky, right?"

He seemed really excited, so we played a round. He kept playing proper nouns like "Spongebob," which is against the rules but I didn't say anything. He won when he played "I (heart) NY" on a triple word square.

"Now THAT was exciting!" said Morpheus. He looked at the shelves "Hey, here's a board game where you sing theme songs from NPR news programs!"

With that, I summoned a great amount of willpower to fully wake up.

akefulness rose up in me. I saw myself floating up and out of the Dreamscape.

Below me I saw the whole land of dreams. Every dream in the universe was in view. I saw naked people in class-rooms, whales with wigs, roads paved somehow with time itself, a city with legs, and a gryphon playing tennis. A marvellous sight, and even more mar-vellous that it was being administered by such a huge nerd!

Lord Morpheus flew up to say goodbye.

"I see you're waking up! No worries! We're cool, right? Like I said, I've been working on my social skills. Did I not ask enough questions about you? Do you think I'm a narcissist? Anyway, see you next dreammmmmmmm!"

I woke up in my room. Maybe it was the cheesy toast, but I remembered every detail. And I felt bad for cutting my visit short. He's not a bad guy, Lord

Morpheus, just a bit much.

That's the end of my tale, reader. Please know that when you've woken up and you feel unrested, like you've had a disturbing dream that you can't quite remember, but you think it was just a little annoying, check your pockets for Scrabble tiles. You've probably had . . .

A VISIT FROM LORD MORPHEUS.

PHOTO N/A

GINO LOMBARDO

GINOVANNI (GINO) LOMBARDO was born on April 20 on Long Island and is an intern at the Earwolf studios, trying to earn credits for his radio major at Nassau Community College, though he rarely shows up to class. He also coaches basketball over Skype. He also has a job as a barback at Mulcahy's.

He is perilously thin, recently achieving 124 pounds. He has to be seat belted in a car if the windows are open because otherwise he'll blow out. He drives a Volkswagen Jetta. His mother, Louise Lomato, is the police chief of Nassau County. His father left him when he was 14 and told Gino to his face it was his fault and his mother got remarried to Gino's stepfather. Then, his father and stepfather found out they were brothers.

It was revealed that he went undercover for the FBI as a bait boy in the Catholic Church but had to be removed for getting "in too deep." He later discovered that he misread an email and the FBI had never sent him undercover; he was compensated with a hundred dollars and a big bag of ketamine (a hundred and k) by James Comey.

He set an empty playground on fire when he was a kid and now he is afraid of fire.

He served some time in juvie for setting the fire. He's got the top record in Bellmore for keg stands—44 seconds. He watches movies by watching only the deleted scenes and sorting out the plot from that.

AGE: [redacted]

INTERESTING FACTS:

1) He has a kidney scar from when his friends played a prank on him by cutting him open while he was passed out drunk to lead him to believe his kidney was stolen.

2) Gino's mom takes him to Dollywood every year on his birthday and her birthday.

3) He is a human dogfighter.

GINO LOMBARDO'S CBB DIARY

Everything that goes into interning/engineering on one of the most chaotic podcasts full of interesting people. A little peek behind the curtain at the glamorous day in the life of GINO LOMBARDO.

WED 5 AM EST
Wake up bright and early to get that motherfucking WORM that early bird is always talking about. Then I smash down a couple No-Xplode pre-workouts to get the heart pumping, the ATP cranking, and the brow sweaty. Eat a breakfast of 12 eggs, turkey, bacon, turkey bacon, and white American cheese. Gotta put on the weight. Doctor D says I have the body mass of a bald eagle, like a real American.

WED 5:30 AM
The 3 S's: Shit. Shower. Shave. I stopped shaving in the shower because the blood in the tub would make me lightheaded, same reason I stopped shitting in the shower.

WED 5:45 AM
Sneak the fraternal twins Maude and Taude that I took home from McHeeb's on Hempstead Turnpike. It was Bladder Buster, so we were drunk AF and definitely had to throw down the ol' tarp. They quickly dress into each other's clothes by accident . . . A charming fraternal twin mistake. And before you EVEN ask . . . yes, fraternal twins ALSO always cum at the same time like identicals.

WED 6 AM
Say goodbye to my family. Cut me some slack, I still live with them. I'm a millennial, I have 10 years of community college student loans to pay back, and I can't stop spending my money on gabbagool toast. I leave while my mom is refereeing a match of gay chicken between my dad and uncle. Kiss them all goodbye (on the lips) and I'm outta there.

WED 6:30 AM
Grab the westbound LIRR at Massapequa (gotta see if I left my debit card at Guido Mulligans) and pass Seaford, Wantagh, Bellmore, Merrick, Freeport, Baldwin, Rockville Centre, Jamaica; transfer to AirTrain to JFK.

WED 8 AM
After an aggressive, invasive, and totally voluntary deep-body search, get all hot and bothered looking at Joe Manganiello on *Men's Health* magazine covers. Listen to a bunch of businessmen take IPA dumps, while I charge my phone in the bathroom outlet. Then, I board my plane to LAX.

WED 8:30 AM

Flight attendant asks me what I want to drink. I order a limoncello on the rocks. They don't have it. She is really pissed at me, and it is kinda hot. I think she is wearing Cool Water as a scent, and it is working on ya boi Gino . . . I gotta crank a quick load into the airplane toilet so I can nap.

WED 8:33 AM

Grab a nap while listening to Jerky Boys on repeat. Being an intern is about energy. You wanna come in HOT to the record, amped up, and ready to derail it at a moment's notice. It kind of seems like what Scottie Ocks wants. A combo of all the pills, the flight attendant's perfume, and my *Men's Health* induced thirstiness cause me to nap-turnally release multiple times (not a problem; I AM wearing a diaper after all).

WED 12 PM PST

Land in Los Angeles, grab my Hofstra pride tote bag from the luggage claim. Get picked up, jump in the front seat of my rideshare driver's Geo Metro as he hands me his *Entourage* spec to read. The C story is that Drama says the N-word. It's HILARIOUS.

WED 2 PM

Arrive at Earwolf for the 2 pm *CBB* recording session. Luckily Engineer Brett had covered for me and got it all set up. He did all the microphones, cables, and the other stuff that goes into it. So I can sit down at a hot mic, check the LUFs, call sound speeds, and start pouring some waters for the "interesting people": Santa, the Chief, Todd, Morpheus the Dream Lord, and Jason Manzoukas.

WED 5 PM

After god knows how long of mostly interesting characters talking to each other, they finally close up the plug bag or some shit. I'm free to go home. I'm not really a "post guy" so I let the other engineers handle that stuff. In all honesty, not exactly sure what else I'm supposed to do. So I walk around the offices, network with my crew, grab some granola bars and some phone chargers, and jump in a rideshare.

WED 6 PM

Sit in the front seat of my Uber driver's Geo Storm, a car released as a tie-in with the Gerard Butler movie, and read HIS *Entourage* spec. The C story is that E and Sloan try pegging (or is that technically the E story?). It's HILARIOUS.

WED 7:45 PM

I can see all the TSA agents laughing at my weird bones on the scanning machine, so I insist on getting a pass to not go through it. I explain that Juggalos have replaced my testicles with magnets at the last Gathering. After an aggressive, invasive, and non-consensual (on their part) search, I pass through security. With a smile and a raging hard-on . . . I enter LAX.

WED 8 PM
Shit blood again, this time in an airport men's room. Really embodying the whole "red-eye" thing. Board the plane in group F, aka "The Bathroom Row."

WED 8:30 PM
Cruise the apps to see if anyone on the plane is DTJTMHC (down to join the Mile-High Club). Only the pilot responds, so I let her finger me somewhere over Illinois. You didn't think the pilot was a woman, did you? Well . . . she wasn't. NOW who's a misogynist.

THURS 6:30 AM EST
Land at JFK, take the AirTrain to Jamaica, and transfer to the eastbound Babylon train line making stops at Rockville Centre, Baldwin, Freeport, Bellmore, Wantagh, Seaford, Massapequa, Massapequa Park, Amityville, Copiague, Lindenhurst, and Babylon. I overslept. I should have gotten off at the Bellmore stop, so I transfer to the Manhattan-bound train and pass Babylon, Lindenhurst, Copiague, Amityville, Massapequa Park, Massapequa (hi, Alec Baldwin's childhood home!), Seaford, Wantagh, and Bellmore!

THURS 10 AM
Finally arrive at my stop, get on my GT Dyno that I have locked up there (front AND back pegs) and ride up to My Hero on Jerusalem Ave. for a chicken club add cheese no tomato. Eat it while riding home, ride past the podiatrist's office on Pea Pond Rd. to see if I can get any glimpses of feet through the window. Then arrive home at my house.

THURS 10:15 AM
Enter my house to see my family hanging out with their friends from the piloting classes they took in Florida in the year 2000. Glad to see they keep in touch.

THURS 10:30 AM
Cruise the apps to see if any of my neighbors are DTFU (down to fuck underground). No responses, so I crank one into the Diet Snapple bottle I keep under my bed. Close the blackout shades (I bought them when I was so drunk I don't remember what they're really called) and drift off to sleep with images of DVR'd radio in my head.

Long Island Rail Road

GINO LOMBARDO'S TRUE HEROES OF LONG ISLAND

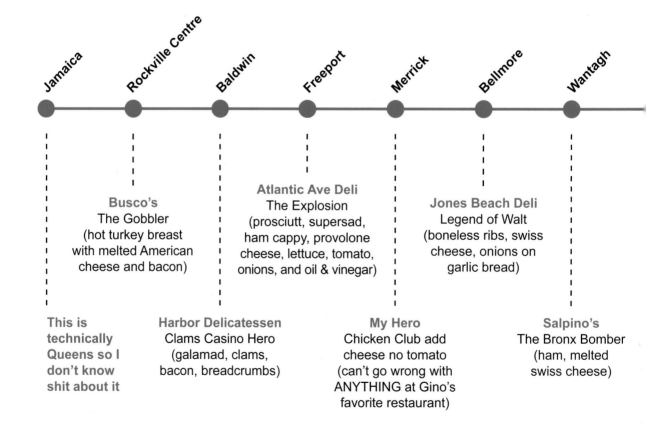

Jamaica · Rockville Centre · Baldwin · Freeport · Merrick · Bellmore · Wantagh

Busco's
The Gobbler
(hot turkey breast
with melted American
cheese and bacon)

Atlantic Ave Deli
The Explosion
(prosciutt, supersad,
ham cappy, provolone
cheese, lettuce, tomato,
onions, and oil & vinegar)

Jones Beach Deli
Legend of Walt
(boneless ribs, swiss
cheese, onions on
garlic bread)

This is
technically
Queens so I
don't know
shit about it

Harbor Delicatessen
Clams Casino Hero
(galamad, clams,
bacon, breadcrumbs)

My Hero
Chicken Club add
cheese no tomato
(can't go wrong with
ANYTHING at Gino's
favorite restaurant)

Salpino's
The Bronx Bomber
(ham, melted
swiss cheese)

Babylon Branch

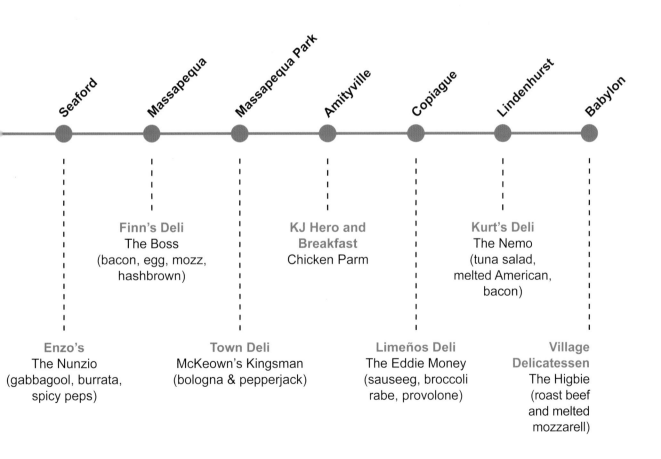

Seaford

Massapequa

Massapequa Park

Amityville

Copiague

Lindenhurst

Babylon

Finn's Deli
The Boss
(bacon, egg, mozz,
hashbrown)

KJ Hero and
Breakfast
Chicken Parm

Kurt's Deli
The Nemo
(tuna salad,
melted American,
bacon)

Enzo's
The Nunzio
(gabbagool, burrata,
spicy peps)

Town Deli
McKeown's Kingsman
(bologna & pepperjack)

Limeños Deli
The Eddie Money
(sauseeg, broccoli
rabe, provolone)

Village
Delicatessen
The Higbie
(roast beef
and melted
mozzarell)

STANLEY CHAMBERLIN

STANLEY CHAMBERLIN is a normal physical therapist who initially studied at Johns Hopkins University medical school. There, he survived a Satanic initiation rite on his first day. First, he was taken blindfolded and naked into a basement and beaten with oak leaves. Then he was taken to the center of the Earth, where he overheard sentient worker bees arguing over pleats. Once he was at the center of the Earth, the dean of the medical school told them they must fight each other to the death to earn a spot on one of the few escape jets that could take them back to the surface (10 spots for 60 students). Before the fight happened, they all ordered Five Guys as a last meal.

He later went to Southern Connecticut State Medical School to have a more normal medical school experience.

Stanley's body has a particularly strong reaction to cigars. One cigar and he can lift a piano and a half. He's also part of the shadow parliament of Belgium. Stanley is currently secretly married to the Princess of Denmark.

AGE: 35

INTERESTING FACTS:

1) Stanley's dad dropped him off at medical school because he dropped him off at college.

2) Stanley is from Connecticut.

3) Stanley personally killed seven people in the Satanic initiation rite. Separate from the rite, he later (accidentally) killed a patient with a mild calf sprain sustained from a blow dart. The patient was actually his mailman and emotional lover and Stanley called him "Skips."

A GUIDE TO
PHYSICAL THERAPY

by
Stanley Chamberlin

whose most notable claim to fame is running
a thriving physical therapy practice in Los Angeles,
and nothing else.

How Can Physical Therapy Help You?

1 gives you **BETTER FLEXIBILITY!**

2 helps **PREVENT HEART DISEASE!**

3 lets you **DETECT PAGAN RITUALS!**
Seriously, lots of places try to
surprise you with these
sort-of dangerous pagan rituals.
Gotta stay sharp!

4 strengthens your **IMMUNITY TO COLDS!**

5 helps you **COMMIT MURDER!**
(self-defense only) (usually)

Ask Dr. Stan!

How important is hamstring flexibility to overall physical health?

So important! "The hamstrings are the gateway to the back" is what Dr. Stan likes to say!

What is your preferred weapon of choice for murdering a room of your peers?

Machetes!

Do you offer discounts for pagans, wiccans, etc.?

Despite his harrowing experience in this area, Dr. Stan is not an expert and isn't qualified to judge who is eligible! All patients treated equally . . . which is to say great! :)

If one has been sufficiently emotionally traumatized, can physical therapy ever totally heal you?

No.

Simple Exercises You Can Do at Home with Machetes

MACHETE SWINGS

Grab any nearby machete and just swing it! Let the weight pull your arm!

SQUATS, WITH MACHETE

Do a simple squat while holding a machete. When you reach full height again, swing that machete forward to stretch the ol' shoulder!

PUSH-UPS WITH MACHETE

Do a push up with your favorite machete lying beneath you. Whisper "you don't own me" as you push yourself away.

ONE-ARMED PULL-UPS WHILE HOLDING MACHETE

Unnecessary.

Programs Available at Dr. Stan's Clinic

BASIC CONDITIONING
A firm but doable regimen of stretching and light weight training. For all age groups.

MURDER TRAINING
How to murder. You hopefully will never have to use this training, but boy howdy is it crucial if you need it! For all age groups.

ANTLER WORKOUT
A series of workouts that all involve wearing antler headpieces. Great for neck strength and intimidation!

WEEPING
An hour of uninterrupted crying is great for clearing toxins AND trauma.

MURDER TRAINING II
By appointment only. Not recommended.

Remember the Four Fs!

FLEXIBILITY!

FORM!

FORCE!

FEMORAL ARTERY
(for murdering, only when necessary, hopefully never)

GOOD HEALTH!

STANLEY CHAMBERLIN
135 Mill Plain Road, Suite 666
Los Feliz, California
555-787-2249

LORD ANDREW LLOYD WEBBER

LORD ANDREW LLOYD WEBBER is an EGOT-winning musical theater composer whose credits include *Cats*, *Jesus Christ Superstar*, *Joseph and the Amazing Technicolor Dreamcoat*, *Evita*, *The Phantom of the Opera*, and, of course, *Starlight Express*. He is a knight of the British Empire. He invented the shrinking technology for the movie adaptation of *Cats*.

He composes his musicals primarily in his dreams. He reviews in his mind's eye the songs he's heard throughout the day and various concepts and then he dreams up a musical. He sometimes sleeps on his feet like a horse.

AGE: 75

SONG HE WISHES HE WROTE: "Cantina Band" from *Star Wars Episode 4: A New Hope*

INTERESTING FACTS:

1) He will appear when you shout "LORD" if your foot is caught in a bear trap.

2) If he could choose his own manner of death, it would be on an airplane crashing into Sir Richard Branson's hot air balloon.

3) He loves all cats, including jellicle, hep, stray, Halloween sexies, and lasagna eaters.

Dear Sir Diary,

Well, that upstart Miranda has now gone beyond the pale. Bad enough he insists upon being a three-namer professionally. But now—presenting the American traitors to His Demented Majesty George III as . . . rap practitioners?! With nary a powder'd wig in the sight lines?! A ghastly nightmare!! Not to mention that it has been massively successful, which is even more of an affront to that jewel-sceptered isle, the place of my birth and eventual death, <u>England.</u>

Well, as Tim Rice clumsily expressed in his board game musicale, <u>two may play at this agreed-upon game!</u> Good Sir Diary, I will go back to the beginnings of my vast lyrical catalogue and <u>add!</u> <u>rappings!</u> to one of the biggest successes in Theatre Hystorie! As my creativity is often fueled by patriotic rage, I believe I'm able to jot a little entire song down here and now . . .

Well my name's Jesus Christ

And I'm here to say

It's fun to rap

In a spiritually ambiguous way

Got a best mate

Name of Judas

Had occasion recently

To say to him, "You des-

picable swine—

You'd betray me to the feds?

See if I ever turn your

Stones to breads!"

I'm just a young G from Nazareth

Now some frontin' pharisees

Want to put me to death?

And for what?

For befriending a prostitute?

Or for giving evil temple moneylenders the boot?

All I'm tryna do

Is rap to folks about love

And to question the design

Of our God above

Well, it's crucifixion time

So I've got to go

Happy Christmas, everyone

And cheerio

Raps!

What do you make of <u>that</u>, Sir Diary? Ha ha ha!

Well, I must sign off for now, S.D. Parting is such sweet sorrow, as Sondheim once failed to adequately communicate. I shall revisit you 'pon the morrow.

Until then I remain,

Yrs most nobly,

Andrew, Lord Lloyd Webber

POWER WHEELS BETH

BETH is a bratty 8-year-old who burst into the show on a Power Wheels she got for Christmas. It's a Jeep Wrangler with no seatbelt and Beth rides without a helmet. The Power Wheels has two speeds—turtle and rabbit. Beth always goes rabbit.

Her mom works in marketing on another floor in Earwolf's building, but she can't control Beth. She tried once to wash her mouth out with soap for cursing, and Beth made her eat a tablespoon of Dawn instead.

She plays pranks like hacking into teachers' bank accounts and donating $5 to charities. She'll also go up to other kids and say "I'm from the future and you're going to die in a week." She's learning the three Rs—wRiting, Reading, and Rapping.

She has confessed on multiple occasions she wishes to one day fuse with the Power Wheels.

AGE: 8

FAVORITE MOVIE: *Silkwood* "Cher is a legend."

INTERESTING FACTS:

1) Beth wishes to never grow up.

2) Beth might be the Grim Reaper.

3) Beth never naps because that's for babies!

THE EXTREMELY AWESOME F

AS DESCRIBED BY BETH

1 — I don't know what this bar back here is called, but usually I like to hold onto it and surfdrive. If I have to explain what that is, then you're old and/or Scott.

2 — Hard plastic seats that are totally uncomfortable for bony stupid butts like Scott's. Easy to wipe off if you squirt your fruit pouch too hard.

3 — Back here you can tie on a jump rope. Then you can tie that jump rope to a skateboard and then your little cousin can sit on the skateboard and you can get halfway to the 7-Eleven before your mom comes to stop you in a big car.

4 — The car has a REAL FLOOR with a PEDAL AND BRAKE. It's not like that flippin' Fisher Price one you move with your feet that babies and Scott like.

5 — I'm gonna put scary spiderwebs on this and trick-or-treat from my car. That will make every house my candy drive-thru. LOOK OUT, LOSERS!

6 — Four wheels with actual tread that I never even used to roll over the Apple remote. I seriously think it was always like that, Mom.

TURES OF A POWER WHEELS

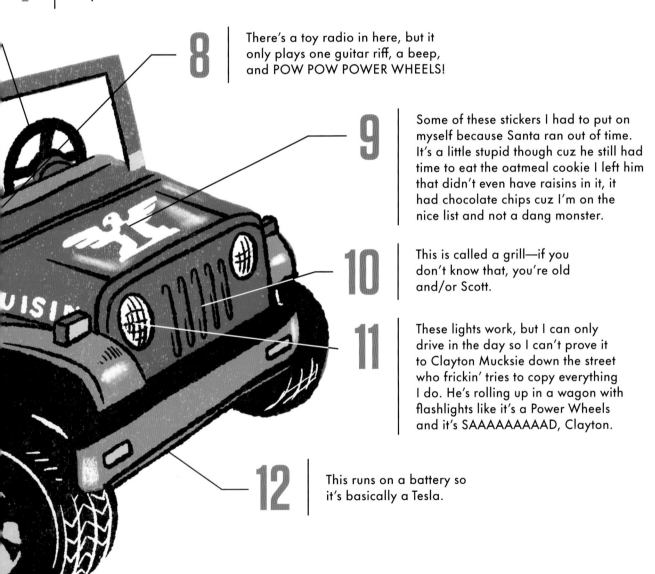

7 — This steering wheel apparently "works" but sometimes I still crash, so I feel like maybe it doesn't?

8 — There's a toy radio in here, but it only plays one guitar riff, a beep, and POW POW POWER WHEELS!

9 — Some of these stickers I had to put on myself because Santa ran out of time. It's a little stupid though cuz he still had time to eat the oatmeal cookie I left him that didn't even have raisins in it, it had chocolate chips cuz I'm on the nice list and not a dang monster.

10 — This is called a grill—if you don't know that, you're old and/or Scott.

11 — These lights work, but I can only drive in the day so I can't prove it to Clayton Mucksie down the street who frickin' tries to copy everything I do. He's rolling up in a wagon with flashlights like it's a Power Wheels and it's SAAAAAAAAD, Clayton.

12 — This runs on a battery so it's basically a Tesla.

MEDICAL CHART

PATIENT'S NAME: Bob Ducca   **DOCTOR:** Jennifer Potatoi

AGE: Early deads   **ADDRESS:** Unzoned shed behind

SEX: Male   the haunted Denny's.

AILMENTS

- Lockjaw
- Gout
- Thrush
- Colic
- Restless Leg Syndrome
- Content Leg Syndrome
- Croup
- The Vapours
- German Measels
- West Nile Fever
- Rocky Mountain Spotted Fever
- East River Shivers
- Oklahoma City Titty
- Great Lakes Diarrhea
- Early-Onset Martin Scorcese Eyebrows
- Lake Superior Inferiority Complex

- Niagara Fallen Arches
- Erie Nasal Canals
- Panamautism
- San Francistic Fibrosis
- Milk Leg
- Inflammatory Bowel Disease
- Upset Stomach
- Spastic Colon
- Irritable Bowel Syndrome
- Angry Brown Star Complex
- Lou Gehrig's Disease
- Lou Barlow's Disease
- Lucy Lou Flu
- Shelie E-Coli
- Robert Plantar Warts
- Cystic Acne
- Gastritis
- Puff Knuckle

- I'm hyper tolerant of Lactose
- Celiac Disease
- Dancing on the Celiac Disease
- Deep-Vein Thrombosis
- Homofelia
- Homophobafelia
- Gallstones
- Sleep Apnea
- Wake Apnea
- Pleurisy
- Shingles
- Depression
- Mania
- Eczema
- Hot tub foot
- Piles
- Dropsy
- Joanie Loves Chachi
- Indoor Toilet Allergy
- Leaky Gut Syndrome
- Fallen Arches
- Crabs
- Sea Monkees
- Alopecia
- Weird Alapecia
- Shel Silverstein's

- The Missing Alapecia
- Dominoes Alapecia
- Dirt Belly
- Carpal Tunnel Syndrome
- Bone worm
- Patella Tendinitis
- Paella Tendinitis (when traveling to Spain)
- Larval Penis
- Carpal Tunnel Syndrome
- Rectal Tunnel Syndrome
- 7-Layer Diptheria
- Loofa Burn
- Post Orgasmic Illness Syndrome
- Urinary Tract Infection
- Urinary Eight-Tract Infection
- Thick Urine Syndrome
- Trickle Nipple
- Stiff Tits
- Parkinson's Disease
- Valet Parkinson's Disease
- Parallel Parkinson's Disease
- Trichinosis
- Dengue Fever

AILMENTS (CONT'D)

- Typhoid Fever
- Yellow Fever
- Saturday Night Fever
- Cabin Fever
- Justin Bieber Fever
- Blue Balls
- Pink Eye
- Inner Thigh Stress Rash
- Melanoma
- Marshmelanoma
- Iron Deficiency
- Social Anxiety
- Anorexia Nervosa
- Type Wilford Brimley Diabetes
- Homophelia
- Bronchial Asthma
- Septic Ulcer
- Tetanus
- Scabies
- Rabies
- Mickey Rooney's Sugar Babies
- Diverticulitis
- Selective Fatigue Syndrome
- Nocturnal Narcolepsy
- Pre-Traumatic Stress Disorder

- Malaria
- Scurvy
- Anglo-Centric Sickle-Cell Anemia
- Swollen Perineum
- Chronic Shame Disorder
- MC Hammer Toes
- Aphasia
- Streptococcus
- Imaginary Vaginosis
- Umbilical Spasms
- Osteoporosis
- Costcosteoporosis
- Supercalifragilisticexpialidocious-perosis
- Miner's Lung
- Black Lung
- Aqua Lung
- Wang Chung Lung
- Thrombosis
- Amoebic Dysentery
- Halle-Berry-Tosis
- Halle-Berry-Berri
- Masturbation-Induced Siezures
- Receding HareLip
- General Anxiety
- Widespread Panic Disorder

AILMENTS (CONT'D)

- Medical-Textbook-Grade Ear Discharge
- Asbergers
- Cheeseburgers
- Tinnitus
- Sinusitis
- My thumb hurts
- Scoliosis
- Myocardial Infarction
- Frequent Shart Attacks
- Bell's Palsy

- Staph Infection
- Moist Tooth
- Gelatinous Cartilage
- Canine-derived Hip Dysplasia
- Selective Albinism
- Prolapsed Navel
- I'm a chocoholic but not in a fun way
- Male Menopause

MEDICATION

- Prozac
- Zoloft
- Effexor
- Itworksall
- Buspar
- Gary Buspar
- Abilify
- Lexapro
- Lexa-amateur
- Alexa . . . How Do You Make A Noose?
- Wellbutrin
- Elavil
- Alphavil
- Alcoholizal

- Marijunazor
- Masturbatkaroten
- NetflixBingemalls
- Luvox
- Hugzall
- Warm Fuzzalene
- Pickled Ayahuasca AKA Psychedelic Relish
- St. John's Wort
- St. Vincent's Zit
- St. Bernardacles
- Martin Shkreli Jelly Beans
- Robert Downey Jr. Mints

Wompler's DiGiorno Cream Cheese Sandwich

BY MARISSA WOMPLER

SERVINGS: 1 | TIME: 20min ★★★★★

INGREDIENTS

2   Digorno pizzas
1   tub of cream cheese

INSTRUCTIONS

1. Take two frozen DiGiorno pizzas out of your step dad's freezer.

2. Pop in toaster oven at 325 for as long as it takes to do ten garbage can runs.

3. Slather one entire tub of cream cheese between and betwixt the crusts and press together as hard as Marissa and Gutters pressed their privates together over the jeans.

4. Eat DiGiorno Sandwich and Womp up Your Jamz.

5. Fall into a deep, unending slumber.

Recipe for Sexual Awakening

BY CHARLOTTE "CHARDOG" LISTLER

SERVINGS: 1 | TIME: 5min   ★★★★★

INGREDIENTS

1   thin white asparagus (9 inches or longer)
1   7.5 oz container FAGE yogurt—open

INSTRUCTIONS

1. Stand in front of open fridge, sans clothes.

2. Drape asparagus tip into open yogurt container.

3. Wait.

4. #turnaround

JOHN LENNON'S BEATLES 1 REVIEW

European guitarist John Lennon reviews his all-time favorite album and reminisces track by track.

1. LOVE ME DO

When Paul came to me with the idea for this song I thought, okay, I think I'll play guitar on this one. George will play another guitar. Paul seems to be pretty comfortable on the bass so he can play that. And Ringo (bless his rhythmic heart) should play drums since he's the only one of us who owns a full set. What I said was, "Paul, I really don't think people want to hear songs about 'love.' I've never even heard of a 'love' song in my entire European life!" I then suggested we go back to working on my song about a secret agent who lost his disguise kit (a pretty obvious metaphor, I'll admit). But Paul (bless his rhythmic heart) persisted, and we wrote and recorded "Love Me Do" in about 15 weeks, and I think it came out pretty damn good. **A**

2. FROM ME TO YOU

This is a fun ditty (ugh, I hate that word), and I'd be a damn liar if I said this one didn't get my hips moving. We got the idea for this song when the four of us exchanged Valentines on February 13, 1963. We were so excited we couldn't wait another day. George noticed all the Valentines had "to" and "from" written on them, and the song wrote itself. After 5 weeks of recording, we nailed it. A little peek behind the scenes: The harmonica you hear was played by a very young, very hungover Geena Davis. She was an old friend of ours. Long before she starred in *Stuart Little*, Geena played blues harmonica in taverns up and down the Yorkshire coast. I'll never forget when she told me all she wanted to do in her life was find a cure for cancer. Such a beautiful person. **A**

3. SHE LOVES YOU

It was my idea to put lyrics to this song. Originally the song was an instrumental played on four grand pianos, and the recording sounded amazing. Part of it was because we had just gotten the pianos tuned, but the other part was because we were having so much FUN. Our record label at the time, which I think was called Bummy Tummy Records (maybe not), said they needed lyrics and we could not all play the same instrument. We said, "Fine but we are gonna wear the same colored suits and you can't stop us." They agreed and even bought us the suits! The song somehow works, though the original is sooo much better. I have a tape of it in storage somewhere, I think. I should find that and ask if the radio wants to play it. **A**

4. I WANNA HOLD YOUR HAND

This is actually a joke song. Someone told us that in Japan couples would hold hands when they walk down the street to show each other affection. Or maybe show others that they were in love? Well, we just thought it was the funniest thing and were like, "Okay, we HAVE to write a joke song about this." The line "And when I touch you I feel happy inside" cracked us UP. It took us 20 takes to get through it without losing our minds. If you're listening to the final version on the right speakers, you can hear George cackle and say, "I'm trying! It's just fucking hysterical." **A**

5. CAN'T BUY ME LOVE

I have a web series idea called *Comedians with Coffees Looking to Buy Cars* where me and a different famous comedian get coffee and try to find a car to buy at a reasonable price. I think this song would make a great theme song. I'd replace "love" with "cars" though. **A**

6. A HARD DAY'S NIGHT

I had a great music-video idea for this song that we never got around to making. It was basically a bunch of dogs working in an office building with humans. We would put shirts and ties on them and sit them at desks and near the

watercooler. Ringo also had the idea to have them running around the office, chasing a ball and stuff like that. I didn't like this idea but I LOVED his other idea to make their boss a cat. I still laugh when I think about that. To be perfectly honest, I'm laughing right now. At the end of the video, the dogs would go home and we'd see them morph into the four Beatles. We sat on the idea for too long and Snoop Doggy Dogg did the morphing trick in his video for "Who Am I (What's My Name)?" which is a good video and song. The lesson here: See if there's a way I can sue Snoop Doggy Dogg. **A**

7. I FEEL FINE

When we were recording this song, Ringo was doing this thing he called "dick cleavage." The idea is kind of like a woman showing some cleavage in a dress or shirt but in this case, a guy pulls his pants down a little bit so you can see some of the shaft of his penis but not the head. He said he got the idea when he was getting out of the shower but I'm pretty sure his cousins told him about it. Regardless of who came up with the idea, it's a pretty sexy look, and we all started doing dick cleavage around this time. **A**

8. EIGHT DAYS A WEEK

I can't remember how this one goes, and it's late right now and all the CD stores are closed. I'd play my own copy but I stupidly left it and my Discman on a horse-drawn carriage in Central Park yesterday afternoon. I've called the park department 4 times and all they can tell me is that it was mostly likely taken by the driver or another passenger or broken by some teenagers. Pisses me off. Funny song title though. **A**

9. TICKET TO RIDE

I'd like to take a quick break from the review to talk about my favorite drink of all time, Mt. Dew. Whether it's in a can or bottle, Mt. Dew is the ONLY neon-green soft drink that I can trust to fully quench my extreme thirst. And speaking of extreme, Mt. Dew sponsors several world-class action sports athletes, including Eli Reed, Paul Rodriguez, and Danny Davis. And take it from me, these guys can really rip. So reach for a

cool, crisp Mt. Dew next time you've got a mondo thirst. I know I will. Mt. Dew: **A+**

10. HELP!

This song was originally called "Welp . . . " It had all the same lyrics as the current version but we sang "welp" instead of "help" on the chorus. It had a passive, resigned attitude that I loved, but Paul thought it would sell better if it was more desperate and needy. I went along with it because Ringo wanted me to. I was pretty bummed about it at the time, but that winter I wore nothing but fur coats so I guess you could say it all worked out. *wink* **A**

11. YESTERDAY

The only thing I remember about recording this was Ringo and I were on a kick of making stupid bets with each other all day long. Like, "I bet you I can throw this banana peel in the trash can from here. Loser has to order lunch in a French accent." Dumb stuff. The day we recorded "Yesterday," Ringo bet me I couldn't balance a broomstick on my chin for 20 seconds. Loser had to wear a tissue box on their head for the rest of the day. I don't think I made it past 3 seconds! So, yeah, I wore a tissue box on my head when we recorded this song. **A**

12. DAY TRIPPER

Fuck! I just spilled Mt. Dew all over my fucking keyboard! I'm so fucked here! FUCK! FUCK FUUUUUCK MEEEEEE!!! I'm such a fucking asshole. DAMMIT! Anyway, this song rules. **A FUCK!**

13. WE CAN WORK IT OUT

This may have been a song George wrote? Maybe Paul and I, I forget. Anyway, I always skip this one. **N/A**

14. PAPERBACK WRITER

There is NOTHING like a good book. Even the best magazine can't beat an okay book. I'll never be able to fully describe the euphoria that engorges my veins when I crack open a book. All the excitement. All the possibilities. All the adventure??? Ooooh and that smell. Pure bliss. A little bit musty, a little bit sour, a LOTTA bit arousing nostalgia. And I need a physical book, ya know? None of this Kindle or tablet BULLCRAP. When I'm on the subway and I see a young person reading an "article" on their "phone," I weep. I hold it together on the train, of course, but when I get home, I curl into a seductive ball and passionately sob until I have an orgasmic headache. I have a favor to ask anyone glued to their devices. PLEASE do a "Google" search for your local library, get a library card, and open your eyes to an infinite world of desirable, unquenched ecstasy. **A**

15. YELLOW SUBMARINE

Ringo wrote this one. I mean, he didn't really, Paul and I did, but I tell people Ringo did because, you know, it is what it is. It's a kid's song. Everyone thought I should sing it and here I'm thinking, "It's gonna be an ice-cold day in Miami, F.L.A., before I go anywhere near this stinker." So I suggested that Ringo do it. Well, he loved the idea. Cut to: the vocal recording session, Ringo's in the booth and he's laying turd after greasy turd on the microphone. Forgetting lyrics, missing cues, WAY off key. It was horrible. Look, I love Ringo. Best friend a guy could ask for, but this song is like, "What are ya doin', dude?" Paul's looking at me like, "What's going on here, John???" I'm looking at Ringo like, "You gotta nail this, man." And George is looking at Paul like, "I'm gonna ask him if he can house-sit for me next week." It eventually got to the point where I had to get in the booth with Ringo and pantomime and mouth the words while he sang so we could get some emotion out of him. Eleven hours later the vocals were done, Ringo thinks he's king shit, and Little Johnny L skates away clean, singing on cool songs ONLY. **B+**

16. ELEANOR RIGBY

Okay, just got off the phone with the lady at the computer shop. My keyboard is gonna cost like 600 bucks to fix, but the laptop "guts," I guess, are all fine so that's a relief. Apparently I'm not their first customer to dump Mt. Dew all over their stuff. She told me about a guy who did that and lost his entire master's thesis.

Can you imagine? Makes me feel less dumb now. I borrowed Ringo's laptop until mine's ready, and he's got some weird shit on here. I went through his vacation photos and the guy can NOT take a picture in focus to save his life! Ha. He also keeps a daily journal. I'm not kidding. I won't tell you much about it because that would be mean but let's just say this dude is OBSESSED with finding something that "truly makes him happy." Haha. What a drama queen. **A**

17. PENNY LANE

Have you ever seen that movie *Wolf of Wall Street*? I always thought this song would have been perfect for that scene where Leonardo DiCaprio's character is selling the penny stocks with all the losers in the strip mall. You know what I mean? Like, they're selling penny stocks and the name of the song is "Penny Lane." It's almost TOO easy of a choice. I bet that's why Marty decided against it. Maybe he'll do a re-edit someday. I think that would be so cool, to have a song in a Scorsese movie??? The guy did *Casino*, man! Classic. **A**

18. ALL YOU NEED IS LOVE

You know what other movie "Penny Lane" would have been great for? *Pacific Rim*. The scene where all the robots or droids or whatever are battling the monsters at the end? The song is so peppy and bubbly that it would juxtapose really nicely with the action, making the scene even more badass. As for "All You Need Is Love," this song's okay. Not my best. Kind of repetitive. **B**

19. HELLO, GOODBYE

Would you believe me if I told you we came up with this song while we were goofing around in a revolving door? **A**

20. LADY MADONNA

I went to a Madonna concert once. Ray of Light Tour, Madison Square Garden. I got some really shitty seats for like 90 bucks way up, behind the stage, but once the show started I snuck down to the floor and got pretty close. In the middle of the show I met a radiologist named Val who was standing next to me. We hit it off and she bought me a beer. On our way out, she also bought me a tour sweatshirt and poster because my money clip fell out of my pocket while dancing during the encore. We exchanged numbers and said goodnight. Over the next month, Val and I went on three or four dates but nothing really clicked. She was also tough to pin down because she was so busy with work. The farthest we got was second base (over the bra) and that was nice. I never paid her back for the sweatshirt and poster and still feel bad about that. But I do still have the sweatshirt. The poster, however, ripped on the subway ride home and I threw it away. So that's my "Madonna" story. As for this song, it's okay. I wish it had more of a calypso sound. Eh, what can you do? **B**

21. HEY JUDE

How many songs are on this fucking album?! **A**

22. GET BACK

I'm on a layover at the Chicago airport. Going down to Disney World for a week. I figured I'd work on this piece but honestly, I'm just so tired. My first flight was at 6 am. That means I was up at 3 am because I always sleep terribly before a flight. And I knoooow, there are prescribed drugs to help you sleep, but I'm not comfortable with the potential side effects. Plus my insurance doesn't cover it. So, this song is good. Glad it made the album. **A**

23. THE BALLAD OF JOHN AND YOKO

I actually didn't write this song. A lot of people think Yoko did, but she didn't either. It was written by my dry cleaner, Bobby Knees. I brought one of Yoko's berets that I was borrowing (and am still borrowing *wink*) for some maintenance work. We got to chit-chatting, and Bobby says it must be difficult for Yoko and I to have a private life. Next thing I know, we're up in my apartment, Bobby at the piano riffing this whole song while I'm running around the place like a madman trying to find a pen to get it all down! The whole song was written in 10 minutes (recording took about 7 weeks. My guitar kept going out of tune.) Bobby said he never wanted any credit. If I took him out to dinner one night to talk Beatles that would be payment enough. I still need to make good on my end of that deal. **A**

24. SOMETHING

I went out to dinner with George one night in October 1988. Ringo couldn't come, he had a karate lesson (he still practices and I think is a green belt now). The place George and I went to was a great little restrauraunt (I don't know how to spell that word) called The Bow Tie Bar Room, and its little quirk was that you had to wear a bowtie

to be seated at a table. You didn't even need to be wearing a collared shirt, just as long as you were wearing a bowtie. Women too. Come to think of it, it's a stupid practice. Everyone looks ridiculous, but they had a VERY good pork chop special on Monday nights, so who cares? And cheap. Damn cheap! So there we are, George and I, sitting in this busy resterant (not it either!) wearing bowties like two fools and I'm thinking, "What the hell are we gonna talk about for the next hour and a half?" We never had great repartee. Then George says he had a terrific time being in the Beatles with me and that he was always in awe of my writing style. He liked how I would take chances like I didn't give a shit and it bloody worked. He went on to say that he felt like he couldn't call it "his band" because he didn't write as many songs. I had never had a conversation with George like this before. It felt very easy to do, though, and I wished I had talked to him like this more. You could tell he really spoke with his heart and listened. I told him he had it all wrong. He was a huge part of the Beatles and OUR success. He wrote some of the most iconic guitar parts of all time. Then I told him "Something" was the most beautiful song I've ever heard. "Written about your first dog?" I asked. "Wife," he said. As I apologized for my gaffe, I spilled raspberry chutney all over my white shirt. Taking off my bowtie to take off my shirt, the resteranteaur (not a chance) sailed over and told me I had to keep the tie on. I immediately told him to hold his fucking horses and cursed him up and down for selling such stain-heavy chutney. We of course got into a physical altercation and I sprained my wrist when I was thrown to the table and then to the ground. We ran off into the night hootin' and hollerin' before we had to pay for the damages. I thought of George often after that night. Mostly about how much we needed him in the band and how his music was so powerful and gentle all at once. Also, on the walk home that night I was scared half to death by a couple jack-o'-lanterns on the stoop of my neighbor's house. **A**

25. COME TOGETHER

In 1978, I was in Madison, Wisconsin, with my good friend Blueberry. We call him that because he has small, deep-set, dark blue eyes that look exactly like blueberries. His real name is . . . I don't remember actually. And I don't know his last name. Nevertheless, we were in Madison for the annual World Champion Cheese Contest. Blueberry is a self-proclaimed cheese connoisseur who goes every year, and I asked if I could tag along. He didn't have a cheese in the contest or anything, he just likes to watch the judging happen live. After a few days of eating everything from Abbot's Gold to Zamorano (and everything else in between *wink*) we found ourselves in a bar without enough money for our bus fare home. As we were talking over the situation, some college kids overheard and said they'd pay us enough for our bus fare if we would go out

back and fist-fight each other for 10 minutes. We agreed, and Blueberry, who is not a big guy, kicked my ass. We left in good spirits with a few new friends and blood all over my white suit. Years later, I was at a middle school graduation party for one of Broderick's kids when Jane Kaczmarek (the TCA award–winning actor who played the mom on *Malcolm in the Middle*) approached me and said she was at the bar that night in Madison! I couldn't believe it. We got to talking, and she said she liked my band's music, and I said I had never seen her show. At the end of the night I accidentally called her Jamie and we parted ways. Haven't seen her since. Anyway, this song always reminds me of that night. **A**

26. LET IT BE

Sesame Street did a version of this song called "Letter B" in the '70s (it's actually pretty funny). In the '90s I went to trial with those PBS sons of bitches for two and half years trying to squeeze every dime they had out of them. In the end, I would say I LOST close to a million dollars and I had to return the custom-made octagon-shaped couch I bought because I thought this thing was a lock. In hindsight I shouldn't have represented myself. That was my damn proud side rearing its ugly head. And

I most certainly shouldn't have threatened the jury on more than 15 occasions. That's my fearful side right there. And I capital "D" DEFINITELY! shouldn't have entered the courtroom every morning to the song, "Here Comes the Hotstepper." But that's just the bad boy in me, baby. *wink* **A**

27. THE LONG AND WINDING ROAD

I wish "Rocky Raccoon" was on this album instead of this song. I don't like this song. I like "Rocky Raccoon" because I picture a raccoon wearing little jeans, a corduroy shirt, work boots, and a leather cowboy hat, and I like that a lot. "Rocky Raccoon": **A**

DARREN MATICHEK

DARREN MATICHEK is the silent cofounder of the National Bobblehead Museum and Hall of Fame in Milwaukee, Wisconsin. He provided the capital to start the museum and hall of fame. The museum's collection currently has over 10,000 bobbleheads and counting. Admission is $8, but it used to be $6, and before that it was $4. The museum honors National Bobblehead Night every Tuesday. If you're ever there in person, ask for the special tour (getting dragged around the museum and hall of fame with a rope tied around your ankle while you drink a beer). Please do not touch the bobbleheads, or you will be banned for life.

The hall of fame is for really good bobbleheads, not just bobbleheads of the players in the sports hall of fames. Bobbleheads in the hall of fame include, but are not limited to: an Ace Ventura bobblehead, a Kal Penn bobblehead, a Nelson Mandela dressed up as Austin Powers bobblehead, and a bobblehead of Penelope Cruz and Javier Bardem kissing on the mouth (when they were dating, before they were married). The only bobblehead in the museum and not in the hall of fame is the Pete Rose bobblehead, which anyone can defile free of charge.

FAVORITE BOBBLEHEAD:
A tie between a bobblehead of Robin Yount of the Milwaukee Brewers (1987) and a bobblehead of Jar Jar Binks doing coke with Chester Cheetah at the Cannes Film Festival (1999).

INTERESTING FACTS:

1) Darren's original collection was 1,000 bobbleheads that he collected during his three weeks of vacation each year from his job of being an actuary, which is a job that analyzes the financial costs of risk and uncertainty.

2) He has been diagnosed with a medium-sized penis.

3) "Bobblehead-booey, bobblehead-booey!"

Darren Matichek's
TOP·TEN Favorite
BOBBLEHEADS
IN THE NATIONAL BOBBLEHEAD MUSEUM AND HALL OF FAME

Hi there, I'm Darren Matichek, part owner/curator and "silent money man" behind the National Bobblehead Museum and Hall of Fame in Milwaukee, Wisconsin. Tourists and bobblehead fans are always asking me, "Darren, what makes a good bobblehead? Is it the rarity of the bobblehead? Is it the depiction of a recognizable character in pop culture, politics, or sports at a signature moment in their lives . . . as a bobblehead?" And the truth is—sure, it can be any of those things! As they say: Beauty is in the eye of the bobblehead beholder. In my own experience, what makes a good bobblehead is any bobblehead that makes you nod at a bobblehead, as if you yourself were a bobblehead, and say, "Now that's a good bobblehead."

With that in mind, here are my top ten personal favorite bobbleheads in the National Bobblehead Museum and Hall of Fame!

JANET RENO
"LAWYERS LOVE SPORTS" SERIES (1998)

Not all lawyers love sports, but Janet Reno sure did!
Here she is doing the Macarena, a popular dance
craze from the mid-1990s, while rocking a very sexy Cal
Ripken Jr. jersey dress in honor of the Iron Man's record-
breaking consecutive-games-played streak in 1998.

Limited edition, very rare.

TOM FROM MYSPACE
"WHAT I'VE BEEN UP TO" WIRED.COM SERIES (2006)

Limited-edition bobblehead from fall 2006 that
highlighted MySpace founder, Tom, almost a year
after he sold his hit social media site to News
Corp. Here, Tom is seen at his desk, with his pants
around his ankles, watching fan-made cartoon
porn from the popular animated series *Family Guy*.
The graphic details are blurred out to make this
bobblehead kid-friendly, but it's clear that Tom has
been making a different kind of "Top 8," if you know
what I mean. (He's been jacking off.)

Limited edition, very rare.

ELLEN DEGENERES
"ELLEN BEING QUIRKY!" SERIES (2014)

Commissioned by NBC, this was #14 out of a 15-part bobblehead series featuring all the fun, quirky things Ellen gets up to behind the scenes of her hit talk show, *The Ellen Degeneres Sho*. Here we see Ellen kicking her assistant in the back for bringing her a coffee with soy milk instead of oat milk, while simultaneously having a laugh over FaceTime with her good friend, former president George W. Bush. Rumor has it Ellen herself spent all of 2020 trying to track down every one of these bobbleheads and destroying them like horcruxes.

Limited edition, extremely rare.

MARGARET THATCHER
"GOING POTTY IS MAGIC" SERIES (2002)

From a 2002 toilet training initiative in the UK aimed at bad little children. Who better to scare the poop from your little behind than Parliament's own Margaret Thatcher?

Limited edition, very rare.

PATRICK MAHOMES
"ATHLETES ROCK THE KATE GOSSELIN HAIRCUT"
ESPN THE MAGAZINE'S FINAL ISSUE SERIES (2019)

When ESPN announced they'd be pulling the plug on their eponymous publication, *ESPN The Magazine*, in September 2019, most people assumed the final issue would be filled with sports nostalgia and behind-the-scenes treats for fans. So it came as quite a surprise when, instead, their cover story was a sloppily Photoshopped series of athletes rocking Kate Gosselin's reverse mullet-bob haircut, from the reality TV show *Jon & Kate Plus 8*. To say fans were disappointed would be an understatement. Longtime subscriber Larry from Connecticut put it best in an ESPN subreddit two days after the magazine's final release: "I regret the money I've given you every month since 1998. You all just took a big juicy shit on the legacy of *ESPN The Magazine* and I hope every last one of you rotts [sic] in Hell." Patrick Mahomes has since said he had no prior knowledge of Kate Gosselin, the reality TV show *Jon & Kate Plus 8*, or his inclusion in this series, let alone the release of associated bobbleheads.

Limited edition, very rare.

MS. CAP'N CRUNCH
"FEMINIZE BREAKFAST MASCOTS"
QUAKER OATS SERIES

Two years after Cap'n Crunch debuted as a breakfast cereal mascot, Quaker Oats attempted to rebrand the cereal for women and girls, after pressure from second-wave feminists. Their attempt failed to gain any significant market share.

Limited edition, very rare.

BRUNO MARS
"STARS: THEY'RE JUST LIKE US"
US WEEKLY MAGAZINE'S SERIES (2019)

Pelosi clap! It wasn't just everyday folks who loved the Speaker's sarcastic clapping at President Trump's final State of the Union address . . . it was also megastars like Bruno Mars! He sued to stop production of this bobblehead after only a dozen were made.

Limited edition, very rare.

SHOELESS JOE JACKSON
"DEAD MLB LEGENDS: WHAT THEY'D BE UP TO NOW" COOPERSTOWN CLASSICS SERIES (1988)

In 1988, the Baseball Hall of Fame released a series of "reimaginings" based on what they thought dead MLB legends would be up to in present day. Someone in Cooperstown must have thought Shoeless Joe Jackson would've been a bad little shoe sniffer! His family sued MLB and Foot Locker to stop production.

Limited edition, very rare.

COLIN JOST

"COLIN JOST DRESSED AS COLONEL SANDERS GETTING A COLONOSCOPY" KFC'S APRIL 2020 AD CAMPAIGN (CANCELED DUE TO PANDEMIC)

"Whether it's the weekend or a weekday, everyone needs to maintain a healthy colon. Why not flush your system with fried chicken and then let a doctor take a look inside your sexy little anus?" That was the marketing angle KFC executives came up with in early 2020, paired with *SNL's* sexy writer/comedian and debonair on-screen personality Colin Jost. Unfortunately, the pandemic canceled production for these ads, but Jost paid out of pocket to make 500 bobbleheads so he could pass them out at 30 Rock.

Limited edition, very rare.

JENNIFER GARNER
"CAPITAL ONE VENTURE CARD SPOKESPEOPLE" SERIES (2014)

Not a rare bobblehead at all. In fact, one of the most overproduced bobbleheads of all time. Darren just really loves Jennifer Garner and believes she does not get enough credit as a triple threat (actress, spokesperson, mother).

Unlimited edition, not rare at all.

MARGIE DONK

MARGIE DONK'S passion is writing fantasy fiction; she has written over 90 unpublished *Twilight* novels, each about 350 pages. She left her husband and three beautiful children to follow her dream of writing in Hollywood, and she is currently looking for a place to live.

She has also written five volumes of a series entitled *The Dark Earth* set a million years in the future in an intergalactic world with no phones. The world is too noisy because of radiation so they've stopped manufacturing phones. The main character is Hanna, similar to the character in the movie *Hanna*. In the movie, the character Hanna learned to kill from her father, and in the book series, the character Hanna learned to kill from a man who might be her father. In this universe, the Milky Way is called Janet's Place. The other galaxies in this universe include Martha's House and David's Backyard. The characters are searching for gold, which is in the middle of the universe.

Her other ideas for books are: *The Apple, Wintertime, Chores.* All of these ideas are registered at the WNBA and they all take place a million years in the future and all of the characters are looking for gold.

AGE: 53 years young

FAVORITE MOVIE/TV SHOW: *Hanna*, the movie

FAVORITE SNACK: Hot beans

FAVORITE SPORT: Water balloon fights

BIGGEST FEAR: Meeting E. L. James; accidentally picking up the phone when her kids call.

WHAT'S IN YOUR PURSE? Band-Aids

FAVORITE APP: Home screen

HEROES: Stephanie Meyer, HBO

INTERESTING FACTS:

1) Margie Donk is invisible in photos.

2) Margie Donk writes all her novels on her computer, which she turns on by screaming "Desktop!"

3) Margie Donk has never seen the Grand Canyon.

[The following is an excerpt from Margie Donk's forthcoming novel *The Dark Earth, Vol. 5: A New Beginning First*]

The Dark Earth
Vol. 5: A New Beginning First

anna looked at the spoon in dismay. She glanced up at Torfburt, who smiled menacingly, his many rows of green teeth on full display.

"You . . . you poisoned me?" Hanna gasped out of her mouth.

Torfburt threw back his horse head and let out a sound that was supposed to be a laugh, but it sounded like a lot of metal being hit together a bunch. Oh, by the way, if you're reading this page, you've just been donk'd. Anyway, so Torfburt thinks this is so funny and Hanna is P.O.'d. "Joke's on you," Hanna said.

"Fruskbo tubyn pul nae?" Torfburt sneered back.

"Because guess what? I'm immortal, and I have been my whole life. My father, who taught me how to kill, is actually one of the Undying. You've heard of them, I'm sure?" Hanna asked inquisitively.

Torfburt's three jaws dropped in shock, and Limel, his mouse, came over and tried to lift them back in place. Torfburt swatted Limel away, and he went cruisin' through the air and landed slap bang in a big ol' mug of mead. Limel lifted his head up above the rim and licked his lips. "I'll have what she's having!" he gurgled, drunkenly, and then collapsed back into the mug.

"Too bad for you that you couldn't dispatch of me, Torfburt. I guess this means the efforts of the Janet's Place Defense Coalition are all for naught. The Undying are the ones who hid the gold in the middle of the universe, and since my father was one of them, only I know the password. And poisoning me isn't a great way to get on my good side." Hanna smiled and rose to her feet. She reached into her chic leather pouch and pulled out six big yabbos. "Here are some yabbos for my applesauce. This one's on me." Hanna put on her fedora and strode with purpose to the front door of the tavern. She took one last glance over her shoulder at the crowd that gathered around Torfburt, who was now crying into a bowl of soup. She touched the rim of her fedora in farewell, opened the door, and disappeared into the night.

nce outside the tavern, Hanna sprinted as fast as she could to her ship. She began coughing and choking, and a bunch of blood started coming out of her mouth and she was like, "Oh, geez!"

As the cobblestones gave way to gray sand, Hanna struggled to keep her footing and maintain her speed. She was dying, and she was dying FAST. Also, hi, you've been donk'd again. Her ship was right there, just a few more yards, but her body started to betray her. She fell to her knees in the sand and looked longingly at the bridge of her ship. Her eyes started to lose focus, and as she drifted off into unconsciousness, she saw a wispy, shadowy figure descend the stairs from her ship. And then she was out.

ut to a couple hours later. In the darkness that swallowed her up, she heard lots of crazy sounds, like talking and beeps and boops. Assuming she was dead, she farted. She wasn't dead! Dead people can't fart on purpose. Hanna attempted to open her eyes, but they only opened just a little bit. Through the cracks, she saw a clearer image of the wispy figure she had seen before she passed out. "Dad?!" Hanna croaked.

"Hi, honey! Wow that was a real stinker, kiddo. Took me forever to find ya, but I should've known you'd be over at Dubray's! You always loved that joint, whenever we swang through Janet's Place. I haven't been around these parts myself since . . . " the wispy figure trailed off. Hanna tried to sit up, but when she did, an invisible force pushed her gently but firmly back down.

"Since you became a ghost?" Hanna uttered with frustration. She's so mad because she hasn't seen her dad in a long time and not just because he's a ghost; he just hasn't been around. "I'm mad, Dad!"

"Oh honey, I know. I really blew it with you. But the thing you have to know is—

ICKYPEDIA

Main page

Contents

Current events

Random article

About Ickypedia

Contact us

Donate

Contribute

Help

Learn to edit

Community portal

Recent changes

Upload file

Tools

What links here

Related changes

Special pages

Permanent link

Page information

Cite this page

Ickydata item

Print/export

Download as PDF

Printable version

In other projects

Ickymedia Commons

Ickyquote

Article | Talk

Leo Karpatze

Sir Leonard Peanut Van Doozer Karpatze IV is an American songwriter best known for cowriting the 1962 Halloween novelty record *The Monster Mash*.

Born	May 11, 1937, Transylvania
Citizenship	American (revoked)
Education	Harvard University Online
Net Worth	$800 million
Spouse(s)	Lydia Karpatze (m. 1974), Bride of Frankenstein (m. 1968, d. 1970), Faye Dunaway (m. 1965, d. 1966)
Surviving Relative	Scaroline Karpatze (granddaughter, b. 1999)

Early Life

Karpatze was born in Transylvania under a full moon to his mother, Natalia Karpatze. His father, a skeleton, was never a part of his life. Natalia fled to the United States, settling in Sacramento, California, with Leo, his six siblings, and their pet bat Flappy.

In school, Karpatze took to music composition, gravitating toward a marriage of the macabre and the erotic, with early songs like "Horny Tarantula" and "Cummy Mummy." Upon graduation, Karpatze was offered a novelty songwriting scholarship to Monsters University, but turned it down to pursue a career in toilet repair.

Music Career

After relocating to Hollywood in 1960, Karpatze booked a freelance job repairing a toilet at Capitol Records, where he met Bobby "Boris" Pickett, there to repair a urinal. The two formed the Halloween-themed group The Boo Boys. Their breakout hit, "The Monster Fuck," made the duo a sensation at the Sunset Strip's legendary novelty song clubs.

The Boo Boys at the Whisky a Go Go with a fan.

Music Career (Cont.)

In 1961, The Boo Boys were signed to a deal with Empire Records, but executives said the imagery in "The Monster Fuck" was too graphic and insisted on a sanitized rewrite. Pickett agreed, over Karpatze's protestations, and the resulting song became "The Monster Mash."

The fallout led to a schism, and Karpatze left to pursue a solo career, touring and performing "The Monster Fuck" as "The Original Monster Mash" to crowds of horrified schoolchildren.

```
For my monster from his slab began to rise        ← LOVE THIS
                                                    IMAGERY!
When suddenly to my surprise            ← DID I MISS SOMETHING??

His trousers dropped right to the floor   ← WHAT DOES THIS HAVE TO
With his bottom bare he ran to the door    DO WITH HALLOWEEN?
                             's MONSTER
I said Frankenstein ← what's gotten into you?

He said my dick is hard and I need to screw  WE CANNOT UNDER
                                              ANY CIRCUMSTANCES PRESS
                                               THIS TO A RECORD!!!!

(He did the Fuck)

They did the Monster Fuck  NO. GOD NO!

(The Monster Fuck)

It was a graveyard fuck  ← THIS IS A VERY LOW EFFORT RHYME.

(The Monster Fuck)

That monster sucked and fucked   ONCE AGAIN YOU
                                 HAVE RHYMED
(The Monster Fuck)               F**K WITH F**K

It was a Monster Fuck


From my laboratory I heard quite the racket

Deep in the castle the vampires jacked it
                              * REMINDER THE CURRENT
                                  YEAR IS 1962!
```

The original typewritten lyrics to "The Monster Fuck," with studio notes

On Television

In 1964, television screens everywhere got a little spookier with the introduction of *The Munsters* and *The Addams Family*. Never one to get lapped, Karpatze invested his modest earnings from "The Monster Mash" into self-producing his own pilot: *The Bone-Aparts*.

The concept saw Frank Steinman (played by Italian pro wrestler Il Trapano) and Vanna Pyra (played by porno actor Jeanie Load) empty nesting with their kids away at boarding s-ghoul, so they rent their castle out to swinging coeds Wolfgang and Lagoona.

One episode aired, after Karpatze cleverly labeled the tape as an episode of *Bonanza* and delivered it to a CBS affiliate wearing a cowboy hat. Families all over the nation were scandalized by the vulgarity, as well as poor writing, shoddy sets, and myriad continuity errors. The tape was destroyed by the bomb squad, and all that remains is an issue of *TV Guide*, completely empty inside as the writers went on strike as a result of having to watch it, and a script page, which was found in a filing cabinet purchased at the estate sale of a celebrity koi trainer.

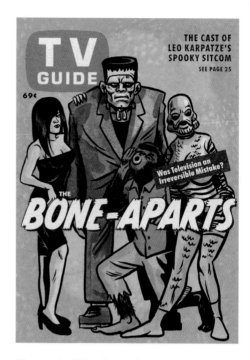

The cast of *The Bone-Aparts*.

Presidential Campaign

On March 14, 1980, Karpatze launched an independent bid for the White House, fueled by his personal disdain for Jimmy Carter's plans to implement the metric system. After a surprise third place finish in the Indiana primary, Karpatze's campaign battled rumors of voter bribery via free passes to defunct theme park Sauzer's Kiddieland.

On May 21, 1980, *Spy Magazine* published paparazzi photos of Karpatze, *Hogan's Heroes* star Bob Crane, and several mummies engaged in a yacht orgy. Karpatze subsequently ended his candidacy and sought refuge in the Transylvanian Embassy, where he would live for the next decade.

Death

Due to declining health resulting from a lifetime of poor choices, Karpatze's death is characterized as "imminent." A designated Ickypedia community editor is on call to update the tense on this page from "is" to "was" at a moment's notice. He's slated to be survived by his granddaughter, failed pop star and aspiring vet tech Scaroline Rose Karpatze-Kennedy.

FRANK and VANNA press their ears up to the cobweb-covered wall.

VANNA PYRA Where is that noise coming from?

FRANK STEINMAN It's gotta be a leaky pipe!

The sound gets louder as they near WOLFGANG and LAGOONA'S room. They pause for a moment before opening the door.

INT. WOLFGANG AND LAGOONA'S ROOM CONTINUOUS

Frank and Vanna enter to see WOLFGANG and LAGOONA fucking hard.

FRANK STEINMAN What did I say, leaky pipe!

SFX: LAUGH

VANNA PYRA What in Baphomet's name are you two doing?

Wolfgang and Lagoona look at each other.

WOLFGANG Aren't you a little old for a bats and the bees talk?

SFX: LAUGH

FRANK STEINMAN Not that, how could you not invite us?

Frank bends over and kisses Wolfgang deeply, with lots of tongue. Vanna sees this, hikes up her skirt, and starts rubbing herself. Lagoona grabs Vanna's ass and pulls her right on top of her face. Frank mounts the woman whose tongue is halfway up his wife's cunt while Wolfgang slathers his dick in lube.

BILL CARTER

BILL CARTER is a certified personal trainer (pending certification) who specializes in raising the heart rate of his clients through untraditional methods. He bills himself as a "trainer to stars" and boasts the legendary Cary Grant as his very first client.

After returning from World War II, Bill was struggling to settle on a career path when he happened to see the film *Notorious* and found himself extremely dissatisfied, to the point of disgust, with Cary Grant's physique. Suddenly, Bill knew what he was meant to do with his life. He packed his bags for Los Angeles, tracked down Cary Grant, and set about trying to convince the actor to hire him as his personal trainer. Grant declined, but Bill was not deterred. He began training Grant for free by breaking into his home late at night and yelling at the top of his lungs in a nonsense language. Grant's heart rate was visibly elevated whenever Bill did this, and a career in fitness was born.

Seventy years later, Bill is still at it. He does not currently have any steady clients or a gym to work out of, though he has an arrangement with the Bally's across the street from Earwolf's studio whereby he will be allowed to work out with a client there as long as the client has a Bally's membership. Bill spends a lot of his time trying to find such a person, and generally promoting his services around town.

One of Bill's promotional techniques involves his friend Victor, who is, according to Bill, "technically classified as a giant." Victor approaches randomly selected people in public, beats them up without provocation, and then wanders off. Bill then appears and asks the victim, "Do you want to win that fight next time?" which is followed by a pitch for his services.

When you sign on to work with Bill, you can expect to have your heart rate elevated in any number of challenging ways.

One of his favorite exercises starts when you give Bill something, or someone, that you dearly love. Bill will then strap explosives to your beloved possession, pet, spouse, or child and put it on the roof of a building with a two-minute timer attached. You'll get up those stairs faster than you ever thought possible.

AGE: 99

INTERESTING FACTS:

1) Bill has a tattoo of a girl he fell in love with and after they broke up, he went back to the tattoo artist and made her blind.

2) Bill has been incarcerated many times for, as he puts it, "doing nothing." He was jailed once for minding his own business while his brother-in-law "popped" someone and once for starting a race riot.

Bill Carter's
WORKOUT OF A LIFETIME

This is a really simple nine-step workout to get you into shape. But before we get into the steps, there's a bunch of things you're gonna need. This is a real-world, environment-based workout, and there's a number of things I need you to get right now, ok?

Some comfortable clothes

A first-aid kit

One mother wolf

Two of her wolf pups, must be at least 10 pounds each

30 tactical knives

A military climbing wall

A can of gasoline

A book of matches

A rifle with a shoulder strap

A ski mask

A sleeping bag

A crown of thorns like Jesus wore

A bottle of water

A friend who is not afraid of dangerous animals

Another friend who really cares about you and your fitness

A third friend who should be the most unstable person you know

Attn: Friend #1, The Wolf Guy

Ok, Wolf Guy friend, I need you to gather all three of the wolves, put them in some kind of enclosure about two miles away from a river. Any river wherever you are. The stronger the current and the wider the river, the better. This is where the workout guy is going to go to sleep in his sleeping bag. When that happens, I want you to wait 30 minutes after he falls asleep, then get really close to his ears and yell, **"WAKE UP! WAKE UPPPP!!!! IT'S TIME TO GET GOING. YOU'RE AT YOUR RESTING HEART RATE WHEN YOU SLEEP AND I JUST JOLTED YOU OUT OF IT. THE WORKOUT HAS BEGUN!"**

Then, give the two wolf pups to your workout friend. Be sure to restrain the mother wolf while you do that!

Attn: Friend #2, The Knife Guy

Knife Guy, get ahold of those 30 tactical knives. Now, I need you to bury the knives blade side up. I don't want the knives to be visible, but the blade is sticking up. Might wanna cover them with leaves. Do this on the other side of the river from where your friend is going to sleep.

He's going to step on these knives with his bare feet, and he's gonna bleed.

You may be saying, "I can't do this to my friend." BUT THIS IS FOR HIS OWN GOOD TO FIND OUT HOW HE RESPONDS TO ADVERSITY SITUATIONS AND CARRIES ON IN A REAL-WORLD FOOT-BLOOD SITUATION. I NEED YOU TO DO THIS FOR YOUR FRIEND. DON'T CHICKEN OUT ON HIM NOW, BECAUSE WE'RE TRYING TO SAVE A MAN'S LIFE AND GET HIM IN SHAPE.

Fine, I think I persuaded you.

Attn: Friend #3, Unstable Person

Ok friend, you have a very important job. You need to find the mother of your friend who is working out. Or a relative he cares about, if his mother is not available. Ideally, his mother. Take her to some location and sit on her.

You're going to get a phone call at a crucial moment, and your buddy is going to tell you, "I have an hour to work out and if you don't hear from me in one hour, then you do whatever you want with the mother." This will all become clear in a little while.

FOCUS! OK FOCUS! Get the mother of the workout guy and sit on her. And at a certain point, you might be able to do whatever the hell you want with her, but maybe not. In the meantime, CONTROL YOURSELF!

 Workout Guy, resume reading here!

START OF THE WORKOUT

Ok, it's the night before your workout, you laid all the groundwork, and you're going to have the workout of your life. What you need to do now is get a good night's sleep. So get in your sleeping bag out there under the stars and go to sleep. Keep these instructions near you but don't read ahead!

STEP 1

Good morning! That was a short nap, huh?! Right now, call your unstable friend. Tell him that you're starting your workout. Tell him you got one hour to do this workout. Tell him, "If you don't hear from me in an hour, do what Bill told you to do."

STEP 2

Take the two wolf pups from the Wolf Guy. Then you're going to turn to him and say, "Buddy, in 10 minutes, I want you to release the mother wolf and say a prayer for me, ok?"

STEP 3

Put on the crown of thorns, grab your rifle and your ski mask and your bottle of water and your first aid kit, and you're gonna run! Are you ready? **RUUUUNNNNNN!!** And while you're running, I want you to do bicep curls with the wolf pups.

Ok, you're running and you got the wolf pups and you've made that call to your unstable friend, and you don't know what that's about and that's got you a little bit worried. And you should be.

And you know in 10 minutes your other buddy is going to release a mother wolf, who is gonna be, let's just say, curious about where her wolf pups are.

Ok, you're running in the direction of the river. Your workout has begun. And hopefully you're feeling excited and optimistic about completing this workout. It's a two-mile run. Could be 14 minutes if you do a seven-minute mile.

STEP 4

Your friend will release the mother wolf. Her sense of smell is far greater than you can imagine. She knows exactly where her pups are and who has them (you). If you're in good shape, you can run about 11 miles per hour. The mother wolf runs 35 miles per hour at a sprint and I promise you she is sprinting. Wolves are very pack oriented. To lose two pups is infuriating. You've got an angry mother wolf and she is infuriated and heading straight for you. If that doesn't help to motivate you toward that river, I don't know what will.

STEP 5

Get across the river. If you're not at the river by now, you're fucked. Because if you're not at the river, you've given the mother wolf too much time to close in on you. And you could be being torn limb from limb right now.

But if you're at the river, then you have a chance. Now the mother wolf is getting angrier the more she runs. And she can get across the river every bit as easily as a person can, maybe even more so. So you continue to be in grave danger.

STEP 6

Now, there's a very good chance you've stepped on a knife by now. And there are 29 more of them. So you're going to be bleeding from the foot, and that's why you have the first-aid kit. If you need to, bandage up the foot. But if you can soldier on, soldier on. The next time you step on one of these knives, dig it up, because you're gonna need it.

Don't give up! You gotta make it! Come on now, you can do this! Dig deep, all the way from your bloody head to your bloody feet — you're bleeding from both ends! And that wolf, by the way, can smell that blood. She knows exactly where her children are.

STEP 7

Slaughter the two wolf pups. Nothing short of that is gonna work. You need to put them where the wolf mother can find them so she'll stop chasing you. It's not enough to let them go because she's still gonna associate your scent with the scent of these wolves. So she might come after you. When she finds her slaughtered pups, she'll have a mourning period. And she'll get over it.

7 STAGES OF WOLF GRIEF

Howling

Yelping

Scratching your butt on the ground

Sniffing, lots of sniffing

Back to howling

Vengeance

Just go "welp," then go wandering off to eat something

If you want to throw the wolf mother off a little bit and make it look like an accident, you can draw up little wolf suicide notes and pin 'em to the bodies. If you end up doing this workout twice, the second time bring a pen and some paper so you can write these suicide notes.

Anyway, slaughter these wolf pups right now because you're headed into a world of problems!

STEP 8

You've come to the military climbing wall. You're going to douse it in gasoline, set it on fire, and climb over it. And you gotta be real fleet-to-foot, my friend, otherwise you're gonna burn alive.

Now focus! This isn't going to be easy! Your feet are bleeding, your head is bleeding, you've made it through the rolling rapids of a river. God only knows what damage you've sustained from that experience. But you've done great so far. I don't know how many knives you've stepped on, but probably at least a dozen knives unless the Knife Guy really screwed up. So you've been through the wringer and the wringer's only just started.

This is the hardest part of the workout. You're gonna set that military climbing wall on fire, and you're gonna climb over it as fast as you can. I mean it, if you take a second too long, you're gonna be consumed in flames. And it may happen anyway! There's a good chance. And you're in no shape to climb anything with what's happened to your feet. And not to mention the crown of thorns. You're in a bad state.

But you're gonna do this and it's gonna be hard so what's gonna help you? A great piece of music. A fantastic workout song. When I say "go," you're gonna throw the match on the wall and you're gonna get yourself over that wall as fast as possible to the tune of "All the Way Tonight Parenthesis Look of the Lion End Parenthesis" by SPYRYT!

THROW THE MATCH

THE END OF THE WORKOUT

Take some time, relax from the burns. But I need you to go to the liquor store and rob it. And that's gonna give you enough money to sign up at TrainerForTheStarsSeekingStars.org to get some personal training sessions. You tell me honestly what you got out of the liquor store, and that's what I will charge you. I will also take lottery tickets and scratch-offs because I believe every one of those is worth something.

After you rob that liquor store, you're gonna want to call that Unstable Friend of yours and tell him to release your mother. And if it's been more than an hour, she might be dead. So you better call him quickly.

And you can take off the crown of thorns now. I made my point with it.

PEOPLE I (LITTLE ORPHAN BOY FOURVEL) HAVE MOIDERED IN COLD BLOOD

(A retrospective on a career of PURE MOIDER)

1. Prince.
2. Leonard Nimoy.
3. Weird Al Yankovic. (?)
4. My parents.
5. Scott. (Bunch of times.)
6. Lil' Lord Andy Lloyd Webby. (Bunch of times.)
7. Anyone who has ever loved me.
8. Jaye Davidson. (Still have the penis!)
9. Tom Sizemore's jeweler.
10. A dude named Dan.
11. Larry King. (Wasn't COVID.)
12. Most of the people who died in 1984.
13. JonBenét Gordon Ramsey. (LONG STORY.)
14. Jaws. (Movie got it wrong.)
15. Kid Cudi.
16. THE Michael Jackson. (Hee hee!)
17. My Brothers, Twovel, Threevel, and Steven.
18. The Anaheim Ducks and countless others.
19. You!

Note to Editor.
Put fancy mirrored
paper here.

Thanks!

KNIFE GRAB!

JACK FURZ

JACK FURZ is a freelance news cameraperson, who spends his free time documenting the vigilante known as The Nite Wolf. Jack is not The Nite Wolf.

While The Nite Wolf has successfully stopped some instances of vandalism and teen loitering, he has been less successful breaking up larger crimes. Jack believes this is more of a PR problem. According to Jack, The Nite Wolf has everything in place other than name recognition.

As skilled a cameraman as Jack is, he has yet to capture The Nite Wolf's identity on video. The footage he does have shows The Nite Wolf to be of medium size and weight, much like Jack, who is not The Nite Wolf.

Jack's parents were tragically murdered, but luckily he was found and raised by wolves.

Jack claims to be totally over it and is not seeking revenge.

AGE: 40

INTERESTING FACTS:

1) Jack has two pet wolves.

2) He has been hospitalized for falling off a building.

3) He's single!

WHAT WE KNOW ABOUT THE NITE WOLF

By Jack Furz

There is a new hero (some might even say he's a SUPER HERO) guarding the streets of Los Angeles. Despite my best efforts I can't get the main stream media to cover this sensational story! Luckily, my skills as a news cameraman have allowed me to study this mysterious force of justice know as... the *NITE WOLF!* While we don't know much about him, there is an alarming amount of misinformation plaguing the young lupine luminary. So, dear reader, let us set the record straight and separate the TRUTH from the LIES about this new defender of the streets.

TRUTH	LIE
No one knowns who the Nite Wolf is!	Jack Furz is the Nite Wolf. *HA!*
TRUTH	**LIE**
Nite Wolf is an original persona, he even has a unique spelling, which he has confirmed with me as N-I-T-E (space) W-O-L-F.	He is being sued for copyright infringement by Midway games who crated the Mortal Kombat character Nightwolf. He is also being sued by Warner Bros who will be releasing the Kevin Hart film Night Wolf.
TRUTH	**LIE**
HE IS A HERO!	N.W. is actually causing more problems by taking justice into his own hands. He is fueling a cycle of systemic violence and not addressing the actual causes of crime.
TRUTH	**LIE**
Has a raspy intimidating voice and is STD free. (He showed me the test result, sadly I wasn't able to get my camera out in time to film.)	Has some kind of throat condition caused by HPV.
TRUTH	**LIE**
Is just a good guy who care about indivuals, myself included.	Nite Wolf is obvioulsy Jack Furz, since he seem to be tracking the killers of Jack Furz's parents.

2

TRUTH
Dons a bad ass and wolf-like costume, which masks his identity.

LIE
Resembles a sick, wet bear or someone in a decrepit mascot costume.

SO COOL!

TRUTH
Is a master of Wolfjitsu, a unique martial art, known only to a small group of practitioners. I am also skilled at Wolfjitsu, which allows me to recognize his mastery of the form.

LIE
Appears to be ungraceful. He often seems to be in pain or hurt/beat up looking.

NO PROOF!

TRUTH
Takes good care of his two wolf pups and they enjoy following him through the city. (Full disclosure: I also have two wolf pups named "Justice" and "Payback". Wolves are wild animals and not easy pets! So, bravo to Nite Wolf for his animal training abilities!) The Wolfmobile seems to be battle tested and safe for animal transport. (Everyone recognizes the Wolfmobile for it's cool wrap around paint job.)

♥ →

LIE
He abuses animals by forcing wolves to walk on rooftops or ride around in his rusty out, sun bleached, aqua blue Pontiac Sunfire. The coupe has "Wolfmob" spraypainted on one side, and "ile" on the hood because he clearly made the letters too big when he started spraypainting "wolfmobile" on the side and realized it too late.

TRUTH
There have been several bad batches of smoke bombs making the rounds on the LA smoke bomb market. I too am known to buy a smoke bomb now and then (adds a nice haze effect to the shot) and sometimes even with the best intentions we are the victims of faulty equiptment.

LIE !!
Nite Wolf set several city blocks ablaze and never took responsibility.

What?! YEAH, RIGHT!

— Payback tried to EAT THIS LOL!

TRUTH

Nite Wolf has loved and lost many times, he's a tortured soul who is doing his best to make sure others do not experience this same pain. (As someone who is also unlucky in love, I for one, applaud his effort.)

~~────────~~

TRUTH

The Nite Wolf and I seem to have a large over laps in our lives, it's true. I take any accusations of myself and the Nite Wolf being one and the same as a compliment and a result of being the sole cameraman who has footage of the elusive hero.

LIE

Nite Wolf is dangerous to be around and seems to have a laundry list of ex-lovers and family members who have died in horrific ways. If he never would've become a vigilante he would probably be happier and the streets would be safer.

LIE

Jack Furz is clearly the Nite Wolf, he fucks up and sometimes says stuff about the Nite Wolf that's way too specific, or sometimes he says stuff about himself and accidentally credits it to the Nite Wolf even though it makes no sense.

PLEASE PUBLISH! —JACK

+

APPROVED BY

NITE WOLF

PAW PRINT FROM WOLF

CRESENT MOON (NITE)

= ~~GOOD~~ AWESOME LOGO!

JUDGE HEAUX BROWN

JUDGE HEAUX BROWN is a self-described judge. He sits on the bench in Central Park and determines whether or not people are heauxs. He is a man but he has big titties. He wears a graduation robe, unless it is hot outside, in which case he just wears shorts. Judge Brown's cousin, Judge O, sits in Griffith Park and tells people if they've had an orgasm.

Heaux-ness is determined by the following criteria:

1) How many times you have orgasmed.

2) How old you are. After the age of 33, you are likely a heaux.

3) If you are in these streets.

AGE: Old enough to know a heaux or two

POSSIBLE COUSIN:
Bobby Brown

INTERESTING FACTS:

1) Judge Heaux Brown has only been paid once to judge if someone was a heaux, and he was paid in cocaine, which he sold for bitcoint.

2) Judge Heaux Brown is not related to Judge Joe Brown.

3) Judge Heaux Brown has irritable bowel syndrome and is backed up like a U-Haul truck.

Judge Heaux Brown
Court Docket

Date Docketed: Today, What's Today's Date?
Lower Ct. Central Park Bench Court
Case Nos. 9135-9145

Date	Proceedings and Orders
March 10, 2018	Elaine - Heaux
March 23, 2018	Barrett - Heaux
April 1, 2018	Charlton - Heaux
May 14, 2018	Tall fella, didn't catch his name - Heaux
May 16, 2018	Cora - Not a heaux (yet)
February 11, 2019	I took the day off to prepare for Valentine's Day
June 15, 2019	Little man with the fedora (didn't leave a name) - No heaux zone
November 28, 2019	Nelly (not the rapper) - Not a heaux
November 29, 2019	Pigeon person - Heaux (pigeons count)
December 9, 2019	Annalise - Mmmmm not a heaux

THE TOP 5 WETTEST TREASURES STILL UNFOUND

By BROCK LOVETT

I'm a treasure hunter who searches *specifically* for underwater treasures. Here are the undiscovered underwater treasures I most would most like to get my hands on!

5.

THE HORN OF THE LAST UNICORN

Okay, look. I don't usually go in for biological items, but how could I not go after perhaps the most ancient wet treasure in history? When Noah built his Ark, he left the unicorn behind. That horn's gotta be out there somewhere, and it's most likely under water (this is assuming God didn't want it found in the earth and didn't anticipate the invention of the submarine). Now you may not believe in Noah's Ark, and you think it's just a story. Well, Indiana Jones is just a story, right? And he found all kinds of religious stuff, and it was a bunch of movies. Just like a movie called . . . *Titanic*? I rest my case.

4.

PONCE DE LEON'S CLASS RING

Rumor has it that when he discovered the Fountain of Youth, de Leon's high school ring slipped off his finger because he'd lost weight on the journey to the Fountain. This is a very common thing with treasure hunters; the longer you spend searching for a specific treasure, the more excited and anxious you get, and you lose like 10 to 15 pounds by the time you find the treasure.

3.

TONS OF WALLETS AND JEWELRY

The Bermuda Triangle has got to be FULL of what we in the business call "casual treasure." This refers to stuff people lose or drop on the ground. If you find twenty bucks on the street, congrats! You are technically a treasure hunter (not really)! All of the people who "disappeared" in the BT are actually just at the bottom of the North Atlantic. Amelia Earhart's down there. The only reason no one admits this is because it's embarrassing to lose a whole ship or plane or whatever. The first guy that made this up was probably a bad captain with a good survival instinct and a real talent for bullshit. Anyway, since then, anytime someone lost something in that area they pretended it disappeared to avoid paperwork.

2.

LA GIOCANDA (THE MONA LISA)

This one is climate-change dependent, but it's looking good!

1.

THE COEUR DE LA MER DIAMOND

Hey, if you KNOW I am looking for a specific treasure that I already looked for underwater and didn't find, and you just, like, have it on you, and you don't want to give it to me, why don't you just TELL ME THAT and I'll be on my merry way. It's yours, lady. It was given to you by your creep ex-boyfriend and he's long dead, so who cares? Did you think I was gonna mug you? Rat you out? And why did I have to sit through that whole goddamned story (where you come off pretty good for most of it, I gotta say, very interesting) and then throw the thing in the ocean?! I'm not even saying you should have handed it to me, because above-water treasures are boring to me. I'm saying you could have thrown it in the ocean with me watching, and then I'd go down and get it! You never threw a quarter in a pool for a kid? Thanks for nothing.

ALBERT ROE

ALBERT ROE is a local grocer who runs Kissy's Local Grocery Store and an outstanding white man.

He tries to set himself apart from larger grocery chains (Albertsons, Ralphs, Vons, Safeway, Gelson's, Pavilions, and Amazon Fresh) by adding "personal touches" like hand-polishing and kissing every item in his store. He will also kiss customers if they ask him "May I Have A Kiss?" There are one hundred bottles of Bud Heavy beer on the wall of the grocery store, which is made of very thin breakaway glass. Kissy's Local Grocery sells veal, which is grown in the back; hot cakes; and box sets, cassettes, and mini discs of the podcast *Serial*. There is no door at Kissy's Local Grocery, but when Albert is not there, he puts a sign next to the door frame that says, "Don't you fucking come in here."

The larger grocery chains are so threatened by Albert's personal touches that they are coming for his neck. The chains are surveilling him from a van that says "Amazon" on the side. But it is also Albert's van that he was given by his father, Jeff Bezos.

AGE: 32

FAVORITE TURN OF PHRASE: Where's the beef?

INTERESTING FACTS:

1) Albert has ten daughters and zero sons, which he attributes to his "feminine cum."

2) Albert is known as the town vandal.

3) Albert has never been kissed and he is also undercover as a high school student.

Space: The Final Frontier for Quitters

Hello, everyone. When I got into the grocery store business, I wanted to offer an experience that no other store had dared to offer before. I wanted to stand out, be my own thing. With nothing but the clothes on my back and inherited wealth, I moved to Downey, California, and opened up Kissy's Grocery Store. I opened Kissy's with this promise: I will kiss every item in the store. I have kept that promise! But to my surprise, other small business owners in the space—such as Albertsons, Ralphs, Vons, Safeway, Gelson's, Pavilions, and Amazon Fresh—all decided they wanted to come for my neck. MY neck! Little old me, the local grocer who started his business with a loan from his daddy that he had to ask for several times. And yet, I persisted. I didn't let these other businesses take me down, and I am happy to say that Kissy's has been a smashing success (we have successfully smashed the storefronts of several of the aforementioned stores, and let's just say our message has been received).

Cut to the year of our lord two thousand and twenty-three, and some of these small business owners can't seem to take a fuckin' hint. They are finding "new" and "exciting" ways to come for my neck, and I will not stand for it. So I have taken to the editorial section of *Kissy's Weekly*, to call out some of my fellow small-business owners: Richard Branson, Elon Musk, and my own canonical father, Jeff Bezos. Space? Really? That's your big move? Having billions of dollars wasn't enough? Bezos and Branson

went to the edge of space, Musk shot a car up there, big whoop, who gives a shit? Not me, that's for sure. Space is for cowards. Anyone can go to space, we've been doing it for years. This is a transparent attempt at coming for my neck, and guess what, fuckers: You ain't shit.

You have forced my hand here and leave me with no other choice, I simply must make an announcement. I, Albert Roe, hereby declare that I will be going where no small business owner has ever gone before. The bottom of the ocean. I will be taking leave from my duties at Kissy's to focus on my expedition to the deepest and darkest depths of the ocean here on Earth. They say that we know more about space than we do the ocean (something about how we're able to use math to predict what more of

space is like and how the pressure at the bottom of the ocean is too severe for any human to withstand), but that will not stop me. Those three dorks have been so hard thinking about space, they missed what was right in front of them all along, and I will be the first one there, at the bottom of the ocean.

I will be using some money from Kissy's to help subsidize the cost of building an underwater transport (shoutout to all the Kissy's customers, you really helped me out with this one, and if I could kiss every single one of you, I would but I have been asked to stop that) as well as dipping into my inherited wealth. My plan is to touch down on the ocean floor, the farthest point down there, leave a message for any beings that might happen upon it saying they can come to Kissy's anytime they want, and of course humiliate Bezos, Branson, and Musk to the point that they must never come for my neck again.

Thank you so much for the continued support, and don't forget to check out our new Kissy's Rewards Program and the New Store Rules for while I am away!

—**Albert Roe**

Kissy's REWARDS PROGRAM

Introducing: Kissy's Second Base, our new rewards program! As loyal customers will know, every single item in the store is professionally kissed by the founder of Kissy's, Albert Roe, and the one thing he loves more than kissing things is slashing prices! Here's how it works: members of the Kissy's Second Base program will get a discount off any item in the store, non-members will pay regular price, and for those of you who wish to NOT have your items kissed by a true professional, you will be paying whatever price I deem appropriate. It will always be more than the normal price, that's the Kissy's guarantee. That is the rule here and if you don't like it, you can kiss my ass. Shop at some other store, I don't give a shit.

Fresh STRAWBERRIES

2nd Base Price

$3.99 /LB

Reg Price **$4.99/lb**
No Kiss Price **$12/lb**

East Coast OYSTERS

2nd Base Price

Less than MARKET PRICE

Reg Price **Market Price**
No Kiss Price **$100 for 3**

Fresh, Loose PANCAKES

2nd Base Price

$9.99 FOR A STACK OF 3

Reg Price **$10.99/3**
No Kiss Price **$1**
for one single pancake and it's gonna be bad

2nd Base Price

99¢ BREAD

Reg Price **$1.99**
No Kiss Price **$6/slice**

Live GOLDFISH

2nd Base Price

$3.75 + FREE FISH FOOD

Reg price **$5**
No Kiss Price **You have to swallow it and throw it up like Steve-O**

A BASEBALL
(We only have one so act fast!)

2nd Base Price

$4

Reg Price **$6**
No Kiss Price **Free but I get to throw it at your crotch**

CAT LITTER

2nd Base Price

$11.99 for 35lb pail of clay litter

Reg Price **$15 for 35lb pail of clay litter**
No Kiss Price **$1 per grain of clay litter**

GUARANTEED. SEALED WITH A *kiss*

HELLO! ALBERT ISN'T IN RIGHT NOW, SO HERE ARE SOME
NEW RULES TO ABIDE BY WHILE HE IS NOT PRESENT!

DO NOT KISS
ANYTHING IN THE STORE
YOURSELF. EVERYTHING HAS
BEEN KISSED ALREADY.
BACK OFF.

DO NOT WIPE
OFF THE KISS
FROM BEFORE. WHY WOULD
YOU DO THAT? IT'S LIKE THE
WHOLE THING HERE.

IF YOU'D LIKE TO WATCH
ME KISS SOMETHING,
YOU CAN MAKE AN APPOINTMENT AT THE REGISTER.
WHAT DO YOU MEAN THIS DOESN'T SOUND LIKE A RULE?

IF YOU HAVE TO
PISS OR SHIT,
YOU CAN USE THE BATHROOM
BUT ONLY FLUSH WHEN THE
BOWL IS FULL.

IF YOU SEE
SOMETHING,
SAY "I SEE THAT" VERY
LOUD TO MAKE IT KNOWN.

HAVE FUN, BUT NOT WITHOUT ME.
PLEASE CEASE ALL FUN WITHIN KISSY'S GROUNDS UNTIL I RETURN.

<u>BOB DUCCA'S</u>
<u>LIST OF HEROES</u>

~~Atticus King~~, ~~Private Detective~~, Remmington
Thunderknife, Omaha Nightblade, Langston
Deveraux, Hank Marlboro, Channing Merchandise,
Dave Navarro, Brick Pudding, Sanjuko
Mamajuloko, Driscoll Mayweather, Devin
Motorcycle, Ponch Gigabyte, Dashell Permanente,
Rodriguo Bloodharvest, Chaz Steadyfist,
Victoria Slash, Larchmont VanDyke, Paul
Workswellwithothers, Maddox Goodtry, Michele
Potential, Norse Regan, Logan Helpful, Hug
Nicemann, Detective Frank Shark, Havercamp
Shatterdome, ~~Dee_____~~, Darius Rucker,
Emelda Cherry, Victor Winning, Delores
Price, Lance Corporal Scott Bukkake, Steven
Truthchurch, Vito Breech, Frank Ocean, Margery
Crossfit, Dominick Assange, Nova Prime, Omar
Throwgood, Magnus Crochey III, Gabe Haliburton,
Clutch Blackwater, The Honorable Teddy Scar,
Beaumont Harddrive, Arlo Crimejustice, Hammal
Loosecannon and Righteous Sebastian

NO LONGER A HERO
DEAD TO ME

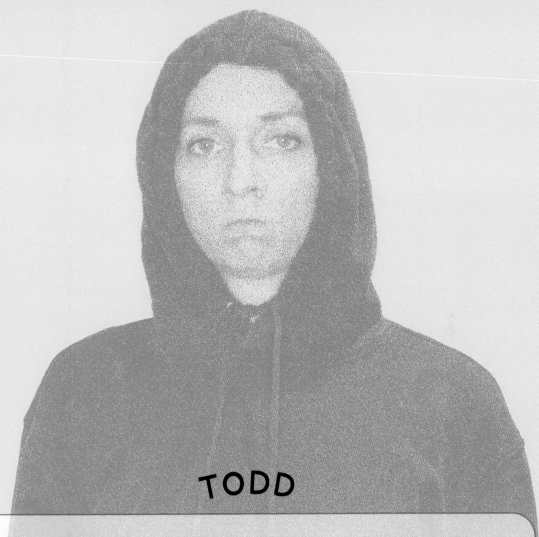

TODD

TODD TYSON CHICKLET is Scott's nephew (Todd's mom is Scott's sister) who is staying with Scott for a while. He grew up in Temecula and one day in 2013, his mom just dropped him off at Scott's house and has never come back for him. Scott makes him sleep on the "mini couch," which is what they call a chair. He also doesn't take Todd to the doctor because Todd's not on his insurance.

Todd is always grounded because he's bad. One time he put on Scott's clothes and peed on the neighbors lawn yelling, "I'm Scott!" Scott got arrested and convicted because Todd didn't show up to court to confess. Among his punishments, Scott keeps him in a closet and makes him fold his underwear.

Once Todd wished to be grown-up at a carnival and was 30 for a day. When he changed back to middle-school age he kept his grown-up size dick.

AGE: Middle school

INTERESTING FACTS:

1) At school, Todd always gets a stomachache before seventh period.

2) He steals drugs from Scott's neighbor.

3) When Scott takes Todd on trips, he puts him in a dog kennel under the plane.

THIS IS WHAT IT IS LIKE TO BE ME, FOR JUST ONE DAY.
LIKE YOU COULD HANDLE MORE!!!!

By Todd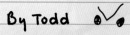

4:54AM - Bang on the side of my crate 'til my Uncle Scott wakes up and lets me out. Then Uncle Scott gets back in bed and makes me cover him with his ~~whole~~ duvet like a burrito so only his face is showing.

5:00AM - Uncle Scott begs me to wash his weekly pair of underwear in the sink "with the no-tears baby soap." I do it or else he makes me face the consequences (eating the same breakfast as Rumpledickskin, my lizard, for one day: a cricket). While I do this, Uncle Scott watches footage of himself sleeping the night before "to make sure it all went okay," he says, with a grin bigger than the fricking moon.

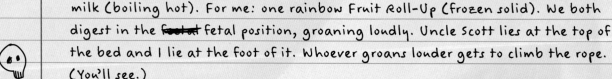

5:30AM - Make breakfast for me and Uncle Scott. For him: Cheerios and milk (boiling hot). For me: one rainbow Fruit Roll-Up (frozen solid). We both digest in the ~~fetal~~ fetal position, groaning loudly. Uncle Scott lies at the top of the bed and I lie at the foot of it. Whoever groans louder gets to climb the rope. (You'll see.)

6:00AM - Time for homeschool! Noooooo! Uncle Scott puts on his Teacher Bonnet and prepares my lesson for the day: First up, where all the states are, as he remembers them. I learned them all! Gorgias is right next to South Dickota and Whyoming is by Delawear.

7:00AM - Math class. Uncle Scott wants me to count 'til I get to the number in his head.

8:00AM - The number was 1. Uncle Scott calls that missionary's favorite position.

8:30AM – It's jim time. Uncle Scott drives me across town and has me climb a rope into Kulap's window, to "make sure she's there." I get up there and see her sleeping. I climb back down, and my glutes are burning. He makes me describe what that feels like. He asks me if I think people will really believe they are married. I say yes and manage to live another hour.

9:30AM – Science class. Uncle Scott shows me how to make a volcano out of three simple ingredients: a bottle of pop and his two hands. He grabs the bottle and shakes it as hard as he can. He actually starts crying while he does it, but he says it's because "it's so heavy." Then he quickly takes off the cap and the stuff goes everywhere. Uncle Scott's so happy to be sticky that he says he needs a nap for a few hours. SWEET!

10:00AM – I scrub through Uncle Scott's Sex & The City DVDs for all of Miranda's sex scenes (yummy yummy she's the babest) and I record a bunch of TikToks where I put those scenes as the background of the TikTok and then I do a dance in front of that. I upload them and always get around one million hits.

2:00PM – Late lunch for me and Uncle Scott. He has lobster with ~~cheese~~ champagne (two bottles) and I have a cheese stick wrapped in a piece of turkey and a glass of stinky milk.

3:00PM – Now it is time for my reading lesson. Uncle Scott sets up a Zoom session using all of the other computers in the house, and he puts his stuffed animals in front of each computer so it's like I have an audience. I get super nervous with a crowd and my reading is really hard so it takes me a second to get through it.

227

sghetti

Gushers

9:00PM - Uncle Scott orders dinner but he's scared to talk to people at the door so I have to answer it and pretend to be grown up. I stand on a chair and put on a really long shirt that covers the chair, and then I put a pair of pants on the front two legs and scrunch them up and put shoes under them. It looks really real. The delivery people never have any questions, which is the same number as they would have for a real guy so I know it works. Tonight he gets some pasta delivered from Cheesecake and I have some Gushers that I found in a hidden section of the dollar store where one of the guys who works there was sitting at a card table looking at his phone.

10:00PM - Time for Uncle Scott's "digestive tuck-in." He lays in the bed and I tuck his sheets and blankets in tightly all around him. He says it helps his stomach push the food down so it goes through him faster. I honestly don't care ~~this~~ because this is my time to practice my skateboard. I hop on it at the top of the hill and fly allllll the way to Venice Beach! WEEEE! All the women and men there love me and want to be with me. I have to sit at a table and sign autographs all over their feet just to get them to relax. I do this allll night as long as I can, then I get a ride home from a sexy nurse in a red convertible.

4:00AM - I get home and look through all the work Uncle Scott has done on his phone: selfies on the porch, selfies on the bed, selfies everywhere, and all nude. God, I love my family.

LOGAN CONLEY

According to our sources, **LOGAN CONLEY** is the news director at KPUS channel 6. He was born in Young Shelton, Connecticut, and attended the prestigious Welton Academy, where he helped get a teacher fired for encouraging the students to think for themselves. He attended Welton from kindergarten through college, ultimately earning a master's in Muckraking. After college he joined the Marines, where he was personally responsible for carrying out a "Code Red" order from his beloved commanding officer, Col. Jessup. Following that, he entered the field of journalism, where he received both a Pulitzer and a Mr. Skin Anatomy Award for his work breaking the Fappening.

INTERESTING FACTS:

1) Loves the beach.

2) Has a dog named "Cronkite."

3) Keeps a torture chamber beneath his house where he imprisons runaways and prostitutes.

MEMORANDUM FOR ALL STAFF

From: Logan Conley, News Director, KPUS Channel 6 News

Subject: Getting a Few Things Straight

All right, everyone. I know I'm new here so I want to make sure we're all on the same page as to how I'm going to run this station, and what our shared priorities are going to be.

Rule #1: If it bleeds, it leads. Does that sound crass and revolting to you? I don't care. My only job is to deliver ratings, and nothing draws in viewers like blood and violence. Simple as that.

Rule #2: If it swallows, it follows. Your second story of the night should be about a python on the loose. You motherfuckers aren't doing your jobs unless you can convince the viewers they will be swallowed whole by a giant snake if they don't tune in. You know what they say: a terrified viewer . . . is a viewer. *What?* It's TRUE! Side note: if no pythons are on the loose, this can be a story about a choking hazard—that also counts. In fact, I would love it if we could cut LIVE to a toddler choking on a quarter every night. Oh, and by the way, I don't care if said tot survives . . . so long as it brings in AD DOLLARS.

Rule #3: If it's about a turd, it goes third. I don't like to be crass, but facts are facts. America loves turds. Don't believe me? Then look up the freaking BOX OFFICE RETURNS for any number of Hollywood films that heavily feature SCATOLOGICAL HUMOR! Oh, what's that? You don't have a lead on a shit-related story? Then point a news camera at your own freaking toilet (post-defecation), *Erica!* "Your third story tonight: someone took a dump." Yeah, I like the sound of that . . . and so do our brainless viewers!

Rule #4: If it's about the Man from the North, it goes fourth. I want the fourth story every night to be about Santa Claus, or as he's more commonly known, the Man from the North. I don't care what time of year it is. Every single day, the fourth news story should be about Santa Claus. What's he wearing, how are his lists coming along, what's he feeding his reindeer? Don't have a story? Then get on a candy-cane phone to the North Pole and dig something up, *Steve!*

And look, I know that nobody who works here is named Erica or Steve. I don't care!

Rule #5: Stories about Mordor go fifth in the order. Stories about hobbits, orcs, ents, or Gimli should be fifth. Any earlier and the ratings plummet. Any later and you'll be plummeting when I throw you out of the fucking news chopper! How did I trick you to get into the chopper in the first place, you ask? Oh, let's just say I lured you in with the delicious scent of Lembas bread!

What? I never said I wasn't a little bitch.

Okay, this next rule actually rhymes, so it should be easy to remember.

Rule #6: If it's about chicks or dicks, then man alive, it's the story one after five. I told you it rhymed! If you didn't believe me, the blame falls squarely on your shoulders, you piss-poor excuses for *journos!*

By the way, look, I know there are a lot of rumors about me. People say I'm unethical, I'm soul-less, I'm a disgrace to my profession. But I'll have you know I'm a family man. Yeah, and my family . . . is the GODDAMN NIELSEN FAMILY!

Side Note: If your story's about a dog, I want to see it on a log. You know logs, right? Trees where the long part is on the ground instead of the circle part?! Anyway, this rule isn't related to air order. It's just another rule of thumb around here. I don't want any stories about a canine unless they include a shot of that dog sitting on a log.

And finally . . .

Rule #7: If Jesus comes back from heaven? That's story number seven. This one is self-explanatory. If Jesus, that old Capricorn, ever returns to Earth, it will be the seventh story of the night. Otherwise, we take a commercial break after the sixth story.

DASH GRABUM'S
POKEYDEX
GOLD COAST REGION

Hello reader!

My name is Dash Grabum. I am 12 years old, and I am going to be the greatest Pokeymon master of all time and also history! I am from the Kanto region but I am currently visiting my friend Scott (Hi, Scott!), here in the Goldcoast region. Scott said, "Dash, I am making a book. It's going to be the greatest book, like no book ever was. To write books is my real test, to sell them is my cause." I turned my hat backward, and got REAL close to him so he could only see my eyes and said, "Scott, does your book include stats, weaknesses, and tips for catching the Pokeymon of the Goldcoast region? Scott replied, "I do not know what that means." "Then leave it to me!" I said as I left immediately. This was super effective and now I am an author. I hope my work here helps you catch, subjugate, and train some of the amazing creatures I've encountered here. PS I have included drawings but DO NOT be mad at me if they are bad, I am NOT an art guy.

#016 - Pigeon
Type: Flying

Evolves from: Pigeoness

This is a Goldcoast variant of a fairly common bird we have in Kanto, but way worse. Pigeoness is extremely weak, and even once evolved it is only effective against breadcrumbs and other people's pizza. I caught mine in the Costco parking lot but honestly they're everywhere. Skip this one.

Note: For some reason they are often missing toes?

#123 - S'Kahlaytor

type: Steel / Electric

Evolves from: S'tairz

S'kahlaytor's can be found in airports and indoor malls.
It has giant, slow-moving teeth, and you can tell
which gender it is depending which way the teeth move.
(Females up, males down. Lol.) Apparently they are a
protected species because the GGG (Glendale Galleria
Guards) chased me when I tried to leave the parking lot
with mine. Trust me, it's not worth the trouble.

#0k9 - Servisdogg

type: Normal (sometimes Fighting)

Evolves from: Normaldogg

Oh boy, people do NOT like it when you try to catch a Servisdogg,
let. me. tell. you. I got screamed at by a lady who claimed it
was "hers" but in my defence, she had it tied to a rope, which
is not a league-approved method of storage. Noob. Apparently
any Normaldogg can evolve into Servisdogg if you take it to a
special office and tell them you are stressed.

#333 - Christree

type: Grass / Fairy

Evolves from: Douglasfir

These only show up in the winter and have no attacks
and bad speed. Very pretty if you're that kind of collector.
About 90% of the people I met catch one every year, but
weirdly they throw it away after a few months! Rude/sad?

#419/#420 - Vaypuh and Dabcloud

type: Steel and Ghost / Poison

Evolves from: Ecig and Lilhit

these two creatures are in a sim-bionic relationship (yeah I read books). Vaypuh is small and metal and looks cool as hell. It hides Dabcloud INSIDE it (woah.) Dabcloud then uses fun smells to lure in its opponents, and destroys them slowly from the inside. Special attacks include: "Juicy Clouds" and "Rip Cotton."

#911 - Arrson

type: Fire

Evolves from: Wyldfyre

the Goldcoast region has a huge problem with both Wyldfyres and Arrsons. Weak against water, but super effective against remote areas and structures built before 2008.

Hides horrible hands?

#??? - Michaelmouse

type: Psychic / Capitalist Legendary

I know, looking at the picture he doesn't seem like much, but reader, believe me when I tell you people LOSE THEIR MINDS for this big rat. there is a whole-ass expensive park that people show up to just to try and catch it, and no one ever has. Wears gloves for some reason. Wild stuff.

#205 Shuttelelon

type: Fire / Steel / Electric / Flying

Evolves from: Musktruck

Here's what this one does: Flies into space for no reason. Honestly it seems like a HUGE waste for something so powerful to do something so pointless, when it could be using its power in much more productive ways. But what do I know, I'm 12! I'm sure the planet will be habitable forever.

- Eats $ for fuel
- very big and stupid
- why tho?

Hair
Glasses give powers?
Ears x2
Soot Suit
6'1"

#??? Andyrichter

type: Co-host

Evolves from: Paulandrewrichter

One of the first ones I caught, before setting him free upon learning he had a family. Didn't have a lot of attacks BUT could basically do anything a person could do. Also he looked a lot like a person. Huh. this might just have been a human man. Oops. Pls don't snitch.

Well, I hope this helps you catch them all, dear reader! I know there are a lot of creatures but remember you can always store them in the internet if you ever run out of room. Are they hungry there? Does time pass for them? we'll never know and we'll never ask! Until next time, stay super effective Goldcoast! (BYE, SCOTT!)

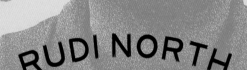

RUDI NORTH

RUDIMENTARY NORTH is a self-described Florida dirtbag from Miami and professional employee who possesses the ability to life swap with people via throat punch (AKA the "dirtbag handshake"). Other dirtbag activities include: cutting people off on the road and not using a signal, parking in front of your house, and playing music really loud. He has a compass in the car that's always pointed north and always pointed to him (Rudi North).

He got his first job in LA by throwing himself onto a car going sixty during rush hour down Sunset Blvd. It was a Toyota Tercel and the driver worked for Postmates. Rudi told the driver, "Let's not have insurance handle this. Just give me the keys," and that's how he got a car. The Postmates driver was mid-order and Rudi delivered it and that's how he got a job. He was eventually fired for punching Neil Patrick Harris in the throat. He was also let go from his next job (security guard at Target) for exceeding the throat punch limit, which is zero.

Through various throat punchings, Rudi has had the following jobs:

- Postmates driver
- Target security guard
- Earwolf engineer
- City of Los Angeles leaf blower
- California Donuts shop owner
- Christmas tree salesman/ "tree guy"
- A reindeer, likely Rudolph
- Santa Claus
- Writer for the TV show Wrecked
- Strip club bathroom attendant
- The devil
- Center for the Detroit Lions

Frequently, Rudi has been known to come in hot. He is a fan favorite.

AGE: Hundreds of years old

INTERESTING FACTS:

1) He is an immortal born in the 1600s and does not live in a human body. Even though he can't die, he does get injured. He made a sacrifice to be immortal.

2) He has been married and divorced at least a thousand times.

3) Rudi and Scott Aukerman became best friends after years spent in the Speed Force dimension together.

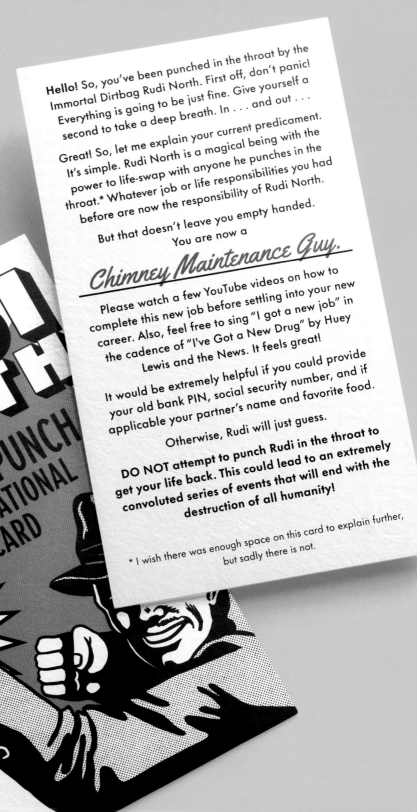

Hello! So, you've been punched in the throat by the Immortal Dirtbag Rudi North. First off, don't panic! Everything is going to be just fine. Give yourself a second to take a deep breath. In . . . and out . . .

Great! So, let me explain your current predicament. It's simple. Rudi North is a magical being with the power to life-swap with anyone he punches in the throat.* Whatever job or life responsibilities you had before are now the responsibility of Rudi North.

But that doesn't leave you empty handed.
You are now a

Chimney Maintenance Guy.

Please watch a few YouTube videos on how to complete this new job before settling into your new career. Also, feel free to sing "I got a new job" in the cadence of "I've Got a New Drug" by Huey Lewis and the News. It feels great!

It would be extremely helpful if you could provide your old bank PIN, social security number, and if applicable your partner's name and favorite food. Otherwise, Rudi will just guess.

DO NOT attempt to punch Rudi in the throat to get your life back. This could lead to an extremely convoluted series of events that will end with the destruction of all humanity!

* I wish there was enough space on this card to explain further, but sadly there is not.

HARRIS'S FOAM CORNER

"WE'VE NEVER HAD AN EDITION OF HARRIS'S FOAM CORNER WHERE YOU DIDN'T HAVE AT LEAST EIGHT TERRIBLE ONES." —SCOTT AUKERMAN

"OKAY, HERE GOES . . ." —HARRIS WITTELS

Harris Wittels was a hilarious stand-up comedian (and coiner of the word "humblebrag") who appeared regularly on *Comedy Bang! Bang!* until his death in 2015.

In addition to playing the seminal character of Jack Sjunior on the "Farts and Procreation" episodes with Adam Scott and Chelsea Peretti, he had a regular feature on the show where he would read jokes he had just thought of—quickly jotting them down into his phone.

This was originally titled "Harris's Phone Corner," but then became known as "Harris's Foam Corner," due to Scott mishearing him. It had a theme song by Reggie Watts and everything!

Harris's sister, Stephanie Wittels-Wachs, and her husband, Mike, generously went through Harris's iPhone and sent us all of the raw pages from his notes app. Here is all the RAW FOAM—including some truly terrible ones—we hope you'll enjoy!

‹ Notes   ⋯

Shout out to pants for keeping buttholes off everything.

I feel like dermatologists and dentists spend most of their days recommending things.

I hate housewarming parties. It's like, gahh just get a heater.

As cliche as it sounds, my favorite feeling is coming home after a long day at work, feeding peanuts to the girl in the basement, and masturbating to a WWII documentary.

Waldo asked me to spot him in the gym. Couldn't do it.

How come credit has to be toward my next purchase, yo? Let's just put it on this one, huh?

Wi-fi? Because-fi.

Remember when everyone in America had refrigerated steaks and would put them on people's faces if they had a black eye? You don't see that much anymore.

I tell ya, I walk around this city now and I don't know what is and what isn't a Banksy. And that's exactly what Banksy wants.

Vampires can't die unless their heart is stopped. But like, same with humans? Just havin' fun with thought experiments, I no know.

It always kinda bums me out when I see a band play a show and none of them have on a wedding ring.

If conservative idiots consider life to begin at conception, then why do they all celebrate their birthdays as the day they were born?

2 legitimately 2 quitimately

Serious question: If you could suck your own dick, would you cum in your mouth? I think I'd try to finish on my tits.

In trailers, I love when they cut right in the middle of someone saying "motherfucker." Hell yeah, I'm gonna see it! Gotta see if they say it!

Sorry to bum you out, but those two otters that held hands broke up and don't even speak anymore. There's kids, too. It's a whole mess.

I just blew a 0.28. His name was Frank.

When I search for something obscure, I feel bad for making my computer "work hard." Then I remember it's a computer. Then I give it a raise.

Wheat Thins? Call me when they're Wheat THICKS! Gimme that wheat!

I wish I was gay. 'Cause I love having sex with men.

I hate smoking sections, unless we are talking about the movie *The Mask* with Jim Carrey. Then the smoking section is my favorite part.

Grossest sentence ever: "Do you want the rest of my yogurt?"

A guy on *The Price Is Right* bid a dollar. How does a chandelier cost a dollar? Idiot.

Coins are worthless. It's gone from "You can keep the change" to "Can you keep the change?"

If God didn't want us to masturbate, why did he give us surgical gloves filled with warm jam?

Forty years ago, I invested in a company called Sunkist. I bought a thousand dollars worth of soda.

It's fun being sarcastic in a drive-thru. "Do you want fries with that?" "Nooooooo." I mean, you're just hurting yourself, but it's a fun experiment.

To me, a girl doesn't have to be hot, as long as she's caring, funny, with a set of kitties. Killer ass and a symmetrical face.

Why is it when a dog licks my face, it's cute. But when I do it, people tell me to put my penis away?

This is my impression of a good dentist with a good family, "Getting my son to clean his room is like pulling teeth. Really easy!"

Hotel checkout is 12, and check-in is 3. Soooo make check out later?

I was having sex with a girl and asked if I could cum on her tits. She said, "just the left one." Most Jewish orgasm I ever had. Haggling while climaxing.

You know old wives tales? Are the wives old, or is the tale?

Why not call half and half "one?"

If you can't find the self-help section at a bookstore, do you ask someone, or....? That joke is called "Shelf-help."

I graduated college early. It was like 7am.

I bet food stamps are delicious.

I stopped smoking when I had bronchitis 'cause I couldn't breathe, and I never felt better than when I had bronchitis. I was like, "Finally I can breathe!" And I couldn't breathe!

You ever have a morning where it feels like you fucked a cat the night before? I woke up today with my dick in a cat.

You ever at a gathering and the homeowner is scrolling through channels and you wanna watch something, but you're embarrassed to say stop? "Hey, wouldn't it be funny to watch *Along Came Polly*?" Then he does for a minute, then it's like, "Wouldn't it be funny to finish it and then discuss it?"

My uncle sold drums and sofas. He charged people per cushion. (Percussion)

My other uncle—his brother—worked at a store that sold Shakespeare plays and brass instruments. "Tuba or Not Tuba."

Then HIS brother took his cue and opened a sushi restaurant called "Tuna or Not Tuna," which is a bad name and didn't make any sense.

An e-mail should be called an e-letter. "I just got an e-mail. I just got a mail." You sound stupid.

My friend can't read and is trying to be a DJ. You wanna know his name? "JD Dyslexic."

Words that sound real but don't mean anything: pontology, memp, dorting, gritch, parthing.

Are you XM, cause you can't be serious?

In movies, where people stay at work late and each get their one Chinese food container? I feel like I'd be like, let's split them instead of committing to one dish each.

Thought about inverse macaroni— cheese inside a noodle. That's ravioli, though, son!

I'm bad at knowing lyrics, but my favorite Grateful Dead lyric has gotta be "What a short, normal trip it's been." So beautiful.

Sucks knowing my kids will never know what it's like going to a Blockbuster, 'cause I'm not letting them go there. The prices are outrageous.

All pets are adopted. No one's shooting dogs out their pussies. Unless you're Mrs. Broadus. Snoop's mom.

"A watched pot never boils." Yes it does.

You hear about that new deal where if you go in on the deal with a cast member of *That '70s Show*, you get a discount on mustard and/or salad toppings? It's a Laura Prepon Grey Poupon Crouton Groupon.

My friend's a real player and a necrophiliac. He fucks anything that doesn't move.

How come the shelves at Bed Bath & Beyond so tall? They should call that place Tall Shelves, Tall Shelves, and Tall Shelves.

If you go into a bank, can you get in trouble for yelling "Everybody get down!" Without a gun or anything? No, James Brown does it every night!

I've seen Julianne Moore's tits more than my own dick. That is a fact.

Grapefruit—it's not a grape, it's not a fruit. Yes it is. That sounds like a joke, but isn't.

I wanna open a Jamaican, Irish, Spanish, small-plate breakfast restaurant and call it "Tapas the Mornin' to Jah."

Instead of trying to desalinize the ocean, they should just add pepper.

I'm not gay, but my asshole is.

Why does cash back exist? Is that just to be nice? It's like if the bank offered zucchinis.

When people genuinely thanked Einstein, do you think it sounded sarcastic?

I've said, "I've said it before and I'll say it again" before, but I'll say, "I've said it before and I'll say it again" again.

I bought a book on how to read. Thing was impossible to get through.

If someone's being egregious, call them Egregious Philbin.

This is a true story. One time I said to a guy that I loved learning new things. I was like, "I'm a bit of an infomaniac." And he thought I said "nymphomanic." So he fucked me. And I said, "No, no, no—I like INFO. I'm an infomaniac!" He said, "Well here's some info, you just got fucked. Now clean yourself up!"

When people say they've read studies, they realistically probably read one study. Let's be honest.

Hey Brussels sprouts and broccolini—enjoy your 15 minutes!

Tip for girls for a funny thing to say. If someone compliments your eyebrows, say, "Hey—my eyes are down here."

What's the difference between Whoopi Goldberg and a tiger? Where to begin? One's a comedian actress, and tigers are animals. Completely different species.

"What am I, chopped liver?" To me that means, "What am I, great?" Chopped liver is delicious!

In the song "Lose Yourself" by Eminem, he says "But this ain't a movie, there's no Mekhi Phifer." But he's saying this is real life . . . so there IS a Mekhi Phifer. Should have said "there's no David 'Future' Porter," Mekhi's character's name in *8 Mile*.

Sometimes I feel like commercials are just ads trying to sell us products.

Sometimes in a restaurant when I order an iced tea I'll say, "A nice tea" and they don't even know.

I got pubes and I know how to use 'em.

Feel like I get how the pyramids were made. Seems easy.

Quit tellin' me to never forget 9/11. It was a terrible day. I'd rather just forget it!

People in relationships call each other "baby." That's gross! Babies are little, young humans! Infants!

A lot of guys play "just the tip." I play "just the shaft." Very difficult. A lot of bending and determination.

I bought a backpack. Woman at register asked if I wanted a bag for it. I said, "Lady, that's what it is," is what I said.

I'm happy when I honk at some bad driver and then see it's a 40-year-old white guy. That is in my wheelhouse for guiltless anger.

LOL'd should be L'dOL

Yoooo why people get ready for bed??

50 percent of the battle is half the battle.

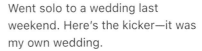

Went solo to a wedding last weekend. Here's the kicker—it was my own wedding.

I haven't eaten iHop in 7 diarrheas.

Scared to have kids 'cause I never want to have the fisting and "water sports" convo. Ummmmm mom can take that one.

What did the fat quarterback do when he wanted to change the play? Called an edible.

Pretty sad, man. Had my first unenjoyable Gotye listening sesh. Knew it was coming, just unexpected. Now it's just somebody that I used to know that I used to know.

I went to a Jack in the Box that was open 24 hours. Got there at the 26th hour and it was closed. It was only open for 24 hours. I don't know how to phrase this.

I'm not getting married 'til gay people can get married. Because I'm gay.

Soon you'll be able to put a computer in your brain. Back in the day, did they think you would be able to put a typewriter in your brain? Or an abacus?

Seeing a Christian girl who loves *My Name is Earl* and I'm Jewish. We call ourselves oyfriend and earlfriend.

Business idea—Hole Foods. It's a donut hole store.

Did I tell you I went window shopping in New York last week? I bought a window.

Swear to God I haven't said a name in 12 years. Too risky. Who can remember 'em all? When I was 10 I knew 7 people. Bam.

He lost three pounds of blood. Wow, three pounds? How's he look? Great!

Where there's a will, there's a Wayans.

Time is the most important thing. We get to keep track of one thing on our wrists, and it's with watches.

Anything's a toilet if you shit on it.

Guy who's only read the word thermometer, but never said or heard it: "What temperature does it say on that thermo-meter?"

My family was super into *That '70s Show* growing up. We used to say Topher Grace before we ate.

Wonder if I'll ever fall down again?

I could find someone uglier that's a better singer than Susan Boyle. Unimpressive both ways.

Here's how to figure out your porn name: Take your first name and change it to "Sir." Then change your last name to "Fucksalot." Sir Fucksalot.

I'm starting a campaign to change bygones into something. Everyone's always trying to let them be bygones.

I've never known what permanent press does on a dryer and I've done fine.

Toothpicks don't really work, man. They don't get in there. Restaurants should have floss. Is it 1800?

"I'm not sick, but I'm not well. I get no respect." —Harvey Dangerfield

Crazy that car radios exist. Only distractions. I'm bored driving this two-ton piece of speeding metal. Need more to do.

I'm not impressed by juggling. Well, okay, whatever—you learned to do that. I could do it too if I learned how. I didn't select juggling to be one of the things I learned.

Good invention I thought of: Food tape. It's like edible, adhesive tape that you can put around ice cream cones, or your sandwiches if they break. Or your tacos. It's edible and flavorless. Oh, but there's a slogan too: "'cause food breaks!"

It's weird that pineapple supposedly makes your semen taste better, yet semen makes pineapple taste terrible!

What do you get when you cross the Holocaust with a baby-clothing store? OshKosh B'g-Auschwitz.

The Burbank airport is called the Bob Hope Airport. That's two things I don't wanna do while flying: "bob" and "hope."

I treated myself to a marathon jerk sesh last night. Not what it sounds like—I watched *The Jerk* twice while masturbating.

Church is just a book club about the Bible.

I think Freud just really wanted to fuck his mom and then was like, "Hey guys, isn't it crazy that we all wanna do that?" And then his friends were probably like, "I don't!" And he's like, "Yeah you do, I'm fuckin' Freud!"

I just saw that Jennifer Convertibles just opened up a car dealership. It's called Jennifer Sofas.

I wonder what vibe I carry when I walk into a room. Lord, I hope it's chill.

FOURVEL'S TIPS
FOR LIVING A HAPPY
AND HEALTHY LIFE

"The secret to a happy life is balance, breathe, and love."

—Your favorite little street rat, scoundrel Fourvel

TIP # WON: Waking Up Right!

YAWN! HAPPY MORNING. You didn't die in your "sleepy.*" Now. Before you even get out of bed each morning you should lie there with your eyes (or eye or whatever) closed. Take a deep, meaningful breath. And FAAAAAAAAAAAAAAAA AAAAAAAAAAAAAAAAAAAAAAAAAAAAAAAAWRT!

2 TIPS 2 FURIOUS: Meditate

Find a lil' corner or a huge hole or whatever the fuck and just sit. Put on some stupid pan flute music and just BE, damnit. Breathe in. And when you are done with breathing in, no matter how good it feels, sexually or otherwise, do NOT forget to breathe OUT. You will die if you stop breathing in or out at any point in the meditation process. Just so you know. If you die, it's not on us.

3 TIPS AND A BABY: Treat people with the same kindness you wish to be treated.

Treat people with the same kindness you wish to be treated. BUT if a bitch starts talking like he knows what he's talking about but he DOESN'T? Then feel free to stab that bitch. Stab him in the neck. The arms and legs. Don't forget those knees. Gotta stab them knees. Stab this bitch in the abs. Stab him in the forearm/forearms. Stab him the butt for fun. The back. The front. The side of the head. The other side of the head. The butt again for more fun. The bottoms of the feet. (RUDE.) The shins. The hands. The mouth. Go for it.

It's YOUR world.

It's NOT on us.

TIP # 4: Stop every once and while and appreciate what you already have.

Like me. I have nothing . . .

Nothing.

And I APPRECIATE that.

Okay. I was lying. I have knives. A lot of 'em. Big ones. Small ones. Others. I love them. It's my "thing." Just like her majesty Missy Elliott once said all the time in her songs once: "Knives, knives, all type of knives. Black, white, Puerto Rican, Chinese knives. Why-thai, thai-o-toy-o-thai-thai Rock-thai,thai-o-toy-o-thai-thai (C'mon)"

Let me put it this way . . .

Me: "I have so many knives."

You: "How many?"

Me: "119."

Let me ALSO put it this way . . .

Got milk?

Good.

APPRECIATE IT.

TIP # Johnny5

"Let it go." **—Pixar movies**

It sounds so easy and it is. Sometimes you just have to move on and not worry so much about where your next meal is coming from, or where you are gonna find shelter or warmth that evening, or who is ever gonna love you and treat you like the kind son you are and adopt you and give you full steaks instead of steak scraps? You know?

You just have to keep moving. Keep going. Never stop. And stab whoever comes within stabbing range. Protect your neck.

Now get LIVIN'! (Or I'll kiww you!)

So sincerely,

Adorable lil' fat child, Fourvel

*cute way of saying "sleep."

DEDICATION

I have frequently been asked who is the most memorable *Comedy Bang! Bang!* guest of all time. And though you may think the competition for that distinction would be fierce, in truth there is none. Because there is only one clear choice:

Ernie Bread.

Though he only appeared a few times, and he never once made us laugh, his impact on the show cannot be overstated. His lack of a distinct voice or funny attitude was unique amongst his peers. His backstory—that he sat by a pond across the street, feeding ducks, and then just wandered into the studio—was uninspired. His "impression" of Major Thackeray was so forgettable that this sentence is probably the first time you thought of it since he introduced it. He made only two appearances on the show, and yet when he passed away during his second visit, it seemed long overdue.

"Does a duck quack?" That was his oft-repeated and stunningly unfunny catchphrase. Audio mixers have frequently written into the show, asking if they can use the silence that resulted after his use of that catchphrase for room tone. (We have always generously obliged, for a hefty fee.)

Several other guests were asked to comment on Ernie Bread's legacy. They all rightfully refused or expressed confusion as to his identity. "Who the fuck is that?" was a common refrain. "Huh?" was another. More than one person simply hung up the phone in disgust, and they were right to do so.

Some say you shouldn't denigrate the dead. But I think we can all agree that those people would make an exception for Ernie Bread. He was awful.

And yet. *Comedy Bang! Bang!* simply wouldn't be the same without him. It would be better, certainly, but it wouldn't be the same.

So if you were to ask me if I'm glad that Ernie Bread is dead, I suppose there's only one way to answer that question:

Does a duck quack?

To be very clear, what I mean by that is yes, I am glad he's dead. Very glad. Honestly, this is maybe the happiest I've ever been.

And that is why this book is dedicated to his memory.

CONTRIBUTORS

CAROLINE ANDERSON is a writer best known to *Comedy Bang! Bang!* fans as Leo Karpatze's granddaughter Scaroline. Her credits include *Comedy Bang! Bang!* (IFC), *Corporate* (Comedy Central), *Yearly Departed* (Amazon), and *This Fool* (Hulu). She's also a certified kettlebell instructor because this industry isn't all it's cracked up to be.

MATT APODACA is a writer and comedian from Los Angeles. He produces podcasts for Earwolf, is one of the hosts of the show *Get Played*, and is a performer at the UCB theater. Matt also really loves the band Weezer.If they see this: Hi, Weezer!

TIM BALTZ is originally from Joliet, Illinois, and was a veteran of the iO Theater, Annoyance Theater, and Second City Chicago before moving to Los Angeles. He cocreated and starred in the critically lauded *Shrink* and currently stars in the HBO series *The Righteous Gemstones*. His other credits include *Better Call Saul*, *Veep*, *Drunk History*, *Parks and Recreation*, *Bajillion Dollar Propertie\$*, *The Conners*, and *The Opposition with Jordan Klepper*. You can also listen to his podcast *HEY RANDY! (a Randy Snutz Show)* exclusively on CBB World.

PAUL BRITTAIN is an actor, comedian, and writer living in Los Angeles. He began performing sketch and improv comedy in Chicago in 2003, and in 2010 he joined the cast of *Saturday Night Live*. In addition to appearances on *Comedy Bang! Bang!* and other Earwolf productions, Paul created the podcast *Mr. Write* for Stitcher Premium. His television and film credits include *Hello Ladies*, *Trophy Wife*, *Kroll Show*, *Hotel Transylvania 2*, and *Killing Gunther*.

NEIL CAMPBELL is a writer, performer, director, and former child model. He was the executive producer and head writer of the *Comedy Bang! Bang!* television show on IFC, and a co-executive producer on *Brooklyn Nine-Nine* on FOX and NBC. By the time this is published it is possible he will have had another job as well.

NICK CIARELLI & BRAD EVANS are a comedy duo who have written for *The Tonight Show*, *Billy on the Street*, *ClickHole*, *Onion News Network*, and projects for Comedy Central and TBS. They were named Comedians to Watch by *Vulture* and New Faces at the Just For Laughs Festival. They created the *Comedy Bang! Bang!* characters Martin Sheffield-Lickley and Memphis Kansas Breeze and write their bits and songs. Nick and Brad wrote, directed, and starred in a bunch of annoying comedy videos that you can watch on the awful website Twitter. Follow them @nickciarelli and @bradfordevans.

ANDY DALY starred in and executive produced the Comedy Central series *Review* and has played regular or recurring roles on *Veep*, *Modern Family*, *Black-ish*, *Silicon Valley*, and *Eastbound and Down*. He's been heard in lots of animated shows including *Bob's Burgers*, *The Simpsons*, *Rick and Morty*, *Big Mouth*, and *Harley Quinn* and is the creator and host of the podcasts *The Andy Daly Podcast Pilot Project* and *Bonanas For Bonanza*. Film credits include *Semi-Pro*, *The Informant!*, and *Kimi*. Andy lives in Los Angeles with his wife, two amazing daughters, and two charming dogs.

BRIAN DALY is an illustrator and graphic designer living in Bloomfield, New Jersey.

SHAUN DISTON is a writer, actor, and podcaster who loves microphones. He is repped by super-producer and mega-manager Sprague The Whisperer.

JON GABRUS is a comedian/actor/podcaster/and now a contributing book author. Readers of this book will know him as Gino Lombardo the Long Island intern on *Comedy Bang! Bang!*, but some other people might know him as "Jon" or "Gabrus." You can see him on his travel show, *101 Places to Party Before You Die*. And you can hear him on his podcasts *High And Mighty*, *Actionboyz*, and *The Movie Buff*.

RYAN GAUL is an actor/writer from the great state of Maine. He has been performing sketch and improv for over twenty years and currently performs with The Main Company at the Groundlings Theater in Los Angeles. His TV credits include *House of Lies*, *It's Always Sunny in Philadelphia*, *Superstore*, and *The Last O.G.* Ryan's film credits include *Identity Thief*, *Killing Gunther*, *The Happytime Murders*, and *Between Two Ferns: The Movie*. He has popped up on *CBB* over the years playing several confused and babbling small business owners.

MITCH GERADS is the multiple Eisner Award–winning comic book artist of *Mister Miracle*, *Batman*, *Strange Adventures*, and *The Sheriff Of Babylon*, and is a podcast obsessive who is just happy to be here.

MIKE HANFORD is a comedian who has made many appearances on the *Comedy Bang! Bang!* podcast and TV show. He is currently embroiled in a "no meat for a month" challenge, but his favorite food is chicken wings.

WILL HINES is an actor and writer in Los Angeles. He's appeared on *Brooklyn Nine-Nine*, *Broad City*, *Crazy Ex-Girlfriend*, *Search Party*, and many other shows. He co-hosts the podcast *Screw It, We're Just Gonna Talk About Comics* with his brother Kevin. He's taught and performed improv at the Upright Citizens Brigade Theatre in both NYC and LA for something like a hundred years. He's learning guitar and feeling optimistic about it.

MARY HOLLAND is thrilled to be a part of this book! She's an actor, writer, and comedian based in Los Angeles. She's a member of the comedy group Wild Horses and can be seen in various film/TV projects. She can be heard on many *CBB* episodes playing an assortment of specific goofballs.

PAUL HORNSCHEMEIER is a writer, director, and animator. He is the author of the graphic novels *Mother, Come Home*, *The Three Paradoxes*, and the *New York Times* bestseller *Life with Mr. Dangerous*. He animated the title sequence for *Comedy Bang! Bang!* and designed the show's logo. He is the art director of Netflix's *Twelve Forever* and a new adult series from the creators of *Norsemen*.

TARAN KILLAM's biggest accomplishments include: Beating *The Lion King* for Sega Genesis without losing a single life, having the thickest brass Pog slammer at Big Bear Middle School, eating two bags of peach rings and three Mountain Dews in one sitting, and purchasing a Super Soaker 300 with his own money. Since seventh grade, he has lived a quieter, simpler life.

THE HIGH ROAD DESIGN, otherwise known as **JON KUTT**, is a self-taught designer/illustrator from Waterloo, Ontario, Canada. He recently shifted to full-time freelance illustration after 20+ years in the graphic design world.

Clients include Naked & Famous Denim, Geoff Rowley, Jimmy Kimmel, Netflix, and many more. He loves napping and spending time with his wife and daughter, as well as drawing copious amounts of dumb, often inappropriate things.

DAN LIPPERT can be seen on screens big and small (depending on the size of your TV) in *Paranormal Activity: Next of Kin*, *American Princess*, *Brooklyn Nine-Nine*, *Son of Zorn*, and *Workaholics*. You can find his improv and conversation podcast *Man Dog Pod* wherever you get podcasts or support it at patreon.com/yourethemannowdog. Go to biggrandewebsite.com for á la carte content like podcasts, animated improvised shorts, and the fully improvised live show *Big Grande: Live on Set*. Or just follow him on social media @danlippertcool.

LAUREN LAPKUS is an actor, comedian, and writer who loves a big round pie. Some sauce. A little cheese. Maybe pepperoni.

JASON MANTZOUKAS – Heynong Man

TATIANA MASLANY is an Emmy Award–winning actress known for her roles in *Orphan Black* and *She-Hulk: Attorney at Law*.

JESSICA MCKENNA is an actor, writer, and podcaster. She's been on TV sometimes (*Party Over Here*, *Curb Your Enthusiasm*, *Modern Family*, *The Goldbergs*, and *Drunk History*). Sometimes just her voice is on TV (*Star Trek: Lower Decks*, *Duncanville*, *DC Superhero Girls*, *The Mighty Ones*, *Craig of the Creek*). Jess and her comedy partner, Zach Reino, host *Off Book: The Improvised Musical Podcast* and write musical comedy for film and TV.

LIN-MANUEL MIRANDA is a Pulitzer Prize, Grammy, Emmy, and Tony Award–winning composer, lyricist, and actor; the creator and original star of Broadway's *Hamilton* and *In the Heights*; and the recipient of the 2015 MacArthur Foundation Award and 2018 Kennedy Center Honors. He lives with his family in New York City.

SETH MORRIS is an actor and writer. He's an improviser and a daydreamer (yuck), a lover, a friend, a husband (booooo!), a dad, and above all (please don't) a grateful doggy owner (unsubscribe).

BOBBY MOYNIHAN loves playing Fourvel and Batman on *Comedy Bang! Bang!* Bobby also loves Scotty Aukerman, his family, Peach Snapple, and the TV show *Lost*. In that order.

EGO NWODIM is a repertory performer on *Saturday Night Live*. She was a mainstay at Upright Citizens Brigade in Los Angeles and performed as a New Face at the 2016 Just for Laughs Festival in Montreal. She was featured in the 2016 CBS Diversity Showcase and in 2017 wrote and performed her first-ever one-woman show, *Great Black Women . . . and Then There's Me*, for a sold-out run in Los Angeles. A 2019 Variety Comedy Impact honoree, Ego can be heard regularly on *Comedy Bang! Bang!* and seen from time to time on television and in films.

BOB ODENKIRK is famous as the guy from *Mr. Show w/ Bob and David* (the one who's NOT David Cross) and from acting in *Best Call Sal* and *The Bad Breakers*, but also a movie about *Nobody* and lots of guest acting "gigs" and just a lotta . . . stuff. He's in SAG! Lately he's been considering retiring but he's not sure from what.

PATTON OSWALT is a writer, comedian, actor, and producer, but not in that order.

GIL OZERI is a comedian, actor, and writer, known for his work on Netflix's *Big Mouth* and *#BlackAF*, Fox's *Brooklyn Nine-Nine*, and ABC's *Happy Endings*. He's also appeared on *Curb Your Enthusiasm*, *Search Party*, and *I Love You, America*, and in the film *Uncorked*. Additionally, he's written on *Borat: Subsequent Moviefilm*, *Another Period*, *Children's Hospital*, as well as feature films for Disney and DreamWorks. Gil is originally from New York City but now lives with his family in sunny and fiery Los Angeles.

LENNON PARHAM is an actor/writer/director/body roll queen whom you may find Womping It Up in a Jersey Mike's. Also known for TV and film like *Playing House*, *Veep*, *Minx*, *Bless This Mess*, and *The House*. Proud UCB alum.

EDI PATTERSON plays Judy Gemstone and is a writer/consulting producer for *The Righteous Gemstones* on HBO. Other films and TVs include *Plan B*, *Knives Out*, *Vice Principals*, the upcoming *Violent Night*, voicing Tom's Mom on *10-Year Old Tom*, and Mertha on *The Fungies*. She's a Groundlings alum and still performs in improv shows there, and is also a member of Impro Theatre.

JACK QUAID is an actor who turned in his introduction way too late. Like VERY close to the deadline. He had to be reminded about it SEVERAL times. Like I know he's a busy guy, but JEEZ learn some time-management skills! We're ALL busy. Everyone's busy! Dickhead.

ZACH REINO is an actor, writer, and composer. He cohosts *Off Book: The Improvised Musical Podcast* with Jessica McKenna.

BEN RODGERS is a writer and performer from Buffalo, New York, who has worked on TV shows like *Workaholics* and *Star Trek: Lower Decks*. He resides in Los Angeles and is currently alive.

PAUL RUST was born in Le Mars, Iowa. He currently lives with his wife and daughter in Los Angeles.

JOHNNY SAMPSON (b. 1974) is an award-winning cartoonist and freelance illustrator based in Glen Ellyn, Illinois. With Al Jaffee's blessing, he has been doing the Fold-In for *MAD Magazine* since 2020 (yes, it is still in print). In his spare time, he can often be found at the local skatepark working on his frontside grinds.

Over the past two decades, **BEN SCHWARTZ** has written and acted in a series of things, but because of Scott, at least once a month someone calls him The Elegant Mr. S and asks how House of Pies is going.

MATT SMITH is a cartoonist and animator who can currently be found drinking various fluids and occasionally thinking about making cartoons in and around Washington, DC! Matt has been known to upload animations of various *Comedy Bang! Bang!* selections to his Youtube channel, Video City Limits, or his Twitter account, @MattLimits.

JESSICA ST. CLAIR is an actor/writer/podcaster who is known for ordering OFF MENU at Jersey Mike's. Along with her ride or die bestie Lennon Parham, she co-created the critically acclaimed comedies *Playing House* on USA Network and *Best Friends Forever* on NBC and is currently stuck in space on HBO's *Avenue 5*. Oh, she also almost got thrown up on in that scene in *Bridesmaids*. She is a proud UCB alum.

LILY SULLIVAN is a comedian and actor based in Los Angeles. She's appeared in *The Righteous Gemstones*, *Killing It*, *Death to 2020*, *Shrink*, and *I Think You Should Leave*. Lily hosts two improvised podcasts: *This Book Changed My Life* on CBB World and *Going Deep* on Stitcher Premium. Follow her online using her very easy, extremely simple, not confusing at all social media handle: @LilyYily.

CARL TART is a comedian/actor/writer born in Mississippi and raised in LA. He has written for shows such as *Brooklyn Nine-Nine*, *Kenan*, and *MadTV* and acted in multiple shows including starring in the NBC show *Grand Crew*.

DREW TARVER is an American actor and comedian from the Upright Citizens Brigade Theatre in Los Angeles. Tarver is known for starring as Cary Dubek on the HBO Max comedy series *The Other Two* and in the Seeso show *Bajillion Dollar Propertie$* and for his appearances on comedy podcasts, including *Comedy Bang! Bang!* and *Big Grande Teachers' Lounge*.

PAUL F. TOMPKINS has been performing comedy in one form or another for what feels like forever. It's honestly pretty wild when you think about it.

REGGIE WATTS is one of those individuals you might see on a train or who might give you some advice on a project you are struggling with. He loves helping out when he can.

JON WHITE is the founder and creative director of his eponymous graphic- and web-design agency (jonwhitestudio.com). He specializes in translating complex material into clear, accessible, joyful new forms, meant to be enjoyed—and understood—by as many people as possible. His clients include Harvard Law School, Northwestern Medicine, Chapo Trap House, Current Affairs, People's Policy Project, The Roosevelt Institute, and The Real News Network. He lives in Seattle.

NICK WIGER (rhymes with "tiger") is a writer, podcaster, and video game designer. He cohosts the chain restaurant podcast *Doughboys* and the video game podcast *Get Played*.

"WEIRD AL" YANKOVIC is the only person in history to debut at #1 on the Billboard charts with a comedy album, and one of only three people (the others being Michael Jackson and Madonna) to have had their own Top 40 single in each of the last four decades . . . but he is probably best known as Scott Aukerman's bandleader on the fifth and final season of the *Comedy Bang! Bang!* TV show.

ACKNOWLEDGMENTS

There are two people who are directly responsible for this book resting in your hands (unless you have a book butler holding it and turning the pages for you—and if you don't, what are you doing with your life? Just consult on a sitcom one day a week, and that will pay for it).

First, to our editor Samantha Weiner, who approached me about doing this project three years ago. She had a vision for what this book could be, which immediately excited me. And all throughout the process, her encouragement and enthusiasm kept everyone moving toward the goal. I hope she's proud of what was eventually spat out (and that she doesn't regret that we didn't end up using her proposed title, *What's Up, Hot Dog?*, which is unfortunately the intellectual property of Al Yankovic).

Second, to Corinne Eckart, whom I've worked with for about a decade now. The fact that this exists at all and isn't still just a bunch of trees sitting in the Amazon rainforest (from what I understand, that's where Abrams Books gets their paper supply) is entirely due to her diligence and force of will. She took it upon herself to make sure this happened— e-mailing all of the participants, pushing everyone to complete deadlines, taking character photos, writing bios, and (unfortunately) listening to my voice much more than she usually has to. This book belongs to her just as much as me (except for financially).

Comedy Bang! Bang! would not exist without the participation of all of the incredible guests who have taken advantage of the open-door policy through the years. I hope this book highlights their collective genius and makes you seek out work in other areas in which they choose to dip their toes (gross).

To you, the fans, who have either come and gone or stuck with the show since it began, the fact that you still listen and care astounds me. Here's to another fourteen years! (Okay, maybe three.)

To my wife, Kulap Vilaysack, thank you for your never-ending support, and for the belief that doing a podcast was a somewhat worthwhile endeavor all those years ago. And to our daughter, Emerald—hopefully, after I'm gone, this book will serve as some sort of treasure map—providing clues as to what your daddy did during all those years before you arrived.

Editor: Samantha Weiner
Executive Editor: Corinne Eckart
Design Manager: Zach Bokhour
Managing Editor: Glenn Ramirez
Production Manager: Kathleen Gaffney

Book design and illustration by Jon Kutt
Additional design by Zach Bokhour and Diane Shaw

Library of Congress Control Number: 2022944492

ISBN: 978-1-4197-5481-4
eISBN: 978-1-64700-301-2
Signed Edition ISBN: 978-1-4197-7029-6

Abrams Image books are available at special discounts when purchased in quantity for premiums
and promotions as well as fundraising or educational use. Special editions can also be created
to specification. For details, contact specialsales@abramsbooks.com or the address below.

Abrams Image® is a registered trademark of Harry N. Abrams, Inc.

ABRAMS The Art of Books
195 Broadway, New York, NY 10007
abramsbooks.com